CULTURE**SHOCK!**

A Survival Guide to Customs and Etiquette

INDIA

Gitanjali Kolanad

Marshall Cavendish
Editions

Photo Credits:
All photos from the author except pages 26,116, 134, 221 (Tejas Ewing),
pages 178–179, 278–279 (Angeline Koh) and pages 186–187 (India Tourism,
Singapore) ▪ Cover photo: India Tourism, Singapore

All illustrations by TRIGG except for page viii (Mickey Patel)

First published in 1994. This edition published 2005, reprinted 2006.
Copyright © 2005 Marshall Cavendish International (Asia) Private Limited

Published by Marshall Cavendish Editions
An imprint of Marshall Cavendish International
1 New Industrial Road, Singapore 536196

Other Marshall Cavendish Offices:
Marshall Cavendish Ltd. 119 Wardour Street, London W1F OUW, UK ▪ Marshall
Cavendish Corporation. 99 White Plains Road, Tarrytown NY 10591-9001, USA
▪ Marshall Cavendish International (Thailand) Co Ltd. 253 Asoke, 12th Flr, Sukhumvit
21 Road, Klongtoey Nua, Wattana, Bangkok 10110, Thailand ▪ Marshall Cavendish
(Malaysia) Sdn Bhd, Times Subang, Lot 46, Subang Hi-Tech Industrial Park,
Batu Tiga, 40000 Shah Alam, Selangor Darul Ehsan, Malaysia

Marshall Cavendish is a trademark of Times Publishing Limited

National Library Board Singapore Cataloguing in Publication Data
Kolanad, Gitanjali.
CultureShock! : India / Gitanjali Kolanad. – Singapore :
Marshall Cavendish Editions, 2005.
p. cm. – (CultureShock!)
ISBN : 981-261-124-X
1. Etiquette – India. 2. India – Social life and customs. I. Title.
II. Series: CultureShock!
DS423
954 -- dc21   SLS2005034500

Printed in Singapore by Times Graphics Pte Ltd

ABOUT THE SERIES

Culture shock is a state of disorientation that can come over anyone who has been thrust into unknown surroundings, away from one's comfort zone. *CultureShock!* is a series of trusted and reputed guides which has, for decades, been helping expatriates and long-term visitors to cushion the impact of culture shock whenever they move to a new country.

Written by people who have lived in the country and experienced culture shock themselves, the authors share all the information necessary for anyone to cope with these feelings of disorientation more effectively. The guides are written in a style that is easy to read and covers a range of topics that will arm readers with enough advice, hints and tips to make their lives as normal as possible again.

Each book is structured in the same manner. It begins with the first impressions that visitors will have of that city or country. To understand a culture, one must first understand the people—where they came from, who they are, the values and traditions they live by, as well as their customs and etiquette. This is covered in the first half of the book

Then on with the practical aspects—how to settle in with the greatest of ease. Authors walk readers through how to find accommodation, get the utilities and telecommunications up and running, enrol the children in school and keep in the pink of health. But that's not all. Once the essentials are out of the way, venture out and try the food, enjoy more of the culture and travel to other areas. Then be immersed in the language of the country before discovering more about the business side of things.

To round off, snippets of basic information are offered before readers are 'tested' on customs and etiquette of the country. Useful words and phrases, a comprehensive resource guide and list of books for further research are also included for easy reference.

CONTENTS

FOREWORD

Once, I performed in Vienna at the house of an architect who was also an avid Indiaphile. He often hosted performances of Indian dance and music, his bookshelves were stocked with beautiful books about India, he loved Indian food—but he had never been to India. He always had an excuse when I or any of his many other Indian friends invited him to come and visit. But after many years, the excuses ran out and he did make a trip to India. He didn't like it.

Another friend, a poet, coming to India for the first time, described an experience of 'coming home' the instant she stepped off the plane. She ended up staying in India for years at a time, and writing poetry 'shaped by India'. She continues to come back again and again, to enjoy 'the kind of culture in which the importance of social relations adjusts the pace of life.'

Someone once said that whatever you say about India, the opposite is also true. Indian systems of thought can handle this kind of paradox. One philosophical argument for such apparent contradictions uses the simple illustration of a room. To someone who enters after a winter's walk, the room is warm. To the person who has been sitting there all day, it is not warm. So the room is warm; the room is not warm; the room is at the same time warm and not warm; and the real nature of the room remains undescribed by any of these standards. That's four possibilities for a room. And for the whole of India? That is very much the dilemma I faced when writing this book. I read many books about India, talked to many people about India, and tried to be fair and accurate in whatever I have included between the covers of this book. But it has necessarily been my viewpoint that colours every statement. You have to experience India, and your own individual viewpoint will make that experience unique. This book is meant to open doors, break down some barriers, clear the way. India then remains for each reader to discover.

I have used Indian words throughout the book. In most cases, they are words used freely by Indians all over India, even when speaking English. As Indians do when speaking, I make the plural or form tenses just as if they were English words. In order to avoid any confusion arising out of this, the glossary at the back of the book gives Indian words in their singular form.

In 1997, Bombay officially became Mumbai, and Madras became Chennai. In all government correspondence, these new names are used. In day-to-day transactions in English, however, even in the cities in question, the old names are often used out of habit. Throughout the book, I have included the old name along with the new. Other name changes are Kolkata (formerly Calcutta), Thiruvanthapuram (formerly Trivandrum), Kochi (formerly Cochin), Pune (formerly Poona), Varanasi (formerly Benares) and Shimla (formerly Simla).

ACKNOWLEDGEMENTS

Many people helped me with this book. Mrinalini and Wilfried Vogeler opened my eyes to the danger of any kind of generalisation about India. Raj Verma gave me introductions to just the right people among her wide circle of friends. Malti Oberoi made herself constantly available to answer carefully and honestly even my most trivial questions. Meena Puetz was, for me in particular, the embodiment of Indian hospitality. Paraj Kakar shared insights about the business world in India today. Prabha Nagarajan invited me to lunches and dinners, where I ate the most exquisite food and learned so much from three generations about modern India, with all its contradictions. So many people shared information and experiences with me; without naming them separately, I thank them all.

The earlier editions of this book had the witty, charming illustrations of Mickey Patel (1941–1994), who died soon after the book was published. I first bought one of Mickey's books for my young son: a counting book of an Indian wedding procession. It has all the qualities which made him one of the best-loved illustrators of children's books: a wry

An illustration by Mickey Patel

insightful sense of humour, together with strong graceful lines and delicious details. Then I found out that he lived just across the street from us in New Delhi! I began to notice his cartoons and drawings in major magazines and newspapers, so I knew he was the person I wanted when an illustrator was needed for *CultureShock! India*. At that time I didn't know of his international reputation and many awards, including the prestigious Noma Concours from UNESCO for 'Children's Picture Book Illustrations'. I just loved the way his illustrations added charm and humour to each chapter.

Lastly, I must acknowledge my debt to my family: My two boys, by being willing to go with anyone—waiters, railway porters, teenage cousins; eat anything offered to them, no matter how spicy, greasy or messy to eat; play anywhere with whatever was at hand—cricket with a crumpled newspaper as a ball and an umbrella as a bat, made it easy as pie to travel all over the country. I met many of my friends through them. My husband Rainer Wolfgramm was Chief of Bureau for German Radio, New Delhi, when I met him. I borrowed shamelessly from his broadcasts on India, and if my German had been better, I would have borrowed even more.

MAP OF INDIA

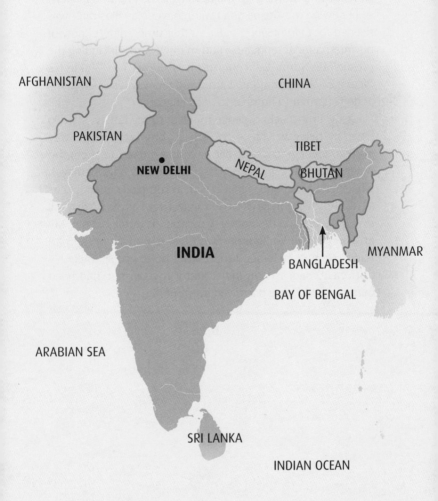

FIRST IMPRESSIONS

CHAPTER 1

'The streets of India are swollen with an embarrassment
of riches, a richness of embarrassments.'
—Pico Iyer, *Video Night in Kathmandu*

MOTHER INDIA

India was never just a country; it has always been a dream, an idea, an elusive vision that attracted travellers from all over the world for thousands of years. The mystique of India impelled the journeys of Alexander the Great, Marco Polo, and Vasco da Gama.

The images that the word 'India' conjures up are diverse and often contradictory, suggesting that one must be the real India, and it's only a matter of finding out which one. If only it were that simple! To understand India at all, you must be able to hold on to completely contradictory images, and realise that both represent the true India.

The Elephant Story

There is a famous Jain story: Five blind men wanted to find out for themselves about that marvellous beast, the elephant. When they were led to the animal, each one approached and felt with his hands that part he found within his reach. The man who felt the trunk said, "Ah, now I know, an elephant is like a snake." The one who felt the body said, "Not at all, it's like a wall." The man who felt the tusk disagreed, declaring, "The elephant is like a pole." The other two, grabbing the tail, and the leg, shouted, "No, the elephant is like a rope," and "The elephant is like a pillar." And so they argued, each one sure that his own limited experience was the reality. Finally, a wise man enlightened them: each one was right, but expressed only a partial truth; a full understanding of the elephant (or India) comes with the perception of the whole beast as the unity of disparate elements.

I remember vividly coming to India when I was 16. I was born in India but I do not remember leaving when I was six, and I also do not remember arriving on an earlier trip when I was ten. But when I was 16, with long black hair, and brown skin, looking like an Indian girl and feeling like a Canadian teenager, India was an exotic foreign land to me.

I arrived with my father at Bombay airport and the first sensation that hit me as I stepped off the plane was the air: it felt like a wall. The heat and humidity gave the air a substance that air does not have in Canada. I felt as if I had to make an extra effort to draw it into my lungs, to move through it.

After we picked up our luggage and exited the airport, the next thing I noticed was the crush of people. It seemed as if every porter in the city wanted to carry our bags and every taxi driver was vying for our fare. They came very close, right up to us, touched us to get our attention, and tried to pull us. They were fighting with each other over us; when my father picked out one driver at random, a different one actually grabbed our luggage and tried to drag it to his car, and the two men exchanged hostile words before the matter of taxis was settled. Then the other drivers lost interest in us and swarmed the next hapless travellers to emerge through the doors.

Our taxi driver set off at a fast clip, in a dented old black and yellow car with the rounded shape of cars from the 1950s. The faster we went, the more it rattled. And all the cars on the road were the same rounded shape: every car looked like a vintage car.

Leaving the airport and going into Bombay, there was a four-lane road with a divider down the centre to separate the two directions of traffic. On our side of the road in front of us was a broken down truck, at an angle so that it occupied both lanes. Instead of slowing down and finding a way around the obstacle on the shoulder, our driver did what no taxi driver in my experience had ever done before. He sped up, went through a gap in the divider, and into the opposite lane, so that we were driving fast, directly into oncoming traffic! I saw my whole short life pass before me as I looked in horror at the headlights of the cars coming towards us. But the cars veered and made room for our seemingly suicidal taxi driver all the way until the next gap in the divider, where thankfully he got back on his side of the road. My father paid him whatever he asked when we reached our hotel, relieved to be alive and in one piece. I think I got my first white hair on that taxi ride.

The new sensations continued as I explored Bombay on my own for the next few days. I picked up some brochures from the front desk at the hotel, and headed out into the streets. So many things seemed surprising: the vibrant colours that both men and women wore—magenta, turquoise, lime green, purple; the baskets, bundles, boxes balanced on heads; the noise—of vendors calling out their wares, of car horns, of bicycle bells, and bells on bullock carts; the enticing aromas of food being cooked right there on the sidewalk. Actually, sidewalk? What sidewalk? Space was at a premium, and the sidewalk was being used for all kinds of activities not normally associated with sidewalks, at least not where I came from: goods were being sold, naps were being taken, hair was being cut, fortunes were being told, ears were being cleaned (yes, you read it right, there are professional ear cleaners, who for a small fee will poke instruments into your ears. I don't advise it.)

One of my earliest lessons was that I had to always look where I was going, to avoid stepping on sleeping bodies, displays of trinkets, men playing cards. Not everything that was going on around me was fascinating and pleasant, though. Men, for example, were often to be spotted unzipping their pants and urinating. I learnt to avoid those stretches of sidewalk.

From Bombay, my father and I went to Trichy, or Thiruchirapalli as it is properly called, to my grandparent's house. It seemed like we were in a different country. This city had plenty of hustle and bustle but on a smaller scale and without the cosmopolitan flavour of Bombay—no wide streets, no big buildings, no obvious remnants of colonial British presence. The people looked different: smaller, darker. The language being talked all around me seemed to consist of only 'r's, 'l's and 'n's. The men weren't wearing pants, they were wearing a sarong-like cloth, which they were constantly unwrapping and rewrapping, and then folding up in half and tucking in so that they look like mini-skirts. The women wore flowers in their long braids. The fortune-tellers on the sidewalks had parrots to help them (the parrot picks out a card from the deck on your behalf). The food at the restaurant was served on banana leaves. But the traffic was equally chaotic, the sidewalks just as crammed, the people just as friendly.

Just Strangers

A boy about my age, wearing a school uniform, struck up a conversation with me at a bus stop in Bombay. My jeans and T-shirt gave me away as a foreigner. He was polite and serious—he wanted to practice his English. So we went through the usual questions: my name, my age, where I was from, what I was doing here and so on. Then he asked where I was going. I answered and he became very agitated. "No, no", he said, "you mustn't go there". But when I asked why not, he wouldn't tell me. In the meantime my bus came and I said, "If you won't tell me the reason, I'm going", and got on the bus. He followed me on and sat next to me. "It is my duty" he said, "to take care that no harm comes to you". Soon after, I realized why he was so concerned. The bus went through the Bombay red light district, where he felt that no young girl should be on her own, even just sitting on the bus. This young boy was the first of many, many casually met strangers in India who went out of their way to help me, even when I didn't know I needed help. I think he must have skipped school to protect me.

If you lay a map of India over a map of Europe, it covers the area from Denmark to Libya, and from Spain to Russia. As different as these European countries are, so are the different parts of India. More than a billion people live on 3,287,590 sq km (1,269,345.6 sq miles) of land. According to the authoritative publication, People of India, these billion are members of 4,636 separate communities that belong to at least four distinct racial groups. They speak 325 different languages and practise more than seven religions (sometimes two or more at the same time). Each area of India has its own distinct culture, and Uttar Pradesh is as different from Tamil Nadu as Finland is from Italy.

Jawaharlal Nehru, the first prime minister of independent India, said that the outward and infinite variety among Indians belied the tremendous oneness. This 'oneness' is hard to recognise in the face of so much diversity, with so much going on, at so many different levels.

India has 25 states and seven union territories, each has its own language, dress, religious rituals, arts and crafts, and food. According to the *Kama Sutra*, a 7th century manual on the science of love, even sexual preferences vary from place to place: 'The women of the central countries dislike pressing the nails and biting, the women of Aparitika are full of passion, and make slowly the sound, "Seeth" …'

As a first-time visitor to India, you begin by noticing the differences between India and your home country. Then you begin to notice the way that one part of India is different from another part: the dress, language, food and customs change as you move across the country. As you stay longer, you become aware of the more subtle markers that distinguish people of the same geographical region, but of different castes and social classes. More time and experience reveal that there are some levels—the most traditional, for example—that may never be fully accessible to you. The lesson that the wise visitor learns is that these hierarchies exist and that they account for the multiplicity of India that confuses, contradicts and defies easy definition.

As you slowly awaken to the complexities of just one place, you may even get the feeling that the longer you stay, the less you know. Don't worry. This is the beginning of the real awareness about India. Now you will be able to sift through the confusion of preconceptions and hasty generalisations and find more accurate and useful perceptions.

I fell in love with India on that trip, and since then, I have been back many times, to visit, to live, to work and to study. In some ways, India has changed immensely since 1970 when I was 16. Bombay is now Mumbai, and Trichy is chock-a-block with big buildings. The airport is air-conditioned, and that wall of hot, humid air won't hit you the instant you get off the plane. There are free luggage carts so you don't have to hassle with porters. At international airports at least, you will find a convenient pre-paid taxi service: you pay according to your destination at a clearly marked counter just as you exit with your baggage. From there, you are escorted without haggling to a taxi. Now there are many more models of cars on the road, Ford Escorts, Tata Sumos, zippy little Xings and battery-operated Revas.

But that taxi may be the same rounded shape, may even be the same taxi, because the Ambassador is a sturdy car which can be repaired and repaired and repaired, and therefore continues to be popular for taxi service. The driving is still hair-raising on occasion, but now there is too much traffic on big-city roads for the driver to pull a stunt like the one I described. The sidewalk still needs to be navigated carefully. The last time I checked, the ear cleaner still has a steady clientele And somewhere, sometime, a young boy will want to practise his English with you.

AN OVERVIEW

'She was like some ancient palimpsest on which layer upon layer of thought and reverie had been inscribed, and yet no succeeding layer had completely hidden or erased what had been written previously. All of these existed in our conscious or subconscious selves, though we may not have been aware of them, and they had gone to build up the complex and mysterious personality of India...'
—Jawaharlal Nehru

THE LAND

India has the world's greatest mountain range, wettest city and longest beach. Indians personify the country as a goddess: her head is crowned by the mighty Himalayas, her two arms outstretched reach from Pakistan to Bangladesh, her life-giving bosom is the fertile Indo-Gangetic plain, and her feet are lapped by the waves of the Indian Ocean. This is Bharat Mata—Mother India.

To the north, Jammu and Kashmir, Himachal Pradesh, Sikkim, and the northern part of Uttar Pradesh lie along the Himalaya-Karkoram mountain ranges, which form a natural border separating India and China. The icy winds from the Tibetan plateau cannot penetrate this mountain wall, and fertile valleys such as Kulu, the Vale of Kashmir, and Zanskar lie protected between the icy slopes. The rain-laden clouds of the south-western monsoon are contained by the Himalayas, turned back, and forced to drop their moisture over the Gangetic plain. Five million hectares of eternal snow are the source for the three great river systems that sustain the Indian heartland.

The great northern plains are in stark contrast to the mountain regions. They extend with uniform flatness from Assam and the Bay of Bengal all the way to the Afghan border. The states of Punjab, Haryana, Uttar Pradesh, Bihar and West Bengal, formed by the basins of the Indus, Ganges, and Brahmaputra rivers, are home to almost half of the Indian population, making it one of the most densely populated areas of the world.

The Great Indian Desert, or Thar Desert, covers the westernmost parts of Gujarat and Rajasthan. Here, there is so little surface water and such scant rainfall that there are children aged seven who have never seen rain. The Deccan, separated from the Indo-Gangetic plain by hills, escarpments and rocky valleys, is a series of plateaus bounded by the Eastern and Western Ghats. The Ghats are low-lying rounded hills that run parallel to both east and west coasts to meet near the Nilgiri Hills in the South.

CLIMATE

While people in Delhi are suffering from the blistering heat of summer, Keralites are being lashed by the first monsoon rains and Kashmiris are waiting for the snows to melt in the mountain passes. India's climate ranges from sub-freezing Himalayan winters with ice and snow to year-round tropical heat and humidity; from 70 cm (27.6 inches) of rain in a single day to 10 cm (3.9 inches) in a year.

Within these extremes, it is possible to distinguish four seasons. In the dry, unrelenting heat of summer from March to May, temperatures in the plains climb to 45°C (113°F) and a hot wind, called the *loo*, raises dust storms. Tempers ignite easily and murder and suicide rates go up. Relief comes only when the first drops of the monsoon rains sizzle on the hot earth. Farmers all over the country wait anxiously for the arrival of the south-western monsoon, which advances across India sometime between June and September. It is the rain, not the temperature, that determines whether there will be good harvest or famine, flood or drought.

The retracting monsoon brings humid, sticky weather from mid-September to November, relieved by the relatively cold and dry weather from December to February, when most of India is at its best. The nights are cold in Delhi and the northern cities, but the days are sunny and pleasant. In the far north, there is snow. In the south, the temperatures can be described as less hot, if not exactly cool.

WILD INDIA

The billion human Indians share the subcontinent with 500 other species of mammals, 2,100 species of birds and 30,000 species of insects, as well as numerous varieties of fish, 500 types of amphibians and reptiles and 15,000 species of plants.

Deer, bears, raccoons and flying foxes roam in the eastern Himalayas. On the plains just below, around Assam and North Bengal, the elephant and single-horned rhino are to be found. The Gir forests of Gujarat have the yellow-maned Indian lions. The dry scrub forests of Ranthambhor hide the tiger. Jerdon's double-branded courser, a bird presumed extinct for nearly 80 years, was seen again recently in the Deccan grasslands. In the south, thick deciduous forests hide the lemur, the sloth bear and the laughing hyena. Kerala's rainforest is home to hundreds of varieties of butterflies, as well as snakes and birds. In the Thar desert, wild asses still roam, and the great Indian bustard walks the sands. They share the harsh terrain with some forty reptile species.

LANGUAGES

The Constitution lists 15 official Indian languages: Hindi, Urdu, Bengali, Marathi, Gujarathi, Oriya, Assamese, Punjabi, Kashmiri, Tamil, Telugu, Karnataka, Malayalam, Sindhi and Sanskrit. English is also an official language.

Sanskrit, the ancient language of priests and poets, forms the matrix for the Indo-Aryan languages of the north, such as Hindi. The Dravidian languages of the south, such as Tamil, are based on a totally different language, despite Sanskritised elements in the vocabulary. As the names of the languages indicate, the country is divided into states on a linguistic basis: in Bengal, Bengali is spoken; in Punjab, Punjabi is spoken, and so on. But since people do move around to work or study, Indians are exposed to many languages in their daily life, and grow up to speak three or more without thinking it a great accomplishment.

English functions as a neutral link-language between Indians

Hindi is being promoted as a national language, but it is useless in South India, where there is often violent opposition to its use.

from different parts of the country. Most educated Indians speak excellent, if sometimes highly individualistic, English; and there is now an extensive literature by Indians writing in English. Contact with India has enriched the English language itself by several thousand words, including bangle, calico, dinghy and juggernaut.

ECONOMY

The currency is the rupee, which consists of 100 paise. The rupee was non-convertible into foreign currency until 1992; it was made partially convertible by the Narasimha Rao government.

India's major imports are petroleum, electrical machinery, food and edible oils, precious stones, iron and steel and fertiliser. It exports gems and jewellery, textiles and garments, engineering goods, tea, iron ore, and leather and leather goods.

More recently, India has added software engineers to the list. During the information technology boom of the late 1990s, an estimated 30 per cent of software engineers in Silicon Valley in the United States were of Indian origin. Major software companies such as Microsoft, Oracle and Toshiba set up offices in Hyderabad and Bangalore, to tap into the highly trained population. With the slowdown of the American economy, many engineers have returned and have further advanced India's technological expertise. Foreign companies are also investing more in India, riding on the wave of one of the world's fastest-growing economies.

HISTORY

A five-star hotel in Delhi has an excellent view on one side of the slum below. A woman makes *chapathis*, a thin unleavened bread, over a clay stove, burning dried cow dung cakes as fuel. Children play a game with sticks. A man squats, utterly relaxed, rocking on his heels, knees at his ears, smoking a *beedi*, a mini-cigarillo.

Reframe the picture: exclude the bluish glow from the TV set, part of life even in the slums, and this could be India in any century. Indian history does not confine itself to the pages of a book. Two thousand years is the distance an Indian travels while doing nothing more than the ritual morning ablutions and then driving to work.

A sense of the forces that shaped Indian history will help you to understand ideas and conflicts that exist even today. At the very least, references in conversation to the great moments or people of history will not leave you completely in the dark.

In the Beginning

The most extensive early Indian civilisation was the Harappa civilisation, which developed along the Indus River valley, in what is now Punjab, northern Rajasthan, and Kathiawar in north-western India. Archaeological remains from the two cities Mohenjodaro and Harappa reveal a civilisation marked by its attention to the utilitarian: organised garbage collection, two-storied brick houses, public and private baths, a drainage system, well-planned streets, granaries, cotton textiles, and metal implements and weapons.

This early civilisation was probably peopled by a prosperous merchant community that traded with people of the Persian Gulf, Mesopotamia and Egypt. The Harappa people worshipped aspects of nature that symbolised fertility—the bull, the tree, the mother goddess. They are still important in Hinduism.

Today, at little roadside stalls, or at the railway station, tea is served in small, unglazed clay cups used just once then thrown away. Indians everywhere bathe by pouring water from a pot over themselves. Harappa excavations indicate the same bathing habits, and pottery shards can be pieced together to form the same kind of clay cups—then, as now, discarded after use.

The Aryans and the Vedic Period

Harappa culture flourished around 2300 BC. By 1700 BC it had declined, no one knows why, making way for the migration of the Aryans about 1500 BC. The Aryans were cattle-breeders searching for new pastures who settled and cultivated the land.

Agriculture led to trade, trade to other occupations—carpentry, metalwork, pottery, tannery, weaving. At first, there were three social classes—warriors or aristocracy, priests and common people. Kings were primarily military leaders, and only later were perceived as possessing divine power, which then became hereditary.

The Aryans' early religion involved sacrifice. Priests offered sacrifices to the gods and goddesses of nature, and each was propitiated by prescribed ritual actions. At dawn or at dusk, you may see men facing the sun, reciting Sanksrit words and pouring water from cupped hands. This is the *gayatri* mantra, directed to the sun, still chanted by devout Hindus as part of a ritual that has remained meaningful for 3,000 years.

The Aryans contributed so much to Indian culture that the Vedic period (1500–600 BC) is regarded as a golden age when gods walked the earth and communicated with men. The four Vedas (*veda* means knowledge)—Rg, Yajur, Sama and Atharva—composed at this time are a collection of hymns and ritual texts. They are the foundation for the Brahminical

This was the time the hymns of the Rg Veda were collected and written down. Once part of the oral tradition, these 1,028 hymns to the gods of the Aryans are the first composition in any Indo-European language.

tradition of Hindu thought. The philosophical speculation of later texts like the *Upanishads*, the Sanskrit language, the caste system that furthered the dominance of Brahmins, various gods of the Hindu pantheon, the rituals of sacrifice—all these evolved from this time and continue to be relevant today.

Alexander

In 327 BC, Alexander of Macedon entered the Indian provinces. After some initial success, he encountered enough resistance from a tribal chief to deter him from advancing towards the heart of India. Although Alexander's campaign in north-west India lasted only two years, he had overthrown and consolidated the small kingdoms and republics of the north-west. His departure left a political vacuum.

The Mauryans

Chandragupta Maurya and his wily advisor, the Brahmin Kautilya, moved quickly to exploit that vacuum, and established an empire that covered the Indus and Ganges plains and extended as far north as Afghanistan. Bold and unscrupulous, Kautilya, who wrote *Artha Shastra* (*The Science of Government*), has been called the Indian Machiavelli.

Chandragupta's son extended Mauryan control to the south as far as Mysore. When his grandson Asoka came to power in 273 BC, only the eastern kingdom of Kalinga (present-day Orissa) still resisted. Asoka conquered Kalinga after a terrible slaughter. At the height of victory, moved by the destruction caused by war, the king renounced warfare and converted to Buddhism.

Asoka's 37 years of benevolent rule established the largest area under one rule in India until the British arrived. He erected pillars where crowds were likely to gather, inscribed with proclamations explaining the idea of *dhamma*, the universal law. Asoka's legacy is the concept of moral and social responsibility, not only to human beings, but also to animals and plants. His decrees creating sanctuaries for wild animals and identifying certain species of trees for protection may be the earliest example of environmental action by a government. The lion pillar of Asoka survives as the official emblem of the Republic of India, and is found on every Indian coin and currency note.

Indo-Greeks and Trade Links

After Asoka's death in 232 BC, the empire fell apart into many kingdoms. The Greeks appeared again, and Menander, the best known of the so-called Indo-Greek kings, expanded their power into the Punjab from 155 to 130 BC. This resulted in greater contact between India and the Mediterranean world. There are references to India in Pliny the Elder's *Natural History*, and Ptolemy's *Geography*. Changing political fortunes in succeeding centuries served to establish varied links between north and south, east and west, which advanced trade and commerce throughout the subcontinent.

South India

South India had its own upheavals, with warring states usurping power from each other over several centuries. The exploits of the warring kings of the Chera, Chola and Pandya dynasties (the Pandyan kingdom dates back to the 2nd century BC) are celebrated in the poems and heroic ballads of the Sangam anthologies, the earliest surviving Tamil literature.

The Pandya kingdom, according to one record was founded by the daughter of Herakles, with the help of an army of 500 elephants, 4,000 cavalry and 13,000 infantry. Early Tamil literature describes Roman ships. Trade with India drained the Roman economy of 550 million sesterces each year. India exported copper, sandalwood, teak, ebony, spices, turquoise, lapis-lazuli, muslin, silk yarn and indigo. Two other well-known Indian exports were chess (to Persia) and Buddhism (to China).

The Guptas

The next long period of dynastic rule came with the Guptas in North India, from the 4th to the 6th century AD. Kings with glorious names—Sun of Prowess, Great King of Kings, Supreme Lord—established themselves by conquest, forming military alliances and marriage alliances between ruling families.

Literature and the arts flourished under royal patronage. Kalidasa, regarded as the finest writer of classical Sanskrit, was a member of the court of Chandra Gupta II. Institutions of learning existed, with subjects like rhetoric, metaphysics and medicine, and veterinary science (mainly about horses and elephants, animals important to the army).

In AD 499, the Indian astronomer Aryabhata calculated pi to 3.1416 and the length of the solar year to 365.3586805 days. Hinduism developed in ways that define it today: concepts of caste purity and pollution, the lowered status of women, and the worship of god through *bhakti* (devotion).

The Moghuls

North India had been invaded by the Greeks, Scythians, Parthians and Huns, and had managed to assimilate these successive waves of alien influx. The Muslim invasions were different in the sense that they forced confrontation, not compromise.

First the Turks and Afghans, then the Mongol Taimur, living up to the title 'Ghazi' (killer of infidels), raided and plundered the northern plains. Before the Moghuls arrived in the 16th century, power was traded back and forth among Muslim invaders and Hindu chiefs. The Hindus were at a disadvantage in war. Their rivalries separated them, their caste system allowed only *kshatriyas* to take up arms, and they battled with elephants and foot-soldiers against the more effective Muslim archers fighting on horseback.

Islamic influences in the south were more smoothly assimilated; from the 8th century, Arabs had been settling on the Malabar coast; trade was their objective, not political power. When the Delhi sultanate tried to extend its power into the south, it was initially repelled.

The great Moghul emperors had grand opera personalities, and they ruled with conviction and brilliance for six generations. Their lives have passed into legend: Babar prayed to God to take his life in exchange for his son's; Humayun, more scholar than king, cracked his skull falling down the stairs of his library on hearing the call to prayer; Akbar created himself as the semi-divine head of a new religion; Jehangir acquired the beautiful Nur Jehan after murdering her husband; Shah Jehan built the Taj Mahal in memory of his favourite queen, Mumtaz, who died giving birth to their 14th child; and the devout Aurangzeb stitched caps to pay for his own shroud.

By the 17th century, Aurangzeb's word was honoured throughout India, but even then the Moghuls had to contend with the guerilla tactics of the Marathas, the hardy people of the Western Ghats. Led by the wily Shivaji, who united both Brahmins and Sudras, the Marathas weakened the Moghul empire and hastened its eventual disintegration.

The Moghuls had never managed to unite the country. With the exception of Akbar, they treated their empire as a Muslim state and Hindus as second-class citizens; the Hindus had no interest in protecting the kingdom. Martial groups like the Sikhs, the Jats and the Rajputs openly revolted, and the end of the 17th century saw the collapse of the Moghul empire.

In the architectural remains in and near Delhi, the fusion of Muslim and Hindu architectural forms illustrates best the nature of the greater relationship between the two cultures: despite the edicts of priests and mullahs who struggled to keep both sides separate, a synthesis of two cultures was created at many levels. The Islamic dome and the Hindu arch, Islamic simplicity and Hindu decorative exuberance, combined to create monuments of that period, including the Qutub Minar, the mosque in Ajmer, and the tombs of the Lodhis.

The effects of 200 years of Moghul rule in North India are still seen today, in the language, literature, painting, music, architecture, and even in the way Hinduism is practised. Their monuments dot the countryside; renowned musicians of Hindustani music have names like Ali Akbar Khan and Vilayat Khan; the Sikh religion takes its form today as a reaction to Moghul rule; the Sufi saints influenced the *bhakti* movements in Hinduism.

British India

The British used Indians and Indian financial resources to conquer India. As the politician Mohammed Ali wryly put it, "It is the old maxim of divide and rule. But there is division of labour. We divide and you rule." The British didn't create the disunity; they merely used it to further their own ends.

They manoeuvred warring Indian princes and chiefs, who, each with only his own interests in mind, eagerly accepted British help to defeat their rivals. The peasants, with nothing at stake, watched with apathy as power changed hands.

The British intruded at the highest level, just as the Moghuls had done before them, but not as a government. They were a commercial organisation (the East India Company). At first, trade, not territory, was the aim. They interfered politically only when their commercial interests were threatened. Then, the combination of political and commercial interests, unrestrained by any motive other than profit, created a climate of corruption, private trade and profiteering.

Initially, British policy was to establish a regime, but interfere as little as possible in the people's way of life. But disinterest did not survive the colonial assumptions of moral and cultural superiority. The new doctrine promoted Western civilisation through the system of education, Christian proselytising, Western techniques and instruments, and especially through the English language.

Sati, the ritual burning of the widow on her husband's funeral pyre, and *thuggee*, ritual murder and robbery, were abolished. English replaced Persian as the official language. The British introduced their own legal systems and procedures. They created a network of roads, canals and railroads, and trained Indians to build and run them. Schools, colleges and universities were developed for 'imparting to the native population knowledge of English literature and science through the medium of the English language'.

At the time the British arrived, India had a strong mercantile capitalist economy. It was a major manufacturer of goods and traded with West Asia, Arabia, South-east Asia, and only incidentally with Europe. British rule restructured the Indian economy to serve British interests: India supplied, at no charge, a large military force to protect British interests around the world, was forced to buy 60 per cent of its imports from Britain (becoming the largest single market for British exports), and helped Britain balance her international trade books by using India's surplus from exports to other parts of the world.

The British dismantled many of the indigenous court, military and religious centres, reducing literacy, freezing fairly fluid social structures and forcing people out of the urban centres and back to peasant life. The British took an even larger share of the resources from labour without reinvesting more than a tiny fraction of the profits.

What the British did do for India, that survives to this day, was to create a bureaucracy that is large, comprehensive and unwieldy. Although it has its drawbacks, it is the machinery of the Indian Administrative Service, and other bureaucratic institutions modelled on British ones, that holds India together. The slow, reluctant movement of the huge bureaucratic structure, created to cement British rule, continued to contain the volatile flashes in one area even decades after independence.

A Change of British Policy

The military mutiny of 1857 started over cartridges rumoured to be greased with cow's and pig's fat (abhorrent to Hindus and Muslims). It turned into a series of loosely connected uprisings in northern and central India that lasted 14 months and involved bitter fighting and savage reprisals.

Although there were brilliant Indian leaders, such as the legendary Rajput queen, the Rani of Jhansi, the mutiny failed for lack of direction. When the British government reacted to the mutiny by buying out the East India Company in 1858, the purchase price was added to the public debt of India. The ultimate irony—India itself paid the cost of becoming a Crown Colony!

The mutiny shook the British into realising that their policy of Westernisation could not be pursued with complete insensitivity to Indian opinion. The Indians realised that the West was here to stay, and the future depended on their own ability to accept and absorb this influence.

The British continued to build. By 1900, India's railway system was the best in Asia, and canals and irrigation systems gave farmers some protection from the caprices of the monsoon. But the British resigned themselves to what they perceived as the changeless, backward-looking nature of Indian society. At the same time, a new rising English-speaking middle-class, eager for change, embraced Western ideas and knowledge with fresh enthusiasm.

Nationalism and Independence

The idea of creating one nation of equal citizens developed out of this interaction of Indian and Western cultures. Western concepts of democracy and liberalism awakened the newly influential middle-class to a growing concern over India's economic backwardness and wretched poverty, the inhumane treatment of untouchables, the persistent injustices of the caste system, as well as to their own treatment as second-class citizens by the same Westerners who espoused ideas of freedom and equality.

The secular nature of British influence made it possible for Indians to question their own moral and religious assumptions without the threat of being taken over by a new religion. This kind of questioning paved the way for the challenge of Mohandas Karamchand Gandhi, and his rethinking of the Hindu religion.

Mahatma Gandhi

Mahatma (meaning 'great soul') Gandhi forged a movement out of old ideas put to work in an entirely new direction. He shaped the Jain philosophy of *ahimsa* (non-violence) into a force for political action that undermined the British administration far more effectively than any armed uprising could have done. *Satya*, or truth, pursued without violence, is *satyagraha*. It is irresistible. The most unreasonable and adamant of opponents would have to give way when confronted with the forces of justice and truth.

The ascetic Hindu pattern of vows and fasting that Gandhi undertook to emphasise his position were more moving and eloquent than arguments. He

When Gandhi visited England, after he had become famous for his revolutionary political ideas, despite the cold he wore his usual *khadi* cloth wrapped and tucked just as he did in India. Winston Churchill found the spectacle 'nauseating and humiliating' and called him a 'seditious, half-naked fakir'. It seems that a reporter asked him, "What do you think of Western civilization?" He replied, "I think it is an idea worth trying."

removed his sacred thread, the mark of his twice-born status, and wore not the saffron robes of the Hindu ascetic, but the plain white homespun cloth wrapped between his legs like any Indian peasant. Such gestures brought his nationalist movement the grassroots support that broke through the barriers of regional, caste and religious differences in a united front against a foreign power.

While Gandhi identified himself with the simple, illiterate villager at the bottom of Indian society, the rising star of the Indian Congress Party, Jawaharlal Nehru, was a well-dressed sophisticated man of the world. Despite differences of opinion, they remained as close as brothers, and together they gave charismatic and far-sighted leadership to the independence movement. Both recognised that there were valuable aspects to British rule, and during crises they were able to rise above the interests of their own groups and effect reconciliation and compromise with both the Muslims and the British.

Partition

Lord Louis Mountbatten, appointed Viceroy of India to oversee the final phase in handing over power, was determined to carry it through quickly and decisively. The Muslim League, headed by Mohammed Ali Jinnah, demanded a separate Muslim state, offering a choice between Pakistan or chaos. Gandhi opposed partition; Nehru and the other leaders of the Congress Party finally accepted it as inevitable. Once over that hurdle, the speed of events accelerated for the British withdrawal.

Just before midnight on 14 August 1947, at the moment of independence, Nehru said, "Long years ago, we made a tryst with destiny, and now the time comes when we shall redeem our pledge, not wholly or in full measure, but very substantially. At the stroke of midnight hour, when the world sleeps, India will awake to life and freedom. A moment comes, which comes but rarely in history, when we step out from the old to the new, when an age ends and when the soul of a nation, long suppressed, finds utterance ..."

Opinions differ as to whether it was the hasty withdrawal of the British, after following a policy of divide and rule, that pitted Hindu against Muslim, or the intransigent attitude of the Muslim, or the Congress Party's overconfidence. Pakistan was torn out of the Indian subcontinent amidst bloody communal riots and a wrenching mass migration of more than five million people moving in opposite directions, Hindus from Pakistan for India and Muslims from India for Pakistan. People abandoned home and land and belongings, families were split up, and terrible atrocities were committed by both sides. By conservative estimates, 500,000 people died.

The drama of independence continued with another tragic note. On 30 January 1948, on his way to a daily prayer meeting, Mahatma Gandhi was assassinated—shot at close range by a young Hindu fanatic, who touched his feet first in the Hindu gesture of respect.

Balancing Act

Jawaharlal Nehru, India's first prime minister, was a brilliant and magnetic man with great personal integrity. Despite his aristocratic background, Western outlook, and strictly secular attitudes, he could command the support of peasants, orthodox Hindus and intellectuals alike. He was deeply committed to democracy, socialism, and the eradication of poverty, and determined to drag India into the 20th century. Nehru's policies led him to walk two political tightropes, starting a balancing act that has brought India to the position it is in today, economically and politically.

One was his policy of nonalignment that put India between America and Russia, suspected by both sides, and often playing one against the other. The West accused Nehru of being too close to the communists, and the Russians felt India was falling into the capitalist trap. But India got aid from both.

The other tightrope was his domestic policy. In his attempts to industrialise India, Nehru tried to balance the interests of a small, educated urban section against those of the rural masses. To do this, he had to go directly against

Gandhi's ideal of village level government loosely joined in a non-industrialised economy. Nevertheless, his policies were based on peasant interests. He believed that only the introduction of modern mechanised industry would win the war against poverty. He had to convince both sides that he wasn't selling out one to the other.

When Indira Gandhi, Nehru's daughter, came to power, she continued with his policies. She annoyed the aid-giving countries by acting like a superpower instead of a developing nation. She not only built a powerful military, but encouraged ambitious space programmes. For some, the final blow came when India exploded a nuclear device. Her economic policies in the 1970s and 1980s led to the influx of rural masses into the cities.

Just one example of the misguided use of government funds was the beautification of New Delhi for prestigious international events like the Asian Games, and the summits of the Commonwealth countries and the Non-Aligned Movement. Slum dwellers and cows were cleared from streets and trucked out to rural areas. Not only did they all trickle back, more came, brought in by contractors hired by the government with taxpayers' money to build the flyovers and work on beautifying New Delhi. They all stayed on.

Rajiv Gandhi, Indira's son, took over after her assassination. Before becoming prime minister, he was a pilot. Educated in the West and married to an Italian, he was enamoured of technology and had no connection to the masses of India. Even his stilted, accented Hindi alienated them. Rajiv Gandhi tried to step up the pace of industrialisation. His political career also ended in his assassination.

POLITICS TODAY

With the growth of films, television and advertising, the magnetism of the cities has increased. As the rural population gets poorer because of population growth, there is little the countryside can offer to keep its people there. Trucking them out is now impossible, and most big Indian cities are sinking under the weight of these people.

The loss of domestic balance was aggravated by the loss of international balance. The end of the cold war also ended India's leverage for international aid. India was forced to play by the rules of donor organisations like the World Bank, International Monetary Fund, and Asian Development Bank. Narasimha Rao's government had little choice but to accelerate industrialisation. Revolutionary (for India) economic reforms were introduced in 1991 to restructure the private sector and attract foreign investment. The rupee was sharply devalued and bureaucratic red tape was slashed.

From Indian independence until the collapse of Narasimha Rao's government, the Congress party survived as the only political party with a national presence. It lost power for only two brief periods: for three years after Indira Gandhi declared a State of Emergency and suspended civil rights in 1977, when a coalition government took over, and from November 1989 for 11 months, when another coalition headed by V P Singh was in power.

But the problems that divided India for centuries have not gone away. The radical change from Nehru's Indian-style socialism created a fertile ground for the divisive politics of the Hindu revivalist movement. In the 1990s, the opposition Hindu-chauvinist Bharatiya Janata Party (BJP) began to gather a national following and challenge the Congress Party. One short-lived coalition government followed another, with no party claiming an absolute majority. The Congress Party could no longer offer a unifying national perspective. In desperation, they turned to Sonia Gandhi, Rajiv's widow, an Italian, for no one else could provide charismatic, viable leadership. The BJP-led coalition, headed by Vajpayee, became notorious when India exploded nuclear devices in May 1998. The Indians took criticism from developed nations as one more sign of their reluctance to recognise India for what it is: the largest democracy, fifth largest economy and seventh largest country in the world.

Despite political changes, the economic policies set in motion by Narasimha Rao continue to shape modern India. While the transformation of villages is gradual, in the cities, the

Decades-old disagreement over Kashmir with neighbour Pakistan continues to simmer. India has fought Pakistan three times since 1947, twice over Kashmir. Both nuclear-armed nations, they came close to a fourth war in 2002, after a deadly attack on India's parliament by Muslim separatist guerillas the year before.

Multi-national companies now have a presence in India.

changes are glaringly visible—billboards advertising Coca Cola, Citibank, Ford and other international companies now dot the urban landscape. Globalisation looks a lot like Westernisation to some. Perhaps it is in response to this that Indians have sought to assert their 'Indianness'. After having survived to celebrate 50 years of independence, India is finally joining the world economy, but the struggles and conflicts are not over.

RELIGIOUS BELIEFS

'Where does the Supreme Being dwell? In what village?
Pandit, tell his name ...'
—Kabir, the poet-saint revered by Hindus,
Muslims and Sikhs

The majority of Indians (more than 80 per cent) are Hindus. Buddhism, which was born here, has been absorbed into the Hindu world view in India, but maintains an identity and a position as one of the world's major religions outside India. Jainism and Sikhism have points of unity and divergence with Hinduism, and are highly visible and influential minority faiths. The Parsis came to India to escape religious prosecution, and have maintained their spiritual practices here unhampered. Islam came with the Moghul conquerors in the north, and with Arabic traders in the south. Christianity, for as long as it has existed as a religion, has existed in India.

In many parts of India the different religious groups have coexisted peacefully for generations. In other places, religious strife has been a recurring theme, and the trend in modern politics has been to aggravate, rather than ease, the tensions that arise out of strongly held, opposing beliefs. Despite the pockets of disharmony, India's reputation as a country of religious tolerance is well founded, for religious tolerance is built into the Hindu religion.

Two groups with very different belief systems and religious practices can live side by side without any problems. Hinduism does not demand that the whole society adopt one uniform set of religious beliefs and practices. But each group within that society has strict rules that must be followed; breaking those rules is not viewed lightly. Even a small transgression of the laws of the group can result in harsh penalties.

> A Hindu community and a Muslim community can live side by side for years without any problems. But should a rumour spread that a Hindu girl was molested by a Muslim boy (or vice versa), tolerance goes out the window, and Hindus or Muslims will commit just as many atrocities as their neighbours.

To better understand your Indian friends and acquaintances, it is necessary to know something of the religious beliefs they hold precious.

HINDUISM

On the banks of the sacred river Ganges in Varanasi, pilgrims sit and meditate; they immerse themselves in the holy water and swallow a handful while reciting Sanskrit verses. Thus they are cleansed of all their sins. A little further down, they squat to defecate; holy water serves the purpose for this cleansing as well. Whoever said of India that it is at the same time the most religious and the most immoral of societies knew that paradox is at the very heart of the Hindu religion.

It is impossible to generalise about a religion that embraces such varied and contradictory beliefs. Hinduism has grown like some gigantic banyan tree, with numerous spreading branches that put down their own roots, and yet remained, however tenuously, attached to the main trunk.

One branch is a primitive animism of spirits, demons and magic; another is the most profound philosophy of monism that sees the whole universe as one transcendent reality. A Hindu may worship a stone, a snake or a rat; god as a person or a person as god; one god or many; or no god at all. A Hindu may worship in a church or a mosque and be no less a Hindu, for no god of the Hindu pantheon would ever declare, "Thou shalt have no other God but me."

The essential spirit of Hinduism may be expressed as the consciousness of the oneness of all life. Gods and humans are subject to the same natural law of karma, the law of cause and effect none can escape. What we see as reality is the merest illusion, a game, a dream, or a dance. The universe goes through endless cyclical repetitions; one day of Brahma, the Supreme Being, is equivalent to 8,640 million years. At the end of one hundred of his years, the universe, including Brahma himself, dissolves, only to be born once again.

The Epics

Ethical teachings are inspired by the two great epics, the *Ramayana* and the *Mahabharata*. Both stories are about the unending conflict between *dharma* and *adharma*. *Dharma* is the law of one's inner being; a moral code, righteousness and duties and responsibilities according to one's nature. *Adharma* is simply to behave against one's *dharma*. This means that good and evil, right and wrong, truth and falsehood, are relative and not absolute terms. The *dharma* of a soldier is to kill, and not to do so would be *adharma*; but for a priest, to kill even an animal would be to go against his *dharma*.

The *Ramayana* and the *Mahabharata* transform the history of the early Indo-Aryan invaders into a vast and potent mythology of wars and strife. Composed over several hundred years, some two thousand years ago, they continue to be a living force for Indians today. When a modern version of the *Ramayana* was produced and televised over Doordashan (the national TV network) on Sunday mornings, life came to a standstill while everyone who could get near a TV set watched it. Buses made unscheduled stops and the journeys did not resume until the drivers had watched their *Ramayana*.

The mass gathering in front of the box was so predictable that Sikh terrorists planted a bomb at a television showroom, knowing that crowds would gather outside to watch the show on the TV sets displayed, even though the shop was closed. It exploded during the broadcast of the *Ramayana*, killing 20 people and injuring dozens of others.

The Ramayana

The 24,000 verses of the *Ramayana* tell the story of Rama, whose rightful place as heir to the throne of Ayodhya was conscripted for her own son by his father's third queen. Rama, his wife Sita and brother Lakshman live in exile in the forest. The demon king Ravana abducts Sita with the help of a golden deer, and Rama battles Ravana to get her back. With the help of the monkey god Hanuman, Rama succeeds. The demigod Rama is an ideal king, Sita exemplifies the qualities of a dutiful Hindu wife, and the *Ramayana* glories in an ideal world, where *dharma* triumphs.

The Mahabharata

The *Mahabharata* is eight times as long as the *Iliad* and the *Odyssey* put together, and 15 times longer than the Bible. It is said that whatever is found in these 100,000 verses can also be found elsewhere, but what is not found here cannot be found anywhere.

The *Mahabharata* is an epic vision of the human condition: it has intrigue, romance, duplicity, moral collapse, shady deals, dishonour, and lamentation. Here there are no ideal heroes. Most of the characters eventually die or are left dying, and victory has the taste of ashes and the smell of burning bodies on the battlefield.

This epic tells the story of the great war between the Pandavas and their cousins the Kauravas. The eldest of the five Pandava brothers, Yudhistira, loses his whole kingdom, his brothers, himself, and lastly, Draupadi, their joint wife, to

Dance, storytelling, theatre, puppetry—in fact all the classical and folk arts of India, use the *Ramayana* and *Mahabharata* for dramatic material, often in the regional languages. Peter Brooks' *Mahabharata* is only one recent interpretation of a work that has been retold countless times without losing any of its fascination.

the Kauravas in a game of dice. They are exiled to the forest for 14 years. At the end of this time, they can reclaim the kingdom. But Duryodhana, the power-hungry head of the Kauravas, refuses to relinquish the throne. The Pandavas and the Kauravas gather their forces to fight on the field of Kurukshetra. It is at this moment, when the two sides stand arraigned for battle, that the third Pandava brother Arjuna directs his chariot into the middle of the battlefield, and seeing relatives, teachers and friends on both sides, refuses to fight. His charioteer Krishna's arguments to remind Arjuna that, as a warrior, it is his duty to fight and kill the people he loves form the Bhagavad Gita, or Song of God.

The 700 verses of this philosophical poem stand alone; it is the best known of the Hindu religious books and is still immensely influential. Some leaders have used it to justify violence, others, like Gandhi, to justify non-violence. Complex and cunning, the Krishna of *Bhagavad Gita* reveals his meaning differently to each reader.

330 Million Gods

The kaleidoscope of exuberant technicolour gods and goddesses, many-headed, many-limbed and fantastical, is the vivid surface polytheism that obscures an underlying monism. They are merely the brilliant, endlessly multiplying refracted images of one transcendent being, called Brahma, Ishwara, or Mahashakti.

The scriptures say there are 330 million *devas* (gods), and one more or less hardly matters. Some are personifications of natural phenomena, evil forces, or even a disease; some are humans deified, or the local deities of town and village. They come into existence as the need for a personal divinity arises. Perhaps now the smallpox goddess will give way to the Aids goddess.

The gods appear as pairs, for the male aspect needs the female, his *shakti* (consort), to be complete. Each god and goddess also has a *vahana*, a creature considered the vehicle on which they ride. They also hold in their many arms the symbols of their power. These are the clues to recognising the deity.

Vishnu, Shiva and Ganesha

The most important gods are Vishnu and Shiva. Together with Brahma, they embody the cycle of Creation, Preservation and Destruction. Brahma the Creator is four-headed and carries a water-pot and a rosary in two of his four hands. His *shakti* is Saraswati, the goddess of knowledge, who rides on a swan, and holds the *veena*, a musical instrument.

Vishnu is often shown reclining on a many-headed serpent, with a lotus emerging from his navel. Or he is shown as one of his ten incarnations, taken to protect the world from the forces of *adharma*. As Rama, he is shown carrying the bow. His most popular manifestation, especially on calendars, is as Krishna, who is blue and plays the flute. Vishnu's consort is Lakshmi, the goddess of wealth. She is seated on a lotus between two elephants with their trunks raised above her. Their *vahana* is Garuda, a man-eagle.

Shiva has many representations, but the most beautiful is his form as the divine dancer, Nataraja. One leg is raised, the other is firmly planted on the head of the demon of confusion. One of his four hands assumes the gesture of protection, one points to the raised foot, one holds the drum that measures the beat of creation and the last holds the fire of dissolution. Shiva is worshipped in the sanctum of the temple known as the *lingam* (phallus).

Shiva's *shakti* is the powerful mother-goddess Devi, whose various forms have different names: Parvati, Gauri, Durga, and the most awesome and ferocious Kali. As Kali, she is black-skinned, her tongue drips blood, she wears a garland of human skulls, and carries a severed head in one hand. Hinduism glorifies the terrible power of the female, the

Three stripes and a Y- or U-shaped symbol, made with sandalwood paste, turmeric or holy ash, mark sects and castes and distinguish worshippers of Shiva (Shaivites) or Vishnu (Vaishnavites).

mysterious, dark, instinctive aspect of the omnipotent Mother, for she is 'the dispeller of the fear of time'.

The most widely worshipped god is Ganesha, the elephant-headed son of Shiva and Parvati. Even the gods must worship him before they assume any undertaking, for he is the remover of obstacles. A journey, performance, business venture, or any Hindu celebration or ritual, must begin with a prayer to Ganesha. He is depicted as dwarfish and potbellied, sometimes seated on his *vahana*, a rat. In one hand, he carries the rice balls he loves to eat; in the other he holds the broken-off piece of one of his tusks, with which, it is said, he inscribed the *Mahabharata*, exactly as the sage Vyasa dictated it.

Flower, Fruit, Leaf or Water

God may be worshipped as a stone, the roots of a plant, a piece of turmeric, a fissure in a rock, an anthill, or a tree stump. And Krishna says in the *Bhagavad Gita* that a flower, a fruit, a leaf or a handful of water offered with devotion will be accepted by God.

But the Hindu who wants all the trappings can have temples, rituals, and a host of intermediary priests, holy men and religious teachers. Most Hindus have both: an altar, simple or elaborate, somewhere in the house, where they perform their own daily *puja* (worship), and visits to the temple, where the priest performs the *puja*. Even in a temple, the ceremony may be no more than offering a flame before the deity, or it may last hours, involve recitation and music, and offerings of milk, honey and other expensive substances.

The ancient scriptures that prescribe the rules of worship say that five elements should come together: the pot containing water that represents the human body, the form of the deity, the flower or fruit or leaf that represents nature, the *mandala* or sacred pattern that encompasses the universe, and *mantra* or the sound that is the beginning of creation. The first four are optional, and worship may use one or all, but without *mantra*, the sacred words, to activate the ritual and imbue the other elements with life, any ritual or ceremony is useless.

Flowers and garlands sold by the roadside for sale to worshippers.

At the end of the *puja*, the worshipper takes the red powder, *kumkum*, and places a dot on the middle of the forehead. A married woman also places some in the parting of her hair. A widow is not supposed to wear the dot, or the *bindi*, on her forehead, only married women and women who have never been married are supposed to do so. But nowadays, the vast majority of variously coloured dots and drops on the foreheads of urban women are fashion statements, meant to coordinate with their saris. The *bindi* does not even mean that the woman wearing it is a Hindu.

SIKHISM

Guru Nanak (1469–1539), the founder of Sikhism, after three days of silent meditation, revealed, "There is no Hindu, there is no Muslim."

Sikhism began as a spiritual, monotheistic and ethical faith which called God simply *ikk*, meaning 'one'. But that message existed already in the philosophy of the Upanishads. What was new was Guru Nanak's concurrent awareness of the diseases of society, and his concern to find an effective cure. Although Guru Nanak may have been influenced by the *bhakti* saints and Sufi mystics, his message of love, faith and equality arose out of his own upright nature; he neither denied any religion nor mixed together opposing faiths. Rather, he rejected the division of people by reason of caste or religion and provided a way for his followers to break down those barriers.

Guru Nanak created a community from among those considered to be the lower professions—farmers, artisans and traders—who accepted his teaching and followed his practices. At the time of his death, he bypassed his own sons and chose from among his disciples, not a successor, but someone to whom he transferred his own special quality. Imagine one flame being lit by another, one spirit moving into a different body. The flame of Sikhism moved through ten bodies, the ten gurus, beginning with Guru Nanak and ending with Guru Gobind Singh. From the last guru, it passed into the Guru Granth, the Sacred Book, which is now its continuing visible manifestation.

The Sikh religion from the beginning tied spirituality to life in the real world, rather than to a path of renunciation. It developed a cohesive social outlook that needed only the catalyst of Islamic persecution to accelerate its politicisation. When the Moghul Emperor Jehangir had the fifth guru, Guru Arjun Singh, tortured and killed, the sixth guru garbed himself as a warrior for the ceremonies of succession, and from then on, taking up arms against injustice became a religious duty.

The martyrdom of the ninth guru in the cause of religious freedom led the tenth guru, Guru Gobind Singh, to create a martial order, the *Khalsa*, or God's Elect. The first five members who offered themselves at Guru Gobind's call, the Five Beloved, wore five physically distinguishing emblems to set themselves apart during Moghul tyranny, and to symbolise their purpose.

These five k's are the marks that give the Sikhs their visible separateness even today:

- *kesa*—hair that is uncut, like the hair of ascetics.
- *kangha*—the comb, for unlike the ascetics with their matted locks, Sikhs have not renounced the world, and keep their hair in order.

- *kara*—a steel bracelet, made of pure unalloyed metal, which symbolises their identity.
- *kachh*—the short breeches, as a mark of cleansing.
- *kirpan*—the sword, like that of a soldier, one who will not initiate violence but will not turn the other cheek.

Guru Nanak has been called the first Marxist, for the religion he founded is egalitarian. All men and women had equal status, and all could become priests. All decisions used to be made by the whole congregation in an open forum. Everyone was called *Sardar* (leader), so everyone was elevated to the same position. Even now, the priests and management of the temple are elected, everyone eats together in the community kitchen, and social and political actions are not separate from spiritual life. The casteism that exists in practice is not sanctioned by the religion. Women are educated and in theory, there is no hierarchical distinction between women and men.

The Sikh temple is called *gurudwara*. The *Guru Granth* is placed in the centre of its inner sanctuary. Ten per cent of a Sikh's earnings are to be given to the *gurudwara*. The *sangat* (gathering together of people) is an important part of religious

A Sikh *gurudwara*.

practice, for God is there among the people. Icons and empty rituals are rejected and the ceremonies and rites for birth, initiation, marriage and death are purposely kept simple.

Sikhs do not smoke or drink alcohol. Although the religion has no taboo against it, many Sikhs do not eat beef, and all other meat should be from animals killed by a single stroke. The traditional greeting is 'Sat sri akal'. The holy days for the Sikhs are the birthdays of the gurus—especially the first, Guru Nanak, and the last, Guru Gobind Singh—and Besakhi Day, which commemorates the initiation of the Five Beloved to the Khalsa on 30 March 1699. Orthodox Sikhs have no last name; all men are Singh and all women are Kaur.

Men and women who follow the traditions of Sikhism maintain their visible physical entity through the five k's, although the sword can now be just an outline etched into the comb. The men with their turbans and beards are so easily identifiable that in the carnage following Prime Minister Indira Gandhi's assassination by one of her Sikh bodyguards, innocent Sikhs could not hide from violent crowds without denying their faith. Not surprisingly, most did not cut their hair even then.

It is a source of pride to the Sikhs that throughout their history, their way of life has been worth fighting and dying for. Although 60 per cent of the population of Punjab, their homeland, is Sikh, they make up only about 2 per cent of the overall Indian population. The disproportionately high representation of Sikhs in the Indian armed forces, business, top management and politics is due in part to the forward-looking, non-exclusive and humanitarian nature of their religion.

ZOROASTRIANISM

Zoroastrianism, the religion of the Parsis, is one of the oldest religions in the world. It was founded by their prophet Zarathustra perhaps as early as 2000 BC, but no later than about 650 BC.

Zarathustra preached a doctrine of morality, monotheism and enquiry at a time when the prevailing forms of worship were sacrifices and rites to placate a multitude of gods. At one time, the religion spread across the Near and Middle East, but religious persecution by the followers of Islam and forcible conversion decimated its numbers and forced them to flee to India. The name Parsi is derived from 'Persia', from where they fled.

The motto of the religion—'Good thoughts, good words, good deeds'—insists upon an actively ethical stance towards other human beings. Their god Ahura Mazda is 'the most luminous of all luminous bodies' and 'clothed in the most glorious of all glorious lights, the sun'. Fire is the symbol of Ahura Mazda, and just as physical fire burns up refuse, but remains itself bright and pure, so the mind must burn up lies, and shine with asha, the truth. Truth and goodness among people strengthen Ahura Mazda in the struggle against Ahriman, the force of evil. The Fire Temple is the place of worship; the fire at the temple in Udvada, about a hundred miles from Bombay, where the sacred fire was brought by refugees from Persia, has been burning continuously since 1741.

Zarathustra rejected blind faith and emphasised freedom of choice. Thus a child of Parsi parents does not become a Zoroastrian until the ceremony of Navjote, or initiation, is performed. At that time, the child is given the sacred shirt, or *sudrei*, of pure white cotton, and the sacred thread, or *kushti*, of 72 strands of fine lamb's wool. The *sudrei* contains a tiny pocket to remind the wearer to offer up every night to God at least one square inch of goodness distilled from the activities of the day. The *kushti's* 72 strands represent the 72 chapters of the most sacred text, the *Yasha*. It is wrapped three times around the waist, as an injunction to think, say and do good, and as a protective barrier from the forces of evil.

The Parsi community, which consists of about 85,000 members, is concentrated in Bombay and Gujarat. This number is doomed to decline because of the hereditary

The Parsis venerate all the elements, and therefore neither bury (for that would pollute the earth) nor cremate (for that would pollute fire) their dead. Instead, the dead body is exposed on a platform in the Towers of Silence, where the vultures pick the bones clean in twenty minutes. After a few days, the bones are lowered into pits at the bottom, layered with charcoal, lime and other minerals, and slowly dissolve without desecrating the earth.

nature of the Parsi religion (only a child with two Parsi parents can become a Parsi) and its rules that bar Parsis marrying out of the faith from remaining Parsis. Parsis are to be found in the upper echelons of business, power and influence far out of proportion to their numbers, and two Parsi names have become household words: Tata and Godrej. They are among the largest industrial organisations in India, and have their name on everything from salt and soap to locks and trucks.

BUDDHISM

Buddha said, "Sorrow is everywhere; in man there is no abiding entity, in things no abiding reality." The truth that he preached was that suffering is the nature of life, desire is the cause of suffering, and that by following the Eightfold Path, one finds the way to end desires, and therefore, suffering.

It was foretold at Prince Gautama's birth, in 563 BC, that he would be either a great king or a great spiritual leader. In order that he might never know the urge to pursue a spiritual path, his father the king kept him from birth in a palace in which only the young and beautiful and healthy were allowed. He never saw, even at a distance, the realities of life. He married and lived happily for 13 years inside his artificial paradise.

One night, he forced his charioteer to take him out into the real world. He saw an old man for the first time, and was told by his charioteer that this was no exception, but the fate of every human being. Next, he saw a man wasted by disease, and learned that this, too, was not unique. He saw a corpse, and realised that he was living in a dream, for death would be his fate as well. Finally, he saw a *sannyasi*, an ascetic, deep in meditation, composed and serene. That very night, he left the palace while his wife and young son slept, and

In 1956, Dr Ambedkar, the great radical leader of the untouchables, or Dalits, more their spokesman than Gandhi, urged his followers to escape their enslavement as Hindus through a revival of Buddhism. He and half a million followers converted in a mass ceremony on 14 October 1956. Today, 3.5 million, or almost 92 per cent of the Buddhists in India, are converts from his followers, nearly all from the state of Maharashtra.

for the next six years embarked on the homeless life of a wandering ascetic. He examined, and rejected, all the schools of philosophy prevalent at the time. Ultimately, sitting under the Bo tree, in Bodh Gaya, Bihar, he realised the truth and became Buddha, the Enlightened One.

During the 45 years of his life, he took this message all over India, expressed in the common language of the people, and without any boring and complicated digressions into the metaphysical realms. He provided a serious threat to the supremacy of the Brahmins, for he attacked the injustice of the caste system, the ritualised worship of deities and sacrifice controlled by the priests, and the idea of pursuing one's own liberation by self-mortification without concern for the rest of society.

Buddhism appealed to the merchant class, who were economically, but not socially, powerful, and the lower castes, who were neither. It provided both groups the means to escape brahmanical oppression, by denying the usefulness of ceremonies and sacrifices and opting out of the caste system altogether. Although Buddhism has established itself as a separate religion throughout Asia, in India it has been chewed up, swallowed, and regurgitated by Hinduism, thereby diluting its message. Buddha, who denied the existence of God, has been added to the Hindu pantheon as an incarnation of the god Vishnu.

JAINISM

There is a Jain saying, 'He who lights fire, kills beings; he who puts it out, kills fire.' Non-violence or *ahimsa*, taken to the ultimate degree, characterises the strict practice of Jainism.

It goes without saying that a Jain must be vegetarian, but a strict Jain even avoids root vegetables, because bugs and earthworms are killed in their harvest, and yogurt, because the bacteria that culture the milk will be killed. Jains do not wear or use any leather products, and will not take up occupations like construction or farming, because small creatures will be killed in the digging of the soil. They avoid harsh words and insults, for these represent verbal violence.

At the time of its revival and reform around 500 BC, under the 24th prophet, Mahavira (22 of the prophets are mythical rather than historical), it was, like Buddhism, a source of empowerment for the lower castes. But unlike Buddhism, it could not be practised by farmers or leather craftspeople, who might harm creatures in their work, so it became an urban phenomenon, a response to the Brahmins from the merchant class. Jains came from the community of moneylenders, traders and middlemen.

Hinduism assimilated Jain ideas of ahimsa and vegetarianism, just as it assimilated parts of Buddhism. Except for the extra emphasis on absolute non-violence, the Jain religion today has few distinctive features that absolutely set it apart from Hinduism. Jainism includes the Hindu concepts of karma, *moksha*, reincarnation, and so on, as well as some Hindu gods and goddesses, and customs and ceremonies. Jains and Hindus may also intermarry.

Jains express their love for their fellow creatures by building and endowing various kinds of animal hospitals and shelters. There are shelters for old cows, a bird hospital opposite the Red Fort in Delhi, and even a home for insects in Ahmedabad; any stray insects that are brought there are sealed up in a small room with enough food to last their lifetime. The name Jain comes from *jina*, meaning 'one who has conquered the senses'. Even the Jain layman is supposed to evolve towards the practice of an almost monastic life, with prayers, fasting and vows of celibacy.

The life of a Jain monk is doubly rigorous. The two sects are the Digambara, or 'sky-clad', and Svetambara, or 'white-clad'. Digambara monks renounce everything not connected with the self; clothes are not connected with the self, therefore they go naked. Svetambara monks wear only white. They cover their mouths with gauze to avoid accidentally swallowing an insect, and their followers sweep the ground in front of their path so that they may not step on any insects.

The three and a half million Jains in India today, mainly in Gujarat and parts of Rajasthan and Uttar Pradesh, continue to work at non-violent commercial occupations. They are to be found in the upper-income brackets and are known for their many charitable trusts and institutions throughout the country. Jain temples are beautifully and intricately carved; before entering, visitors must leave anything made of leather outside, including wallets and belts. Despite their small numbers, they play an influential role in the economy and social life of India.

ISLAM

Islam is the largest minority religion in India, with more than 75 million followers (close to 10 per cent of the population), making India one of the largest Islamic nations in the world.

The first Muslims came to North India as invaders and to South India as traders, so the history of Islam is different in different parts of the country. In Kerala, for example, there is a large Muslim population, but religious conflicts are few, and the various religious communities have coexisted peacefully for centuries. In the north, the Arabs, Turks and Moghuls came as conquerors; they sometimes converted Hindus by force, destroyed Hindu temples, and imposed taxes and laws against Hindu customs. At one point, even the gesture of greeting, the namaskar, was banned. Old grudges and animosities have been passed on through generations, and can erupt unexpectedly with violence.

The parts of India that have come under Islamic rule have been profoundly influenced by Islamic culture, whether in food, architecture, music, dancing, social life, attitudes towards women, or dress. The attitude towards women has had a great impact on the areas of its influence. Although the Islamic holy book, the Koran, itself opposed female infanticide, protected women's rights in marriage, divorce and inheritance, and limited the polygamy of men (to four wives at any one time, and only if they could be taken care of and treated equally), the traditional Muslim attitude that now prevails is that women are the property of their husbands, unfit for learning, and a constant temptation to men if not restrained.

The custom of *purdah*, keeping women covered and away from the gaze of strange men, although followed by only about 15 per cent of women, had the effect of isolating women socially, psychologically and economically. Only a rich man could afford to keep women in this style, so *purdah* became a symbol of affluence and prestige, affecting the classes with the most influence on societal norms. Although women are no longer kept in strict seclusion, *purdah* as a concept has come to coincide so much with the traditional Hindu view of modesty that women in all strata of society are affected by it, and especially in the way that men and women relate to each other.

One has only to say, "There is no God but Allah, and Mohammed is his prophet" before an official of Islam to convert to Islam. The messages Prophet Mohammed received from God are recorded in the Koran. The sayings of Mohammed that did not come from God are collected in the Hadith, the second most important source of Islamic teachings.

A Muslim is obliged to perform *namaz* (ritual prayer) five times a day; undertake *roza* (ritual fasting) during the month of Ramadan; perform *zakat* (contribute a portion of income every year for mosque officials to distribute to various causes); and go on a *hajj* (pilgrimage to Mecca) at least once in a lifetime. Muslims do not eat pork and amphibians, and meat must be *halal* (ritually slaughtered). They are not supposed to drink alcohol. The Muslim holy day is Friday, when a special prayer is offered at the mosque.

During the month of Ramadan, Muslims who undertake the fast can only eat, drink, or smoke before dawn, which is defined as the time when there is enough light to distinguish between a white thread and a black thread. After dawn, they must pass the whole day without even drinking water until the light fades in the evening. Another important month is Muharram. Like Easter, it is observed rather than celebrated, for it marks the sombre occasion of the Prophet's grandson's death. Shia Muslims especially may have 12 days of prayers and singing in their homes.

The message of absolute monotheism and the unity of mankind as one family no doubt exercised a powerful appeal for the lower castes. The practices proscribed by Islam create the feeling of fraternity and equality before a just God, who rewards good deeds and punishes evil in the eternal life after death. A young Muslim, when questioned by V.S. Naipaul as to what his faith gives him, replied, "Brotherhood. Brotherhood in everything. Islam doesn't teach discrimination. It makes people help people. If a blind man is crossing the road, the Muslim doesn't stop to find out what creed he belongs to. He just helps."

CHRISTIANITY

India has one of the oldest traditions of Christianity in the world. It is believed that one of the disciples of Jesus, St Thomas of Syria, the one who initially doubted Christ's resurrection, sailed to India and landed at Malankara on the Kerala coast in AD 52. He converted several members of the high-caste Brahmins, established seven churches and even ordained priests—three hundred years before Christianity gained official recognition in Europe. According to the legend, St Thomas then went overland to the east coast, what is now Tamil Nadu, where he was martyred and buried.

Early members of the Syrian Christian community in Kerala were prominent in business and trading, and enjoyed an equal status with Hindus, perhaps because of their conversion from the high castes. In dress, language and customs, they made few concessions to Christianity, even continuing with such un-Christian practices as recognising untouchability. In Kerala today, they fit into the hierarchy like another caste, and marry within their own community, just as the Hindu sub-castes do.

Although only about 2.5 per cent of the overall population is Christian, they form a quarter of Kerala's population, a third of Goa's, and the majority in the easternmost states of Mizoram and Nagaland. Most of the recent converts come from the lower castes, but Christianity's ethical stance and practical application

When Vasco da Gama landed in Calicut in 1498, he told the Indians he met that he came to seek Christians and spices. The Portuguese were enthusiastic missionaries who left behind a large Catholic population in Goa. Later, French, Dutch and English missionaries rushed to save the souls of the idol-worshipping Indians. The humanism of the Christians, who protested against social injustices and set up hospitals, homes for lepers, and schools and colleges, attracted the Indian converts.

in philanthropic work has influenced even Hindu revival groups. Mother Theresa is only the latest Christian to have pricked the collective Indian conscience.

YOUR RELIGIOUS SENSITIVITY

The visitor should approach each situation with attention to religious affiliation, in order not to offend. A good Sikh is not going to appreciate a box of cigars or a bottle of aftershave. A Muslim may not be impressed with your gracefully executed *namaskar* and well-pronounced 'Namaste'. A Hindu is likely to feel the same aversion to your remarks about a delicious steak that you might feel if someone talked about eating dog.

On the other hand, Sikhs and Muslims are not supposed to drink, yet many of your Sikh or Muslim acquaintances do. Should you offer them a drink? It is pointless to offer sweeping generalisations for these and other situations. As long as you remain aware that religious taboos do exist, act as the circumstances appear to warrant. When in doubt, you will not offend if you ask an Indian for advice.

In Places of Worship

Temples, *gurudwaras*, mosques and churches are, first and foremost, places of worship. If they happen to also be places of interest to tourists, then it is up to the tourist to interfere as little as possible with their primary function. This means observing the rules of the religion. Some of these are clearly stated: that shoes must be removed, for example. Most Indian places of worship require this, including many Christian churches.

Some temples do not allow non-Hindus in at all, most notably the Jaganath Temple in Puri, Orissa. Some temples allow foreigners everywhere but in the sanctum sanctorum, the innermost heart of the temple where the deity is kept. Other temples allow foreigners even in there, where for a small donation you can have a *puja*, offer flowers, and come away with *kumkum* or sacred ash. In many temples, in South India especially, the priests will take you around and explain the shrines and ceremonies.

It is better to err on the side of conservatism in the matter of dress in the temple. Bare arms and legs may get comments; in a mosque and *gurudwara*, as well as in some churches, the head should also be covered. Non-Muslims will not be allowed into mosques at the times of worship, and women will not be allowed in certain areas. At a Jain temple, you must remove every bit of leather before entering, including belts, wallets and camera cases.

Some temples allow you to take photographs of everything except the interior of the sanctum sanctorum. You may have to pay for the privilege; this applies to both still and video cameras.

Children, or rather the normal high spirits of children, are usually not a problem in any situation unless their noise or behaviour is directly disrupting a ceremony. Small children will be forgiven almost everything.

Some ancient temples that are no longer in use as temples—that is, they don't have a priest and all the paraphernalia—are still considered sacred, and people may be doing their own personal worship. Such historical sites may, like the temples, require that you take your shoes off.

THE INDIANS

CHAPTER 3

'May all beings look on me with the eye of a friend;
may I look on all beings with the eye of a friend.
May we look on each other with the eye of a friend.'
—Yajur Veda

THE SIMPSONS, A HUGELY POPULAR ANIMATED TV SHOW, has an Indian character—Appu, owner of the Kwiki Mart. One episode involves Appu's arranged marriage: at first he tries to avoid it by pretending that he is already married, then when his overbearing mother makes clear it is inevitable, he goes through with it, and actually ends up liking it, behaving exactly like several of the real Indian men I know. Stereotypes become stereotypes for that very reason: they express a certain truth.

But the stereotype is never the whole story. Starting with the Beatles, the West has been exposed to a variety of Indian stereotypes with varying degrees of underlying truth. For example, from the way that *yoga* has proliferated in the West, you might get the impression that everyone in India does *yoga*. Not true, if by *yoga* you mean exercises on plastic mats wearing '*yoga* gear'. *Yoga* has a very different meaning and purpose here where it is often a part of one's daily religious practice.

In the West, 'Dharma' is a character in a sit-com, 'Samsara' is a perfume, and 'Nirvana' is a rock band. In India, these are words for important philosophical concepts. In this chapter, I try to get past the stereotypes, and closer to the underlying truth.

CHARACTERISTICS

A popular misconception is that all Indian women wear *saris*. Some do, but the *sari* is not the definitive word on Indian dress. Indian women wear many kinds of draped clothing, different kinds of pants and trousers, over-blouses, blouses, jackets, full, long skirts, fabrics that are woven, brocaded, embroidered, tie-dyed. It looks like a wonderful freedom and variety of dress at first; only later do you realise that an Indian woman's dress reveals her individual conformity. It is restricted by considerations of region, religion and caste.

Indians can see from the way a woman is dressed which part of India she comes from and therefore what language she speaks. Indians can make assumptions from that as to what she eats for breakfast. And once Indians know the woman's name, they are clued in on other assumptions. Of course, they may end up being wrong in some particulars, but this is the way Indians break through the jumble of people and recognise pieces of the jigsaw puzzle that is India.

This is only the beginning. As you read, you will realise that this theme keeps recurring: vast differences across the broad fabric of Indian society, but a surprising sameness within each little piece. It will take you some time to learn to recognise these clues yourself, and even a lifetime of travelling from one end of India to the other may not unravel all the secret codes. Even Indians from one part of India or from one strata of society may know very little about Indians in another part of India or from another social class. Nevertheless, this one casual observation of the way women dress shows you how much you can find out.

Take the woman wearing a draped costume, off-white, with a gold border. It looks like a *sari*, but is actually two separate pieces wrapped and draped over an underskirt and a blouse. This is the *mundu*, the dress from Kerala. The way the *mundu* is tied and its colour also tell us her religion and her caste. If the *mundu* had been white, instead of off-white, and had a little fan hanging out at the back, then there is a very good chance that the woman is not only from Kerala, but is a Syrian Christian. She would probably have eaten something different for breakfast than her neighbour with the gold-bordered *mundu*.

The woman, dark-skinned and small, with flowers in her hair, wearing a heavy silk *sari* with a contrasting border worked in gold is probably from Tamil Nadu. She wears the *sari* as it is universally understood, but even here there are many different ways to wrap it. Traditional Brahmin women wear a nine-yard *sari* instead of the usual six yards. Poor women wrap it without the underskirt that middle-class women wear.

Moving up the west coast, to Coorg in Karnataka, you find the women wear the *sari* so that it stretches tightly across the front, like a sheath, and then hangs down the back without any folds. On the eastern side, in Orissa, tribal women wear a short version of the *sari* that drapes just below the knee. There is a distinctive quality of silk, called *tussar*, made with the threads of wild silk cocoons.

In Maharashtra, some women also wear the nine-yard *sari*, but they have a way of wrapping it that brings one part

Modern young women wear a mix of ethnic styles.

through the legs, like loose pants, revealing the calves and outlining the hips. The fisherwomen of Bombay pull this part tight, which is very attractive. In Gujarat, the women wrap the *sari* so that the *pallav*, the more intricately worked part, drapes in pleats across the front rather than the back. Some Rajasthani women wear a skirt heavily embroidered and decorated with mirrors, with a bare-backed blouse. Many fabrics are covered in *bandnas*, or tie-dye designs. In Punjab, the women wear loose trousers and a long over-blouse called *salwar kameez*. The many styles of this across northern India include the full loose over-blouse worn in Kashmir, the fitted and tied versions found in parts of Uttar Pradesh, and the tight-fitting trousers reminiscent of the Moghul courts.

Concealing these visible clues of identification, the modern young Indian woman adapts and picks up little bits from one costume or another to create a stylish ethnic look. That, too, places her somewhere on the social and cultural map. Even the ubiquitous jeans and tee shirt will mark her.

How about the men? Take the man wearing a sarong-like lower garment, in a pattern of blue and green checks, with a shirt. He is most likely from Tamil Nadu. If you see him reach down, pick up the hem of the lower garment and give it a quick flip up, and then twist it at his waist, so that it is now above his knees, you can bet on it. The tall man with the full beard and a turban is a Sikh from Punjab. You even know his name from looking at him—he is sure to be Mr Singh. But be careful, there are other kinds of turbans (and Singhs, as you will see below). The man with the elaborately wound white turban, fine moustache, and a kind of draped lower garment pulled up between his legs is from Rajasthan. There are many kinds of turbans worn all over India.

Names

Although you do see many variations of dress even with the men, they have been quicker to switch to Western clothes, which makes them a little harder to figure out—until you know their names.

By now you know that all orthodox Sikhs are Singhs. But not all Singhs are Sikhs. There are Singhs in Uttar Pradesh,

Bihar (where they are usually from a land-owning caste), and Rajasthan (where they are from the high-caste royal families). Chatterjee, Banerjee and Mukherjee are from Bengal, and the names are high-caste ones. Bose, Ghose, and Gupta are also from Bengal, but from other castes. Mazumdar could be a Gujarati or a Bengali.

Kar and dey—Gavaskar, Ranadey—are typically Maharashtrian endings, the first high-caste, the second low-caste. Cherian, Kurien, and Jacob are all names from the Syrian Christian community of Kerala. Menon and Nair are Kerala Hindu names. Typical Tamil names are Srinivasan, Padmanabhan, and Krishnamachari. A name with many syllables is very likely to be from South India.

After reading all this, don't be surprised if every Indian you meet is a Sharma, Gupta or Malhotra. You move in certain circles, with Indians of a certain level, and in that circle, you will encounter surprising conformity. In this country of so many names, everyone seems to have the same name.

Indian Names

My name is Gitanjali Kolanad, but it is not the name I was born with. I was born Gitanjali Susan Charles. Gitanjali has a lovely meaning: *gita*—song, *anjali*—offering. It is the title of a book of poems by Rabindranath Tagore, the Nobel prize-winning Bengali poet. Susan is for my great-grandmother on my mother's side, and it is a common name among the Syrian Christian women of Kerala. Charles was my father's name, a name given to him by his parents, who had been converted to Christianity by British missionaries. My original name reflected my origins, as the daughter of parents who had gone against tradition and the wishes of their parents, and married outside of their own communities. But when I became a dancer, and wanted a name more 'Indian' than Charles, I changed my name. I adapted the last name Kolanad from the name of the house where I was born. Because I invented my name, Indians hear it, but it doesn't help them to figure me out. They can't tell what part of India I'm from, my caste or religion, and so they can't fit me into an appropriate little hole in the jigsaw puzzle.

As a foreigner coming to India, you can observe and participate on many different levels, move geographically and through the hierarchy with a freedom many Indians do not have. Your foreignness places you outside the rules defined by ethnic group and hierarchy. Ironically, you can experience an India that the Indian will find it hard to discover

THE JOINT FAMILY

The multitudinous family exerts the primary influence in the Indian's life. It extends its tentacles in all directions, tying the individual into the bondage of mutual obligation; the same knots that hold together the only safety net there is for man, woman or child in a country beset with natural calamities and disease, the ever-present threat of poverty, and no pension scheme or health insurance.

Terms of Kinship

The relevance of kinship ties is revealed by the extent to which they are named. In English, where two words—'grandmother' and 'grandfather'—serve the purpose, Hindi and most other Indian languages need four: the mother's mother and father are *naani* and *naana*, and the father's mother and father are *daadi* and *daada*. The relationships that in English are lumped together under the terms 'aunt' and 'uncle' are clearly spelt out with ten words in the Indian languages. In Hindi:

- the mother's sister is *mausi*, and her husband is *mausaa*
- the mother's brother is *maamaa*, and his wife is *maami*
- the father's sister is *bua*, and her husband is *phuphaa*
- the father's elder brother is *thaya* and his wife is *thayi*
- the father's younger brother is *chaachaa*, and his wife is *chaachi*

Indians differentiate between the mother's side of the family and the father's side for many reasons. The *gotra*, or line of descent, is traced through the father's line for boys, while it changes to the husband's line for girls. The custom among most Hindus is that girls must marry out of their own gotra. In some communities of the south, the mother's brother and cousins are considered suitable marriage partners for the girl.

The ties of obligation and duty are different for the mother's side and father's side of the family. In many communities all over India, the mother's brother has a special relationship with the children; he and his wife may take over the role of parents should the necessity arise.

Despite the number of names for 'aunt' and 'uncle', in Hindi and Tamil there is no separate term for 'cousin'. The words for brother and sister (in Hindi, *bhayya* and *bahan*) are used for cousins. Cousins are as close as brothers and sisters, are treated with the same affection and are subject to the same demands. Brothers have obligations towards sisters, but sisters have none towards each other. Age confers respect, and the younger sibling should correctly call the older 'elder brother' or 'elder sister', rather than by name. It is common to call someone who is younger or of almost the same age by their name.

The traditional Indian joint family grew out of the needs of an agricultural community. The oldest male member was the head, and all his younger brothers and their wives and children lived together under one roof, ate food cooked in one kitchen, and shared the produce of joint labour. In urban India, the joint family does not make the same kind of sense. But even in the cities, where the nuclear family of just parents and their children is the norm, the joint family remains the emotional reality. It exerts pressures and extends support from any distance. The ancestral village home is the heart of the family; its members return there from all over the world for important events and celebrations.

Family Ties

The carpenter came to the house, listened and smiled, his head oscillating continuously in a fluid movement of agreement with all my plans. He took measurements, made complicated calculations, and came up with a wild and unrealistic estimate. Systematically, I reduced it to a reasonable figure, with which, considering his lamentations during the bargaining, he now seemed inordinately pleased.

Against my better judgement, I gave him a sizeable advance to buy the wood. He promised to be back the next morning to start work. He does not show up the next day, and I wait in vain for another two days. I give up hope, convinced he's made off with the money. On the fourth day, he shows up with the wood, ready to work. His explanation: "I had to go back to my village for the haircut of my mother's elder brother's daughter's first son."

Sons and Daughters

A man is incomplete without wife and children, but there is thought to be a particular type of hell, called *put*, from which only a son, *putra*, can save his parents.

Almost all families wish for a male heir to continue the lineage, provide support in old age, and do the last rites at the funeral to ensure that the parents' souls make the journey to the home of the ancestors without difficulty. The birth of a daughter is not always celebrated with the same jubilation that greets the birth of a son. This is more true of poorer families, where the economic reality is that the boy grows up to earn money and will take responsibility for his parents until their death, while the daughter must be provided with a dowry, and marries out of the family. From then on her allegiance is with her husband's family, to the extent that if her father comes to visit her, he is supposed to pay for even a glass of water.

The marriage practices in the south until recently favoured a cross-cousin or even the maternal uncle as the husband, so that the girl moved into a family she already knew. Her mother-in-law was also her aunt, and she may well have played in childhood with her future husband. Even though such practices are considered old-fashioned now, generally the relationship between husband and wife in the south is closer and more intimate.

In many parts of the south, a matrilineal system was practised, and so daughters don't necessarily suffer the same kind of second-class status that they do in the north. Their history did not include the gender segregation of *purdah*, so women are relatively more relaxed.

Childhood

An Indian proverb dictates that for the first five years, a son should be treated as a prince; for the next ten years as a slave, and from the 16th birthday as a friend. This much is true: early childhood in India is a time of great indulgence, even for the girl child, if the family can afford to be so fair. Babies are never allowed to cry, are picked up and breastfed on demand, and go around bare-bottomed, peeing wherever they like.

Children in the extended family grow up with almost constant, but rarely undivided, attention from someone or other—if not the mother, then a surrogate from among the women of the household. The role of care-giver is so diffuse that the child may call one of the many aunts 'mother' and call the real mother 'aunt'. There are always ready-made playmates among cousins, and children are encouraged to play in groups rather than alone.

No demands are made on them to become independent in any way—they are fed and dressed and bathed by others long past the age when they can handle these tasks themselves. Children sleep first with their parents, then with their siblings, so they are rarely, if ever, alone. They are not 'taught' to walk, talk or use the toilet. They learn from watching, and quickly come to understand and fit into the hierarchy of the family, observing when and how to use the terms and gestures of respect.

Sometimes, because of economic circumstances, children, especially girls, grow up without much childhood at all. Mothers often carry bricks at construction sites, pull heavily-loaded handcarts, work in the fields, and do many other physically taxing jobs while carrying a small baby. Or the

Children start young in their traditional professions. A young boy plays the drums for a puppet show.

child is put into a makeshift cradle, made from a piece of cloth knotted and hung from a tree, or left on a mat in the shade, while the parents work. The oldest girl is responsible for her younger siblings, and it is common to see one child carrying another almost as big as herself, while leading yet another by the hand.

Most Indians of forty and above have grown up within a joint family. Today, without the supportive joint family network, the strictures of urban life, even for the relatively wealthy, make it more and more difficult to allow children five years of regal living, and even disposable diapers are finding a market. But the ideal of indulging children remains, and if the economic conditions allow, small children continue to have someone, if not a grandmother or an older sibling, then a servant, at their beck and call.

Mother and Son

It is inviting contradiction to generalise about such things, but studies of the urban Hindu family have shown that, on a scale of intensity, the relationship between mother and son is the strongest, way above that of husband and wife, which is next to last, just above sister and sister.

The young wife's first duty is to bear a son. If she fails, it is often considered her own personal failure. Her status in the joint family and in society comes to her through her son, and he is her key to power. It is no surprise that she invests most of her emotion in him, or that he reciprocates with equal ardour. Even well-educated modern men show a marked dependence on their mothers, and respect their wishes in regard to marriage and career at the cost of their own happiness.

Mother-in-law

The mother-in-law is the villain in many joint family situations. She treats her son's wife in the same way she may have been treated by her mother-in-law when she entered the family as a new bride.

The list of abuses goes all the way from actually murdering the new bride, usually by setting her on fire in a 'bride-burning' to preventing the young couple from having any time together and poisoning the relationship with lies and innuendoes to the son about his new wife. This is a stereotypical view which has grown out of a harsh reality. There are of course also perfectly wonderful mothers-in-law to be found all over India.

VALUES

> 'That religion which allows one to touch a foul animal
> but not a man is not a religion but a madness.
> That religion which says one class may not gain
> knowledge, may not acquire wealth, may not take up
> arms, is not a religion but a mockery of man's life.
> That religion which teaches that the unlearned should
> remain unlearned, that the poor should remain poor,
> is not a religion but a punishment.'
> —Extract of a speech by Dr B R Ambedkar,
> from *Sources of Indian Tradition*

At the entrance to a temple in India, there are beggars. They sit in two long rows on either side of the path to the inner courtyard, patient as corpses under the merciless sun. The stone gods look down with unwavering serenity on the blind, the maimed, the deformed, the lepers, the widows with shaven heads, and the holy men in saffron robes.

To achieve the sanctity of the cool, dark inner sanctum, one must first run the gauntlet of outstretched hands. Graceful Indian women in resplendent silk do this with equanimity, dispensing a few coins at random before proceeding to their worship. Not one expresses emotion over this display of suffering, injustice and renunciation. The foreigner encountering this scene for the first time is doubly shocked—by the wretchedness and by the indifference to it. What is this composure? Is it callousness, apathy, stoicism? It seems inhuman not to be moved to tears.

Karma

If there is a philosophical basis to this equanimity, it is to be found in the doctrine of *karma*, which means both 'action' and 'the result of the action' because the two cannot be separated. *Karma* is a law as pervasive as gravity, as indisputable on the moral plane as 'For every action there is an equal and opposite reaction' is on the physical plane.'

Karma is the law of cause and effect. Our thoughts, words and deeds have repercussions, the effects of which follow us throughout our lives. A necessary corollary to *karma* is reincarnation. Actions in a past life secured fortune in this one; similarly, actions in this life will affect future reincarnations. Hindus use the analogy of the archer—the arrow already shot is out of anyone's control; this is *karma* from past actions, and it must run its course. Even the gods have no power to change the results of acts already performed. Over the arrow held ready and aimed (present actions), and over the arrows still in the quiver (accumulated merit from past actions), the archer has perfect control.

Karma in Everyday Life

When we were living in New Delhi, we had a maid named Susan, which means she was a Christian. I had not known she was pregnant when I hired her, because Susan was quite chubby, but over the next two months her condition became quite clear. She continued to come to work, and seemed to be having no trouble coping with her chores. Then one day garrulous Susan turned up subdued, and no longer pregnant. She had lost the baby. When I asked her about it she said, "It's good. The loss of this child has wiped out my bad *karma*. The next one will survive." Though she was Christian, it was the Hindu concept of *karma* that made sense of the miscarriage for Susan.

Another time, I was visiting an Indian friend in Germany. One hectic day, every traffic light she came to was red, she just missed the only free parking space, and then the escalator going up was broken and we had to walk up. She grimaced and said, "What bad *karma* did I accumulate to deserve this?" Not only miscarriages, but traffic lights, parking spaces and escalators are governed by the law of *karma*.

Karma has dominated Hindu thought for more than two thousand years. Whether it is excuse, apology or deep understanding of the nature of the universe, it allows the Indian to face any eventuality and shrug, "It's my *karma*." The worst misfortune is acceptable because it is deserved. What seems to be injustice—when bad things happen to good

Beggar girls in New Delhi. Neither beauty nor intelligence is likely to advance their position in society.

people—is only so because of the limitations of knowledge: we can't remember our past lives. Yet human beings are not victims of fate or destiny or the whims of gods, for good actions in this life will influence a future birth.

Caste

The caste system, with all its evils and abuses, has *karma* as its philosophical justification. The Sanskrit word for caste is *varna*, meaning colour. It evolved as a way for the invading Aryans, with their fair skin and chiselled features, to avoid assimilation with the indigenous dark-skinned people of the Indus valley.

One of the later hymns of the Rg Veda describes the mythical origin of caste, from the ritual sacrifice of the primeval male, Purusha:

'When they divided the Man, into how many parts did they apportion him?

What do they call his mouth, his two arms and thighs and feet?

His mouth became the Brahmin; his arms were made into the Warrior.

His thighs became the People, and from his feet the Servants were born.'

Caste evolved to serve the same purposes that the medieval workers' guilds had served in Britain, and that the workers' unions are supposed to serve today. They protected the workers from unfair competition, and preserved the knowledge of each community. If a potter's daughter married a potter, she would know already where to get the clay, how to prepare it, what wood to use for the kiln, and so on. If she married a blacksmith, where would her knowledge go?

In an age when antiseptics and antibiotics did not exist, there were entirely practical reasons to have one group of people to do the dangerous (for health reasons) work of carting away carcasses and making leather from the hides. One theory is that the caste that was 'untouchable' developed immunities over generations, and the other castes avoided them for purely health reasons.

Once caste became hereditary, taboos against eating together and intermarriage came into existence. There arose a vast network of subcastes, called *jatis*, intimately linked to occupation, with relationships based on work and economic interdependence. Trapped in this net, the individual is effectively prevented from moving up in the

A *dhobi* (washerman) belongs to an occupational caste.

hierarchy of castes, but the subcaste as a group can gain status as the nature of the work acquired new relevance in changing times. Each new ethnic group to arrive in India became a separate subcaste and was assimilated into the larger caste structure.

The hundreds of *jatis*, or caste-groups, are graded on a scale of 'purity', with the Brahmins at the top, and the untouchables right off the scale at the bottom. Only one generation ago, untouchables in some parts of the country had to wear bells to signal their presence to the higher castes, because even the shadow of an untouchable was polluting. They had to live outside the village proper, use a separate well for their water, and do dirty work such as removing human waste and animal carcasses.

The only way to escape the degradation of a low-caste status was to convert to one of the religions that rejected caste, such as Buddhism, Christianity or Islam. But even these religious groups became stratified into hierarchies, so the caste system survives the defections.

Gandhi tried to reverse the stigma of untouchability by naming the untouchables *Harijans*, meaning 'children of God', but now they refuse to be patronised as objects of sentimental piety. They prefer to emphasise their identity by calling themselves *Dalits*—oppressed.

The Indian Constitution in 1950 destroyed any quasi-legal basis the caste system might have had until then, and made all citizens equal before the law. The principle of one man, one vote led to 'casteism', political representation on a caste basis, and for the first time in the long history of the caste system, the dominated castes have the means to benefit from the shrewd manipulation of caste conflict. Not surprisingly, they are making use of it.

In the cities, caste has much less importance than in rural societies, where disobeying caste rules can still get one killed. It is not possible to control who sits next to whom on a bus, in a factory or in a restaurant. An 'affirmative action' approach by the government, which reserves a percentage of government jobs and university admissions for the lowest castes, further destabilises the caste system by encouraging upward mobility.

The caste system and its horrifying abuses are unjust, evil and morally and ethically without any justification. In my opinion, it is worse than apartheid, being applied by Indians against fellow Indians. Many Indians feel this way.

Resistance to the caste system is not new; Buddha and Mahavira, the Jain leader, rejected it in the 6th century BC. In the 15th century, the *bhakti* movements stressed man's direct relationship with god, circumventing the mediating Brahmin, and many of its leaders were low-caste men and women. Sikhism, influenced by Islam, promoted a fraternal order, where eating together became an important tenet of the religion. Modern Hindu revival groups consider caste to be evil.

But caste has not gone away. There is a story passed around about a prominent political figure who was from one of the 'scheduled castes'. He went back to his small village to open a hospital and was welcomed like a hero by the people who had formerly shunned him. After the speeches and the fancy lunch, he was getting ready to leave, when another untouchable came in the back way into his room. The politician told him, "You don't have to come in by the back way now. I was once like you, and see what I have made of myself." The other replied, "I just came to get my plates. They borrowed them to serve you your lunch."

A story that is true is the one behind the tragic suicide of Dharam Hinduja in October 1992. The only son of a wealthy Indian businessman living in Britain, he was nevertheless brought up in a conservative Hindu family. He did not drink, smoke or eat meat, and his parents expected to arrange his marriage. But the young man, only 22 years old, fell in love with and secretly married without his family's knowledge. His bride was an Anglo-Indian woman, who, according to the reports, would be considered a half-caste and therefore unsuitable by families like the Hindujas. When it seemed as if newspapers would make public the details of his marriage, Dharam Hinduja set himself on fire.

Caste continues to raise its ugly head again and again in modern India. It still determines who gets ahead and who does not for the majority of Indians. Most Hindus would find it difficult to imagine a casteless social system. A glance at the matrimonial page of the newspaper is enough to confirm that. Even the ancient association of caste with colour remains, and everyone wants a fair-skinned bride, for the equation 'black skin = menial status' has not changed since the time the Aryan invaders despised the indigenous dark-skinned people they called *Dasas*, or servants.

Dharma

Dharma translates badly into English, the best equivalent being 'natural law' or 'universal justice' or 'duty'. Even the planets in their orbits follow their *dharma*. *Sva-dharma* is one's own moral code, something like our conscience. In popular terms, *dharma* means 'doing what you are supposed to do according to the position into which you were born and according to your stage of life.'

Dharma varies for the individual according to caste, and changes according to age and situation. What is correct behaviour for a priest is not necessarily correct behaviour for a weaver. In ancient times, the punishment for crimes was fixed according to the caste, in a kind of reverse discrimination: a Brahmin thief suffered eight times the punishment of a low-caste thief. This quality of relativism makes it difficult to pin down the standards of Hindu ethics. The traditional values, as expressed in popular religious works in the regional languages, are generosity and selflessness, truthfulness, respect for one's elders and the capacity to live with the minimum of harm to fellow creatures.

Dharma Practised

While waiting with a friend at a bus-stop in my ancestral village in Kerala, a man stopped his car and asked us to get in. Only when we were inside did he ask where we were going. Then he drove us all the way to the train station in the nearest town. When I thanked him, he replied, "Don't mention it. It was my duty."

He did it not to be helpful to strangers waiting for a rare bus in that small place, or because he guessed where we were going and it was on his way, but because it was his duty. Why was it his duty? Because, he explained, I was related to him; my mother was his grandmother's sister's daughter's husband's niece. His sense of duty extended to me, although he knew very well that I did not know who he was.

Karma and *dharma* are not just ancient philosophical concepts; they are freely used in everyday life to explain the most mundane actions. Politicians use the terms all the time to elevate their arguments. Movie plots hinge on coincidences that are explained as the result of past *karma*, and heroes act heroically in the fulfilment of their *dharma*. It is simply the way many Indians perceive the universe to be structured.

TRADITIONS
The Stages of Life
There are four basic life stages. As a child, one should concentrate on studying and learning a skill. This is the first stage, or *ashrama*, which is supposed to be spent as a celibate student. Later, as a householder, one's duties are different. Now is the time to marry and start a family. During this life stage it is correct to pursue wealth and *artha* (power) and *kama* (pleasure).

After seeing one's first grandson, it is time to retire from the world and, ideally, live in the forest. Finally, after living a productive life and fulfilling all one's social obligations, it is time for religious pursuits, to seek God and attain *moksha* (liberation).

Sex, Love, Marriage
There is no puritanism in the ancient Hindu view of sex. It was considered normal and necessary, and therefore worthy of careful research and study. The *Kama Sutra* (*Scripture of Pleasure*) is only the most famous of a vast literature on the subject. At the end of his treatise, which describes, among other things, 12 kinds of embrace, 17 kinds of kisses and eight kinds of nail-marks to be used while making love, the author writes, 'The *Kama Sutra* was composed, according to the precepts of the Holy Writ, for the benefit of the world, by Vatsyayana, while leading the life of a religious student and wholly engaged in the contemplation of God.'

Somewhere along the line, between the writing of the *Kama Sutra*, about AD 600, and modern times, Indians have developed inhibitions. Premarital sex is forbidden, with varying degrees of severity in the different strata of society, there being more license at the top and bottom ends of the social scale, and the most restrictions in the middle. The double standard definitely applies—for women the code of conduct is stricter than the men's at every level.

Even in the *Kama Sutra*, the ideal of sexual happiness was to be found within the marriage bond. The arranged marriage between partners who may have only seen photographs of each other is the norm. Marriage is first of all a social contract, as much between two families as between two individuals. Love is important, but it is believed to happen naturally during the course of a life lived together and to grow stronger over the years. It is not necessary to be 'in love' before marrying. In fact, the 'love marriage' as opposed to the arranged marriage is frowned upon as it suggests a union dominated by emotions rather than the carefully planned union based on matching horoscopes, caste and subcaste, economic status, education, etc.

Old Age

The four stages of life are not empty of meaning today. A hard-driving businessman told me about his cottage in the mountains. "That is where I will go when I have fulfilled my duties. Now it just remains for me to marry off my youngest daughter. When I have seen that they are well settled, then I can go on to the next stage. I want to take care of the spiritual side."

Not all Hindus are in a position to renounce paid work and concentrate on their spiritual growth in their old age; and not all who can afford it, do it. But the ideal of old age as a time not of decay, but of the active pursuit of an all-important goal is very much a part of the consciousness. The passing of youth is not to be mourned, nor is advancing age to be hidden or avoided. Older family members in the community are treated with respect and deference.

With age, women come closer to equality with men. The middle-aged Indian woman does nothing to hide the grey, contain the spread or slow down the wrinkles.

She is comfortable with her aging body, and finally free of some of the conventions that direct the lives of younger women. If she wishes, she can be remarkably independent and outspoken.

Holy Men

Sannyasin is a stage of life that everyone is supposed to go through when they are old and renounce the world. Those who do become *sannyasis* are considered to be holy men by society and, as such, treated with respect.

Society's laws, strictures and ceremonies mean little to a *sannyasi*, or one who has renounced them. The *sannyasi* embarks as a wanderer in search of truth. There are many religious orders of these holy men and women, each with its own philosophy and practices. Many demand celibacy, but not all. Some religious orders require that initiates spend some time as wandering beggars, living off only what they can collect in their bowls. Modesty and cleanliness are valued as social attributes. Holy men or women, having renounced the world and its value system, may go completely naked. Some have matted locks of uncut hair or bodies covered in ashes.

There are also religious practices that subject the body to pain: walking on fire, piercing the cheeks and tongue with metal skewers, walking on the knees, or rolling. These are tests to prove that the senses have been conquered by the mind in the cause of religious experience.

An Indian story illustrates how strongly the pull of the senses is felt. A man chased by a tiger falls over the edge of a precipice. He saves himself by clinging to a vine. Two rats are gnawing through the vine. At the bottom of the precipice a crocodile waits to devour him, and at the top the tiger is still pacing. At that moment, a drop of nectar starts to fall from a flower. The man puts out his tongue to catch that drop. Even in the face of certain death, man will seek the pleasure of the senses.

Samskara refers to the human condition itself, through the endless cycle of rebirths. Only the ascetic can hope to escape.

Death

Death has no finality in the Hindu world view. It is the door to yet another beginning. The endless repetitive cycle of birth and rebirth knows nothing of hell or heaven. There are no rewards or punishments, only the inexorable working out of the law of *karma* through infinite lifetimes.

The only way to break the cycle is to attain *moksha*. Hindus are not dogmatic about how this liberation is to be achieved. For different people, different personalities, obviously different paths may be followed. Some people may practise yoga exercises and meditation; some may worship a personal deity, such as Krishna, with songs and rituals; others may take up some kind of charity work, called *karma yoga*, for good hard work can also lead to realisation.

The Inevitability of the Life Stages

The concepts of *karma* and *dharma*, and of *artha*, *kama* and *moksha* create an ordered path for the individual. Accepting the path, finding happiness in a career and marriage shaped by other people's choices, and taking one's proper place in society are the natural responses shaped by an Indian upbringing that encourages interdependence and cooperative effort within a group, and discourages independence and individual effort on one's own behalf.

Sometimes the pressures on the individual to conform are too much. The only course that society leaves open to those who reject its values is that of the *sannyasi*, the ascetic. The ascetic avoids the problems of career and marriage and the demands of family and society by renouncing them altogether. But for the man who simply wants to be a doctor instead of heading the family cement business, or the woman who wants to continue to perform as a dancer after her marriage, there are no easy solutions. Sometimes, as for Dharam Hinduja, suicide seems to be the only way out.

SUPERSTITIONS

It would seem that in a universe that revolves according to the law of *karma*, there is little use for superstition. But not everyone who uses the terms talks or thinks about these concepts in the highest philosophical sense, or considers the logical outcome and acts accordingly. Who is without contradictions?

Some are able to fit the position of the planets and the lines on the palms of the hands into the *karmic* scheme of things. For some, reading horoscopes and palms are just a digression, hardly more meaningful than reading one's horoscope printed in the daily paper. Or maybe it is like buying insurance; as long as it is not too inconvenient, what's the harm? And then there are those who will do nothing of importance without consulting holy men, the stars or other oracles.

Auspicious Days

Auspicious days are decided according to the movement of the stars and the planets. Indira Gandhi had her astrologers and holy men to advise her. It is said that all her trips were planned according to auspicious times. Even Queen Elizabeth had to comply with the rules of these astrologers: when the

Queen visited India, her plane had to touch down at precisely 5 minutes to 12:00 pm or 5 minutes after 12:00 pm, rather than at 12:00 pm, as previously planned.

Auspicious Days and Times

You can buy almanacs that give details of auspicious and inauspicious days and times for a whole year. Once, in Mahabalipuram in South India, I was using a telephone at one of the many little telephone offices to call my father in Chennai (Madras) about the details for registering a piece of land in my name. The man who ran the phone booth quickly looked up the days I was considering in a dog-eared almanac. He was not at all happy when I chose an inauspicious day. As soon as I got off the phone, he tried to convince me to opt for another day. When I wouldn't, he went back to his almanac. A few minutes later, he said triumphantly, "Do your registration between 10:05 am and 1:35 pm. See, even inauspicious days have auspicious times."

Auspicious days and times are chosen not only for registering land, but also for the first day of school, for weddings and other ceremonies, for opening businesses and even for journeys. If you want to plan your trips around auspicious days, my book tells me that, in general, Mondays and Saturdays are inauspicious for journeys to the east; Tuesdays and Wednesdays are inauspicious for journeys to the north; Fridays and Sundays are not good for travelling west, and Thursdays are not good for going south.

Marriages are the mainstay of the astrological profession in India. When they predicted that 8 February 1984 would be the best day of the century for weddings, 2000 couples tried to get married on that day in Punjab alone. Unfortunately, there was a general strike on that very day, and the marriages could not take place. (One wonders if this explains India's climbing divorce rate.)

Fortune-tellers of many descriptions abound on the streets of India. Astrologers need your time of birth in addition to the date to be accurate. You can also have a parrot read your fortune; these birds will pick a card from those offered, and their master or mistress will interpret it for you. Omens are to be found everywhere. The chirping of a lizard is auspicious or inauspicious on particular days of the week. The cries of

Horoscopes guide every major life event, and some minor ones as well.

certain birds, seeing certain animals, meeting certain people (a man with matted hair, a woman carrying fruit) can all be interpreted by those who are learned in reading the signs.

THE WOMAN IN INDIA

If one were to look for an image that best exemplified the Indian woman, it would not be the gracious, sweetly smiling beauty with folded hands on the travel posters. It would be a strong wiry woman, straight-backed under some heavy load balanced on her head: bricks, water pots, firewood, or grass for fodder.

Poor women work out of necessity. There are proportionately more working women than in any other country. There is no known occupation in India where women are not involved.

Women break stones in quarries, go down into mines, weave, make pots, plant paddy, plough land and harvest crops—in addition to the daily household chores of carrying water from the well, collecting firewood and grass for fodder for the animals, cooking, cleaning and childcare. In the cities, Indian women can be seen at construction sites with a head-load of bricks, one child balanced on hip, climbing a precarious bamboo ladder. Women do the same backbreaking unskilled jobs as men, but for smaller wages; and while pregnant, nursing, or carrying a child.

Do Indians take these things seriously? Some do. A friend, well-educated, well-travelled, left a high level media job to start her own company. The astrologers picked the time for the signing of the papers, and even changed the spelling of the company name to bring it better fortune. The company is doing very well, and the first big project was a resounding success. Another Indian friend said, of palmistry, "Everyone says I have a good fate line, so where is my good fate?"

These are not the women you are likely to encounter socially. Women are not a homogeneous group, and there is an enormous degree of variation due to class, caste and regional perspectives. Nor is everyone living in the same historical epoch: parts of Rajasthan remain medieval, and a woman was recently burned on her husband's funeral pyre, supposedly in accordance with the highest ideals of an ancient tradition; in modern urban India, brides are burned without even the masquerade of ideals, but for VCRs and refrigerators, at the rate of more than one a day in New Delhi alone.

To the extent that it is possible to generalise at all, North India, which came under the influence of a strong Muslim ruling class, is more feudal and patriarchal, and South India is more egalitarian. Tribal societies show the greatest gender equality, often more than in the West. Poor and low-caste women, while facing the oppression that goes with their low caste, may have more power for self-determination in relation to higher-caste women, because the status of the family is often determined by the extent to which they can keep their women subservient, idle, and confined. Loss of freedom is the price women pay for prosperity and leisure.

Pervasive image of the Indian woman—with a load on her head.

High-caste women suffered the most from traditional practices that oppress women, such as *purdah*, *sati*, child marriage and the degraded position of the widow. *Purdah*, meaning 'curtain', refers to the custom of keeping women secluded. Although it may have been borrowed from Islam, it extended to the higher-caste Hindu families in North India. Even today, many women will hurriedly pull the upper part of their *sari* to cover their face in the presence of a male stranger. Also, only high-caste women were expected to practise self-immolation on their husband's funeral pyre in order to become a *sati*, a virtuous woman. High-caste women are married at a younger age, and are less likely to be able to remarry if widowed.

Female infanticide, or its high-tech version of aborting female fetuses after using amniocentesis to determine their sex, reflects the Indian obsession with having a male child. Only a son can continue the line, or perform the funeral rites that insure the soul's safe passage through the Hindu purgatory. And only a son brings dowry, the gift that the bride's family must pay. Daughters must be provided with dowry, in amounts that can bankrupt the family. Even in tribal communities, where it used to be the tradition for the man to pay a bride-price, the system of dowry is catching on, bringing the abuses that go with it.

In parts of South India, because of a greater affinity to the pre-Aryan cult of the mother-goddess (in some places, because of a matrilineal system), the preference for boys is not as pervasive. Men and women mix together more freely, women have equality in family relationships and a strong presence in the society. In the urban centres, including Mumbai (Bombay), Delhi, Calcutta and Chennai (Madras), there are many highly educated, articulate and independent women who do not have to carry bricks or cover their faces. They are doctors, lawyers, journalists, movie-makers, artists. They are able to combine fulfilling and demanding careers with marriage and children because of the infrastructure provided by the joint family, or with the help of numerous servants. Their lives may be fuller, freer, and more satisfying than the lives of their Western counterparts.

There are many women in positions of power, but to what extent is this because of their relationship to a man? Indira Gandhi became prime minister of India, but she was the daughter of Jawaharlal Nehru. Jayalalitha is a political force in Tamil Nadu, but she was the on-screen and off-screen heroine of movie-hero-turned-politician MGR, the late chief minister of that state. Maneka Gandhi became Minister of State for the Environment, but she was the widow of Sanjay Gandhi, Indira Gandhi's son. Sonia Gandhi, the

India encompasses every extreme: if there are forms of all-male theatre to be found, there are also all-female theatre forms; if there is polygamy, there is also polyandry; if there are patrilineal societies, there are matrilineal ones. It is therefore especially important not to draw simplistic conclusions.

Modern Indian women playing baseball.

Italian widow of Rajiv Gandhi, became the leader of the
Congress party. So far, for the woman without the man in the
past or in the background, power has been more elusive.

According to the Hindu religion, the woman is both the
object of worship (as a mother) and a source of ritual pollution
(when she menstruates, has given birth, and is widowed).
The old menstrual taboo required that a woman retire to an
outhouse and stay secluded there for three days. Even now,
in many orthodox families, a menstruating woman should
not enter the kitchen, touch the salt, go to the temple, or
participate in any religious ceremony.

In the family, the woman has her position. As a wife, she
keeps up the traditions and rituals that maintain the caste
purity. In Vedic times, a woman had equal status with a
man, could be a priest, and remarry if she was widowed.
But though her position has deteriorated since then, she is
still required beside her husband at important sacrifices and
ceremonies. As a mother, she is revered, and as the mother
of sons, she has power through them. She has unquestioned
authority over her daughters-in-law, who can be subjected
to any humiliation until they in turn give birth to sons and
gain power through them.

The mythology represents God as the male, passive principle, activated only in consort with his *shakti*, the female, active principle. Hinduism provides a potent image of female energy as Kali, the black goddess, wearing a garland of skulls, tongue red from drinking blood, who destroys the world at the end of its cycle, and sets in motion the process of creation once more. But in contrast to the dark, forceful and frightening majesty of Kali, is Sita, the ideal wife, selfless and devoted, who follows her husband Rama to the forest, and undergoes a trial by fire when her chastity is questioned.

The position of the woman in India, in the family, in society and in religion, exemplifies the characteristic Indian ability to hold two contradictory viewpoints without undue inner conflict. As one Indian woman put it, with a certain succinct bitterness, "Indians are mother lovers, but women haters".

FITTING IN

CHAPTER 4

'Thou hast made me known to friends whom I knew not.
Thou hast given me seats in homes not my own. Thou hast
brought the distant near and made a brother of a stranger.'
—Rabindranath Tagore, 'Gitanjali'

On my last trip to India, I had to advise a young French couple on what to take as a gift to a wedding. On the train from Madras to Cochin, they had shared a berth with a young man on his way to get married; what could be more natural than that he invite them, two complete strangers, to the ceremony? Marriages, birthdays and special festival days are all opportunities for family, friends and sometimes even fellow train passengers to come together, the philosophy being, 'the more the merrier'.

There is a pervasive sense all over India that a stranger to the country should be made welcome. Along with that there is curiosity about you, the foreigner, and therefore you have entertainment value. As a visitor to India, you will no doubt be invited to celebrate in many ways with Indians you know well or not so well. Here are some of the important events that Indians celebrate, with the background behind the rituals.

THE LIFE CYCLE

I have given the rituals of the Hindu religion here, since India is predominantly Hindu. The life-cycle events of Jains, Buddhists and Sikhs, and some rituals, are also similar to the Hindu ones. Muslims, Christians and Parsis have their own celebrations, which I have referred to briefly in Chapter Two, in the section on religions.

The Hindu rituals that mark the significant life events are called *samskaras*. The ancient scriptures prescribe 12 to 16

Details of ceremonies are often complex and minutely prescribed, with rules as to who should sit on which side of whom, in which direction they should face, at what time the ceremony should be performed, what kind of wood should be used for the sacrificial fire, and so on.

such ceremonies, but nowadays most urban families don't have the time or the inclination to perform all of them. The correct rituals involve both high and low castes in the event. Besides the Brahmin priest, who recites the sacred verses and oversees the other aspects, there may be a barber who purifies the person by removing the hair, the washerman called in at births, and the drummers who use animal skins and are therefore impure. A special community of eunuchs who appear at births is a feature in some parts of the north; like the evil fairy at the birth of Sleeping Beauty, they must be appeased or they will spoil everything with their curse.

Birth

The first ceremony takes place when the woman is seven months pregnant. She is equated with Mother Earth; each family member approaches her and puts flowers in her hair, her arms are loaded with bangles, and she holds out a part of her sari, which is filled with rice to symbolise fertility and plenty. Before the birth, nothing is bought or planned for the baby. The first clothes that the newborn wears should not be new, so they are borrowed from an older sibling or cousin.

After the birth, mother and child are secluded for between six to ten days. Friends may not even be informed that a child has been born. These are perhaps customs that arose because of the high infant mortality rate. On the sixth or the 11th day, a priest will be summoned for the naming ceremony. The name will be chosen according to the baby's horoscope, keeping in mind such things as auspicious numbers. The priest will 'blow' the name into the baby's ears, and write it on a plateful of raw rice. This may well be a social event.

When the baby is six months old, there is a ceremony, called *anna praasana*, when the child is given solid food for the first time. The first step and the first birthday may also be observed with a religious ceremony of some kind. But the first haircut, when the head is completely shaved, is an especially significant event. Some families perform the shaving ceremony within a month of the birth, especially if it is the first baby, and a boy. Others do it at one year, or after the first step, or at odd years, say at age three or five. There may be reasons to delay the ceremony, including simply not being able to afford it, because priests, rituals and celebrations cost money. Until then, even boys will have their hair long and braided. The father is actually supposed to do the shaving, but sensibly, he just cuts a few hairs while reciting the appropriate Sanskrit verses, and then the task is handed over to the barber. The first hair is offered like a sacrifice to the gods.

Birthdays

In the cities, among well-to-do Indians, birthdays may be celebrated with parties, presents, cake and ice-cream, just as in the West. Members of what Indira Gandhi called the 'five-star culture' try to outdo each other with original and extravagant events held at five-star hotels, featuring elephants, bands and the latest fads.

Most Indians take little note of birthdays other than the first, and if they do, the child may get new clothes, and distribute sweets among school friends. A more traditional extravagance that may be performed for boys is to weigh the child and distribute the equivalent amount of wheat or rice to the temple or some charity. During my mother's lifetime, even when she lived in Canada, she arranged a feast for the poor children of her ancestral village on my son's birthday, and gave gifts to them on his behalf.

Out of the big cities, gifts are still very often given by—rather than to—the person having the birthday. A token of that kind of gift-giving still remains.

A coming-of-age ceremony for girls when they reach puberty is still celebrated in some villages and tribal areas, signalling to the whole community that another girl is available for marriage. In

When my son went to a typical Indian school, even in Chennai (Madras), the birthday child would show up with a box of sweets to be handed out to the other children. And at my son's birthday party, the only ones who brought presents were the non-Indian children and my relatives.

the cities, the change may be marked by a change of dress: the girl may go from skirts to Indian dress, either *sari* or *salwar kameez*, the long tunic and wide gathered pants worn in the north.

Menstruation

Even in well-educated families, menstruation can still be a time of ritual impurity. Nowadays, women may stay out of the kitchen during those days, and leave the cooking to the servant, or an older daughter, or even the husband if no one else is there to do it. Menstruating women are not supposed to touch salt, go to the temple, or perform any rituals. Some girls from orthodox Hindu families even take birth control pills to regulate their period, in order to be able to take part in important ceremonies. As a foreign woman, unless you are in the unusual position of participating in the ritual in some significant active way rather than as an interested spectator, your own menstruation is not an issue. In most circumstances, if you were being asked to participate, some woman in the family would ascertain your condition. My advice is to never bring up the topic yourself, but be understanding if you are ever excluded for this reason.

Marriage

The biggest and most important celebration is the wedding, the public display of a family's wealth and status. Wedding customs vary from community to community, but the arrangements are usually as extravagant as the bride's family can afford.

The Price of a Wedding

The *dhobi*, or washerman, working for a German family we know, earning less than US$ 50 a month, spent more than US$ 3,000 dollars on his daughter's wedding, including gifts to the groom's family and a reception for at least two hundred people. At the wedding feast, seven different dishes were served, the bride wore a *sari* heavy with a brocade of real gold, and every significant moment in the ceremony, which lasted several hours, was recorded for posterity on video. The father will be in debt for ten years.

About 95 per cent of Indians who marry go through an arranged marriage, including university-educated, 'foreign-returned' young men and women. For some, the decision is the parents' and they have no choice in the matter. Others may exercise a right of veto after seeing a photograph, or in more progressive families, after meeting the potential partner. Usually, it is the woman who must be viewed by the man's family, who will judge her on her looks, deportment, homemaking abilities, and any special skills she may have. The tradition remains, but it uses modern technology to further its aims: newspaper ads, computer matchmaking, and the latest trend, videos of prospective partners and the Internet.

The marriage is considered to be a ritual gift-giving, in which the father bestows his *kanya* (daughter) as a *dan* (gift) to the other family. *Kanya dan* is the biggest donation a father can ever make.

If you are unmarried, watch out. Indians will consider you an object of pity. In my brother's case, everyone he met while he was in India felt sorry for him and tried their best to fix him up with a suitable bride. They placed the blame squarely on my parents for not arranging his marriage. No one paid

Modern day matchmaking through a newspaper advertisement.

the least bit of attention when he said he preferred being single. After all, the saying goes, 'No life without wife'.

The Wedding Ceremony

During the wedding season, the time of year when it is most auspicious to arrange weddings, wedding processions in Delhi constantly disrupt traffic. Headed by a motley group of musicians, dressed in Western-style band uniforms complete with black boots and white spats, playing disco tunes loud enough to make up for any other inadequacies, a crowd of relatives and well-wishers jiggle and gyrate before the white horse or fancy car, or even elephant, on which the stoic bridegroom sits as they snake towards the bride. The heavily decorated bride waits with equal stoicism for his arrival, and throughout the ceremony, neither one looks particularly happy.

The traditional celebrations around marriage can involve days of festivities, the most popular of these being the *mehendi* party, where the palms of the bride and the female guests are decorated with intricate henna designs. This used to be a tradition only in parts of North India, but has caught on through its depiction in movies to the point where it is a part of marriages all over the country. Henna is ground into a fine paste, and then applied to the hands and sometimes the feet of the female relatives and friends of the bride and groom. The henna colour dyes the skin according to the 'heat' in the person's body, some people being considered to be more 'heaty' than others; the colour can be intensified by leaving the paste on longer, and continually re-dampening it as it dries. The design lasts for a few days, and then slowly fades.

The marriage ritual itself doesn't take long, and is usually performed at a time chosen for being auspicious, and so is not necessarily convenient. First, the father of the bride proclaims that this is indeed his daughter, and that he is giving her to the groom. Then the groom takes the bride's right hand with his right hand, or the hanging end of her *sari* is tied to his upper cloth, and the two of them walk around the sacred fire seven times. Each round represents a blessing—food, strength, wealth, happiness, children, cattle, and devotion. The Sanskrit verses that the couple recite to each other express the intention that they will be friends and partners throughout their life.

The verse and the walk around the fire make the marriage sacrosanct and irrevocable, for the fire god has witnessed their vows. The man and the woman are in a sense transformed by the purification and rituals, so that the spectacle is actually a marriage of the gods. He represents Vishnu, she his consort Lakshmi, for now they are to be progenitors, the preservers of life. There is no way to dissolve the marriage, and in neither Tamil nor Sanskrit is there a word for divorce.

Cars, refrigerators, TV sets and VCRs, as well as cash, are often demanded by the groom's family, and the demands often escalate after the marriage ceremony. When the bride's family can no longer meet the demands, the young bride may be doused in kerosene and burned alive so that the young man can try again for that new motorcycle or TV set with a new bride. This is not some rare and heinous crime committed by illiterate people in backward rural areas; it happens regularly among the Indian middle-class in big cities.

> Dowry, the amount that the bride's family must pay to the groom's family at the time of marriage, is the dark side of the marriage ceremony, and bride-burning is its ugliest deformation.

In 1975, in Delhi alone, bride-burnings were happening almost daily. By 1983, the figure had risen to 690 deaths in Delhi, and in 2001, there were 7000 cases of registered dowry deaths in the whole of India, but only a handful of convictions. Since it happens within the family, there are usually no witnesses, and as many cases are often treated as suicides or accidents with a kerosene stove, these figures only hint at the immensity of the problem. Police have a difficult time proving such murders, and the culprits, usually the groom and his mother, get off scot-free.

Recently, women's groups have started taking action against bride-burning families, even after the courts have dismissed the case, by plastering their houses with banners announcing the alleged crime. The stigma attached to the accusation makes it more difficult for these families to find another victim.

Turning 60 or 80

The 60th birthday is the next milestone in a person's life. Just as 12 months make a year, 12 years make another unit, and five of these units make a complete cycle. If a man completes the cycle as a married man, it is very auspicious. Making it to the 80th birthday is as good as reaching a hundred, and the celebration is even called by the name for one hundred—*sathabishekam*.

Death

Death is viewed as a release. The soul throws off the mask and costume of the body and is free for a time before becoming involved in the next masquerade. The act of dying is a positive event in the individual's life, as the words used to speak of death show: *samadhi*—absorption into the Supreme Spirit; *moksha*—liberation; *shanti*—peace; *kaivalya*—total equanimity; and *paramapada*—the ultimate place. One of the duties of the individual is to prepare for death.

The rituals performed at the time of death reflect the same concern with the soul's journey and its safe passage to the land of the ancestors. Cremation must be performed as soon as possible after death, but at an auspicious time. The body is prepared like an offering to the gods. It is bathed, cleaned, and dressed in fresh clothes. The particular customs vary from community to community. In some communities, the colour of the shroud cloth varies. A married woman is decorated as for her wedding and her shroud is orange. Men and widows have white shrouds. The son or nearest male relative purifies himself in order to do the rituals for the cremation, by which he will acquire religious merit. At the cremation grounds, Agni, the god of fire, is worshipped at the altar with chants that beg him to accept the sacrifice of the dead person.

The very young child, because it has not prepared itself for the sacrifice of death, and the ascetic, having been burned up internally already by the inner fire of *tapas* or spiritual practice, are not burned, but buried or thrown in the river.

The funeral pyre uses about a third of a ton of wood. For eminent people, such as Indira Gandhi, and those who can afford it, sandalwood is used. In Kerala, the wood of the mango tree is popular, and people are supposed to plant a mango tree in childhood, to be cut and used for their funeral pyre at the time of death. Nowadays, wood is difficult to get, and very expensive; funeral pyres are made of cakes of cow-dung.

The body is placed on the funeral pyre, which the son lights. It takes about six hours for the body to turn to ashes. The skull should explode from the heat; otherwise it must be broken by the chief mourner. Only then is the soul released. Then Agni, who destroys the corpse as matter, takes the soul as an offering to the god of death and the ancestors. If the rituals are performed properly by the mourners, the soul, after remaining as a ghost for between ten and 30 days, will progress to the next stage.

Death pollutes the dead person's relatives, and mourners must follow certain taboos. Among the orthodox, very close relatives are not supposed to shave, comb their hair, use footwear, wear rings on fingers and toes, cook food in the house, or attend or give a celebration for a period of time. Those who know of the death in the family will not send around the traditional sweets on festive occasions.

Special ceremonies mark the fourth, tenth and 14th days. After the mourning period, there is *shubasvikaram*, the 'acceptance of what has happened and return to the auspiciousness of life'. This includes a purification ceremony that allows mourners to re-enter the world, albeit in their new roles: a wife becomes a widow, an eldest son, the head of the family.

Legally, from 1856, widows were allowed to remarry. The custom of *sati*, where the wife was burned alive on her husband's funeral pyre, was banned in 1859. But the law has not removed the stigma of inauspiciousness that attends the widow throughout her life. No lawyer can increase her chances of remarriage. Tradition prescribes that she is not allowed to wear bright colours or flowers in her hair, or bangles, or the dot on her forehead, or the *sindoor*, the red powder in the parting of her hair that marks her auspicious married state. She may be required to shave her hair, or have it cut in a way that does not show a parting. No restrictions are placed on a man whose wife dies.

GIFTS

Gift-giving is an important part of joyous ritual celebrations. The gifts that one has given during one's life will ease the journey of the soul after death. It is a privilege for the person who gives to have the gift accepted, and it is the giver who traditionally expresses gratitude, not the receiver. Instances of sumptuous gifts to mark ceremonial occasions are recorded on the stone walls of temples; gifts of gold, elephants and horses have been bestowed.

The giving of gifts is strictly prescribed. At weddings especially, it is hard work to fulfil all the obligations to everyone's satisfaction. The groom's mother should get the most expensive *sari*, the groom's sisters and sisters-in-law slightly less expensive ones, and so on down the line.

Births and marriages are primarily family events. Indians know what is expected of them by each person in their own circle of obligation, and will give accordingly. Foreigners who are invited to a life-cycle ceremony by friends, servants or colleagues do not have a place within that circle, and their obligations are not clearly defined. It is important to remember that if you give lavish gifts, the recipients may feel obliged to give you lavish gifts in return, even if they can't afford them.

The safest gift is cash. At a wedding, the cash goes to the family, to help offset the huge expenses incurred, and not to the newlyweds. Cash is usually given in an auspicious number—101, 501, 1001 rupees are considered more auspicious. If they are your friends, and you want them to have a gift from you, then a household item that is practical or decorative is an appropriate choice.

The custom of giving presents at children's birthday parties has caught on in the cities, perhaps because the children themselves find it such a good idea. Go ahead and bring a gift, or send one with your child if he or she is invited to the party of an Indian friend. Cash is an acceptable gift on this occasion.

On festival occasions, there may be traditional gifts that are appropriate—for example rice balls on birthday of the elephant-headed god Ganesha. But nowadays sweets, flowers, cakes, and for those who drink, a bottle of wine, are welcomed and accepted gratefully.

ALTERNATIVE LIFESTYLES

Homosexuality is illegal in India, and some religions are very vocal in condemning it; which is not to say it doesn't exist. In most cases, homosexuals try to stay under the radar, and are very discreet. In some situations there is a sense that it

Men hold hands as a sign of friendship.

is better neither to ask nor to tell. I have very dear friends whom I have known for years who I suspect may be gay, but they have not chosen to share that with me, nor have I ever asked.

Since there is little sexual experimentation between young men and women, there is a kind of sexual activity that happens between adolescent men which is not considered to be homosexual at all, and the young men would be deeply insulted if anyone suggested that it was. It is expected that they will get married and have heterosexual relationships, and leave that kind of sexuality behind.

Men holding hands with each other is not a sign of homosexuality either. I discuss it further in chapter 8, in the section on body language. Nor does 'gay' universally mean what it does in the West: Gay Travels and Gay Man Tailors, in Chennai, just want to suggest a carefree shopping and travelling experience. Be very careful when approaching the topic, because there can be serious repercussions in some circles.

Below are some tips to help you settle into Indian society:

- Do expect to be invited to a variety of social events, even by people you hardly know.
- Do take a gift, keeping in mind religious sensibilities, eating and drinking habits and your relationship to the recipient.
- Do enjoy the special characteristics of the celebration: henna designs, holi coloured powders, flying a kite etc.
- Don't feel compelled to accept every invitation.
- Don't give very lavish presents to people not well known to you.

THE PRACTICALITIES

CHAPTER 5

'In India, 'cold weather' is merely a conventional
phrase and has come into use through the necessity
of having some way to distinguish between weather
which will melt a brass door-knob and weather
which will only make it mushy'
—Mark Twain

FORMALITIES

It used to be that one's first taste of Indian bureaucracy came with the trip to the Indian embassy or consulate to apply for the visa. When I went to the consulate here in Toronto, there were no applications forms—they had run out. I had to wait in line for 20 minutes for that piece of information, and no one was even a little apologetic about the inconvenience. I had tried to call before going to the office, but only got an answering machine or a busy signal. It was as if the embassy was trying to say, 'if you can't handle this, maybe a trip to India is not for you.'

India has streamlined the visa application procedure, and now you can even download visa application forms over the internet. The website address is provided in the resource guide at the end of the book.

There is not one formula for visas which is valid for everyone, as India, just like any other country, has bilateral agreements with different countries. The best plan is to contact the consulate or embassy near you. Consular staff can help you figure out which is the best visa for your requirements. But all visas are entered into the passport, so the application forms along with a valid passport, photos and supporting documents must be submitted to an Indian embassy or consulate. Besides the tourist visa and transit visa, visas are granted in the following categories: business, employment, student, research, missionary, journalist and conference. All these require longer to process, with additional supporting material, so please consult the website, which is very clear about the conditions. Visas for spouses are usually granted for any long-term stay.

All foreigners staying in India for more than six months at a stretch need to fill out forms and get a piece of paper from the Foreigner's Registration Office, which can be found in

Types of Visas

- Tourist Visa: Normally given for six months, depending on the country of residence. You may have to produce documents to prove your financial standing.
- Business Visa: Valid for one or more years with multiple entries. A letter from sponsoring organisation indicating nature of business, probable duration of stay, places and organisations to be visited, and a guarantee to meet maintenance expenses, etc. should accompany the application.
- Student Visa: Issued for the duration of the academic course of study or for a period of five years whichever is less, on the basis of firm letters of admission from universities/recognised colleges or educational institutions in India.
- Journalist Visa: Issued to professional journalists and photographers visiting India. The applicants are required to contact the External Publicity Division of the Ministry of External Affairs in New Delhi or in other places, the Office of the Government of India's Press Information Bureaus.
- Employment Visa: Issued to skilled and qualified professionals engaged or appointed by companies, organisations, economic undertakings as technicians, technical experts, senior executives etc. Applicants are required to submit proof of contract/employment/engagement of foreign nationals by the company or organisation.

If you stay in India for more than two years you are supposed to undergo an Aids test at a government hospital. No one can explain to me the logic of this requirement. India has a serious HIV/Aids problems, true, but foreigners have a negligible impact on the situation.

most big cities. The procedure is not complicated, but is long and tedious, so take a good book. The piece of paper or booklet you receive allows you to pay the Indian rate on airline tickets and luxury hotel rooms (foreigners pay about 15 per cent more). If you are working or doing business in India for more than six months, then you have to get clearance to leave, a 'No Objection Certicate' from the tax authorities, or else you may get hassled at the airport.

CITY LIVING

Only 30 per cent of the population of India lives in the cities, but 30 per cent of a billion means that, although there may be more people somewhere else, there sure are a lot of people right here. Urban structures lie shipwrecked in the sea of humanity and a flowing, sinuous, teeming mass enlivens the streets, causing what Erik Erikson calls 'sensory and emotional seasickness'. Every space is filled, and just as on temples, where carvings complicate every surface, there is

City contrasts—shanty dwellings are a common feature.

no background, only the endlessly shifting patterns of the human form in all its postures.

The fastest-growing part of the cities are the *bastis*, the shanty towns filled with those from the villages lured by Pied Piper promises of a better life. More than one-third of the population in the four major cities lives below the poverty line. The slums encroach on the pockets of affluence from every side so that the compound wall of the house with five air-conditioners is the only stable part of the thatched and resourceful construction that shelters five people on the other side.

ACCOMMODATION

In the big cities of India, there are neighbourhoods where most foreigners live, in big houses with beautiful gardens surrounded by high walls. Here, it is possible to create a cool, serene oasis amid the noise and bustle and strangeness of India. It is natural to try to create a refuge, with familiar things in their accustomed order. Harsh realities can be shut out for a time.

To some extent, it is desirable and possible to create such a sanctuary. But ideas of normal life must be adjusted to Indian standards. No matter how posh your neighbourhood, and how insulated you are in your beautiful house with the high compound walls, Third World realities will sometimes intrude. It is usually the woman, the wife and mother, who must cope with the conflicts that arise between the expectations of husband and children, and the realities of life in India.

The telephone doesn't work. The power's just gone off. The water won't come on until 4 o'clock. The gas cylinder for the cooking stove has run out, and the man at the gas supply promises a replacement in two days. Two days! How does anything ever get done in this country? In developed countries, electricity, telephone and constant running water have come to be accepted as the bare necessities of life. But only one quarter of the world's population, using 80 per cent of the world's resources, is able to achieve that standard of living. For the other three-quarters, such things are still luxuries, and not to be taken for granted. Welcome to the Third World.

Renting a House
Posh

Every city has its better neighbourhoods. In Delhi, where many foreigners live and work, there are areas well known to be where the foreigners find their homes. These areas have houses that are up to Western standards of convenience. Many of them are very grand, with marble floors and attached bathrooms and well-equipped (with ovens, for example) kitchens.

In Bombay, apartments are the general rule. The rent situation is so tight that most companies bringing in foreign executives have long-term leases on apartments for their use. The company apartment is a welcome perk also for Indian executives in Bombay. Not many foreigners live in Madras and Calcutta; there is neither the number of foreign service staff as in Delhi nor the personnel from foreign companies as in Bombay. Even the posh houses may not have Western-style conveniences and fittings, although nowadays, most have Western-style toilets rather than the squat kind.

Houses and apartments can be found both furnished and unfurnished, but unfurnished is the norm for long-term rental.

A house in a top residential neighbourhood usually has a security guard.

Unfurnished may mean without even air-conditioners and refrigerators. Fans and lighting fixtures may be included.

Many landlords prefer foreign tenants because they know that eventually you will leave. The laws in India make it difficult to evict long-term tenants. For the same reason, landlords may also prefer a company lease rather than a private one. It is customary to give several months' rent in advance as a deposit that is refundable as rent for the last few months of your stay. If you are staying only for some months, you may have to pay the whole amount before you move in. Many, if not most, landlords give a receipt for only that part of the rent they intend to declare for income tax purposes. The rest, as much as 90 per cent of it, is 'black'.

Indian Style
It is also possible to live in ordinary middle-class neighbourhoods for a fraction of the cost of the posh colonies. Of course, you have to give up the American or European notion of what constitutes reasonable living conditions. Indians may be used to having running water for a couple of hours every other day; it may not be so easy for you to structure your life around those hours. Are you prepared to wake up early and fill huge buckets, and then wash dishes

A truck delivers water to a middle-class Indian neighbourhood.

and bathe according to your reservoir of water? Can you live without a telephone? Without an air-conditioner? It is best to consider these things seriously before moving into a middle-class house.

If you do move into an Indian middle-class neighbourhood, then your neighbours will be able to tell you about the hours of water supply, what the electricity situation is, and so on, because these are problems that affect the whole neighbourhood at once, not just you. There are advantages as well as problems. All your marketing will be cheaper. The locations may have more convenient access to markets and public transportation, as most Indians there don't own cars. You'll never be lonely, as there will always be people around. And your experience of India will be closer to that elusive 'real India' than in a neighbourhood where every house has a high wall around it and a guard at the gate.

Finding a House

Houses are advertised in the newspapers, but are usually to be found through agents. The agents are not always aware of your expectations, and it is sometimes difficult to convey these expectations to them in a way that is convincing. A new breed of agent is emerging, in the big cities— usually a well-educated woman with good contacts, who moves in the same circle as foreigners. She understands their needs and is well-versed in the intricacies of dealing with an outsider's expectations.

The agent's commission is usually one or two months' rent. Rents in Bombay and Delhi for above-standard accommodation can be as high as in New York or London, in dollar terms; that comes to an exorbitant amount in rupees. In Madras and Calcutta, prices are much less at the moment, but posh houses in prime neighbourhoods are not cheap in those cities either.

Below are some tips on finding a home:

- Ask people who will give you an unbiased report about potential problems—colleagues, Indian acquaintances, your predecessors in the country, or foreigners who have lived some time in India.

- Indians may assume that you are only interested in the most luxurious accommodations, so be clear if you are willing to look at Indian style places.
- In Bombay and Calcutta, check whether the roads in the neighbourhood you are considering get flooded.
- Ask about power supply—some neighbourhoods experience more frequent power cuts.
- Ask about telephone lines; if they are already installed in the neighbourhood, it will be easier for you to get a phone quickly.
- Expect Western-style toilets, and showers, but not bathtubs.
- Check the traffic on the roads; the urban centres in India have serious traffic problems. Carefully check plumbing, electrical outlets, lighting fixtures, fans, air-conditioning, etc and be clear on what is working, not working, before paying the security deposit, which is usually very steep.

APPLIANCES

There are stores selling everything you might need for a long stay in India. The quality and selection may not be perfect, but the appliances bought in India are made for Indian conditions and can be fixed by Indian repairmen. There are washing machines, ovens, microwaves, blenders, irons, etc. The only things that I have brought into India with me are an espresso machine and an electric waffle maker.

Furniture design may leave something to be desired, but even here there are boutiques with interesting furniture, not all of it very well made. There are stores in the posh neighbourhoods which sell heavy upholstered pieces, as well as stores where you can have your own designs realized with the help of trained staff. You can also buy beautiful antique and colonial pieces at very reasonable prices.

ELECTRICITY

Normal life in India includes power cuts, euphemistically called load-shedding, that disrupt the electricity supply for minutes or hours throughout the day and night. At times when power demands are too high for the city power supply to meet, the supply to areas without hospitals or factories—and therefore largely residential—is cut off. When the air-conditioner or fan suddenly fades off in the middle of the night, and you lie in an ever-widening pool of perspiration in the oppressive heat, this is merely a nuisance. Power cuts also disrupt work schedules, meetings, movies and performances.

At night, children may be frightened by the sudden darkness of a blackout. It does become very dark, for even the street lights in the neighbourhood go off. It is important to keep torches and candles (with batteries and matches) in convenient places. Usually, blackouts last only minutes, but once in a while, minutes stretch into hours. Even when there is power, the supply is erratic and the voltage fluctuates alarmingly. All major appliances, such as refrigerators, television sets and computers, require a stabiliser to regulate the current and prevent the surges that can cause severe damage. When there is current, it is 230–240 volts, 50 cycles, alternating current, as in Europe.

The Electrician

The electrician's tools of trade are a very large pair of rubber gloves, a key-ring holding an array of keys suitable for opening any main circuit-box in the city, a light-bulb with two wires attached to detect current, and an assortment of wires. The fuses are generally the old-fashioned ones wound with wire, and the wiring in the house may be aluminium running in metal pipes. If a fuse blows, the tendency is to increase its capacity by winding more wire around it, which in turn increases the flow through the wires in the house. Moisture in the pipes and a weak cable can lead to a nice fireworks display emerging from the living room socket.

The solution to constant problems and repairs is to keep an electrician on a monthly retainer, rather than paying separately for each job as it comes up. Then it is in his interests to maintain good working order, instead of coming up with the dangerous quick fix.

TELEPHONES

It used to be very difficult to get a phone in India. But in April 2005, India passed the 100 million mark for phones installed, making it the fifth largest phone population in the world. The phone density is still low: only about ten people in a hundred have a phone, which is hard to believe, since the vegetable vendor, the auto-rickshaw driver, the carpenter, all carry around cellphones these days. Many people who have land lines also have cellphones, and prefer to give out that number as it is more reliable.

The increased competition has made the process of getting a land line much simpler, and without the long wait. Service is more consistent, and there are fewer breakdowns and crossed connections. The two companies providing connections for landlines are Bharat Sanchar Nigam and Mahanagar Telephone Nigam. They both provide information on applying for a phone on their websites, and promise a connection within one week

Cellphones are easily available everywhere in the big cities, but not all the companies offer the same services. Only by asking the locals can you find the phone company that offers the best rates and service. There are prepaid and post paid services. For the former, you buy a rechargeable card with as much money as you want to spend, and then top it up as you need. The post paid service requires that you have proof of a fixed address, and you are billed on your usage every month.

There seems to be no such thing as cellphone etiquette in India; not only do cellphones ring in concert halls, but the person actually answers, and talks while the musicians are playing! People take calls in almost every social situation with no inhibition whatsoever.

Public Telephones

Nowadays there are also public phones for local and STD calls all over the cities, which usually have well-maintained phones and clear lines. STD stands for Standard Trunk Dialling, and it means a long-distance (including international) call. The sign for this facility is usually very big, and can be found in all kinds of obscure corners. When you enter, you find little cubby-hole offices, with from one to several phones, and

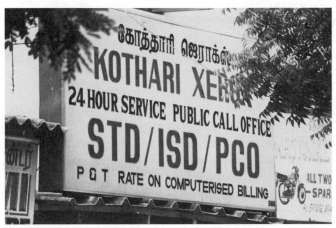

A 24-hour public call office makes it convenient for one to contact friends and loved ones.

a helpful man or woman who runs the place. Sometimes faxing is also possible.

There may be a booth where you can make your call in private; sometimes there is just one phone, with you on one side of a table, the person who runs it on the other, and a whole bunch of people waiting all around. It is not so easy to have an intimate conversation with the love of your life—unless you speak in a foreign tongue like Mandarin. People are not shy about listening in on your conversations, and may even give you advice, as happened to me when I was trying to finalise the details for buying a piece of land.

Usually, the charge is calculated electronically on a little LCD display, so you can see how much each 'I love you, darling' costs. At the end, a small commission is added. It is a very convenient way of making long-distance calls, as even if you have a telephone, you may not have long-distance dialling facilities on your line.

INTERNET

It is possible to get Internet connections through the telephone companies, but as yet the service is not fast and reliable. There are Internet cafes in even small villages in India and you will see all kinds of people using the Internet, to keep in touch with grandchildren in the US, to find a bride or groom, get astrological information, and access porn.

WATER

Both the quality and the quantity of tap water in India may present problems. Municipal water supply can be erratic and insufficient to maintain water pressure at more than a dribble for much of the day. In some parts of India, houses have underground or overhead storage tanks that fill up during the hours of supply. Then water flows to meet the family needs as if there was indeed constant running water.

Madras and Bombay regularly face water scarcity, when access to water depends on one's ability to pay for it. The poor queue for hours in the streets; those who can afford it have it delivered in big tankers. In Madras, there is underground water in parts of the city, where houses may have their own well from which water can be pumped into an overhead tank as needed.

Drinking Water

If the well and the overhead tank are kept clean and covered, well water may be safe to drink without any further treatment. Municipal water is not. To be on the safe side, wherever you are in India, boil and filter drinking water. Water must be kept at a rolling boil for 10 minutes to be safe from bacteria, and even then, it should be filtered as well.

The most common type of water filter uses a ceramic cone through which the water passes drop by drop. The ceramic cone of the filter must be removed, scrubbed clean, and boiled regularly. How often depends on the quality of the water being filtered through it. It starts to turn brown or grey as it traps the dirt, so it is easy to see when it needs to be cleaned. Once every week or two weeks is usual.

Nowadays, bottled drinking water is available almost everywhere. Drinking water can be purchased in large plastic jugs, some which have a little tap built in, and some which fit onto a dispenser. These can be ordered and delivered to your door, or can be bought as needed from the general shops. There is a deposit on the plastic jugs, which is paid back when you leave.

CRIME

Houses in India usually have high compound walls around them and watchmen at the gate. The windows and doors often have metal grills or prison-like bars. This may give you the impression that there is a lot of crime in India. According to the latest statistics, the crime rate in the cities is going up, but senior police officers say it is only the result of the rising population. According to Delhi's police commissioner, most of the crimes take place in the squalid shanty towns that have become a part of every big city.

In Delhi, the main roads have checkpoints manned by armed police almost every half mile. Since the criminals must be aware of the location of these checkpoints, there is nothing to stop them from travelling by some other route. Still, they do serve to remind Delhi inhabitants that a serious problem exists and it pays to be careful.

Most houses are equipped with low-tech burglar protection: sturdy padlocks and heavy bolts. But lowest tech of all is the neighbourhood *chowkidar*, or watchman, who keeps watch through the night, assuring you of his alertness on the job,

Tight security on the streets.

and warning off potential thieves by walking around blowing a whistle intermittently, and banging with a big stick. At first, the periodic shrill blasts and percussive accompaniment keep you awake; after a while you only notice it when he stops, and that's when you can't sleep.

Street Crime

Until recently, Indian cities were among the safest in the world for a woman alone. One might worry about having one's pocket picked, but that was about it. Now the crime rates are going up, including rape.

Pickpocketing and petty theft are a problem in Indian cities, but no more than in other big cities elsewhere in the world. Be careful where you put your wallet or purse in crowded situations. This is just common sense, and that is what is most necessary in India. Chain-snatching is another possible crime. Someone (sometimes a young man on a motorcycle) grabs the gold chain from around your neck, breaks it and runs off. Indian women find this a serious problem, because often their *taali*, the chain symbolising their marriage, is gold. On the streets, women either don't their gold, or they tuck the chain under the *sari* where it will not be so easy for the thief to secure a grasp. I did have a gold chain snatched once. In Rome.

> Don't attempt anything illegal, like meeting attractive young ladies through intermediaries. That puts you into direct contact with the kind of people who commit crime, which is what you want to avoid.

SERVANTS

If modern technology is not at your beck and call, people certainly are. Servants are there to do the work you don't like, or can't do, or don't have the time for. This is putting it strongly, but if you so desire, you can hire a servant to tie your shoelaces every morning. In India, no sense of pride attaches to doing things for oneself; rather, manual work of any kind lowers one's status. So every Indian household that can afford it has a multitude of servants: a cook, a maid, a gardener, a *chowkidar* to guard the house, a driver, an *ayah*

In a country where the one overwhelming resource is human beings, it is almost a sin not to take advantage of the possibilities that having servants provides.

to mind the children, a *dhobi* to wash the clothes, a bearer to fetch and carry and do almost anything except clean the toilets. Cleaning toilets is a task that only untouchables will do in India.

Getting the work done is only one of the benefits. More important is the fact that they know this country, and their knowledge will often make up for your ignorance. The cook knows where to buy good quality beef in a country where eating the meat of the cow is taboo, and how to solve the problem of the gas cylinder's non-availability. The *ayah* will find playmates in the neighbourhood for your children. The cleaner will clean your house from top to bottom without the benefit of a vacuum cleaner, mop, or any advertised miracle spray, powder, liquid or wax.

For what amounts to a pittance in Western terms, you provide several families with an income that allows them to send their children to school, eat and dress properly, and pursue a profession they view with some pride. You are an employer, and in a country with high unemployment, you can make a small contribution to keeping the economy going. Your servants represent the part of India you might otherwise never come into contact with. Very often, they will live in the servants' quarters attached to your house. Their families and their lives will become an important part of your experience of India.

The Master-Servant Relationship

The employer and the servant are linked by mutual ties of obligation. As *sahib* and *memsahib*, you will be expected to attend weddings, name newborn babies, give loans, fill in application papers, and perform a multitude of ceremonial duties better suited to members of the royal family.

The master-servant relationship is a remnant of an old feudal system. The servant has little protection if you choose to hire and fire on whim. Take your time to hire full-time live-in servants, and do not have them coming and going through your house as if you've got a revolving door. Small mistakes early on must be corrected and forgiven, and are not justification for firing. Servants need as much time to adjust to you as you need to adjust to having them.

There is no union for servants, no health insurance, no dental plan, no unemployment benefits of any kind. You take on these responsibilities when you hire a servant. This is not stated, but it is understood. Reason and conscience must guide you to an equitable arrangement in unforeseeable circumstances, such as death or serious illness.

You will undoubtedly find yourself at some stage (sometimes the very first day of work) put in the difficult position of having to decide whether to lend your servants money. Take the request seriously, for it is sure to be a matter of great importance—usually to do with weddings. Treat it as a loan, no matter how negligible the sum when translated into dollars or pounds; get a signed receipt, establish a repayment schedule, and sign for each sum deducted from the salary towards repayment. A request for a loan is not a hint for a gift, and should be handled just as a bank would. You should not, of course, charge interest.

Lending money has never been a problem with me, and every servant I have ever had has borrowed money. Large or small amounts were paid back meticulously over the years. I think the correct attitude on the part of the employer is important. For the servant, the loan represents a substantial sum of money; for you it may be less than the amount you spend on a meal at an expensive restaurant. If you don't take the loan seriously and keep track of the repayments according to the schedule you've both agreed on, if that trouble seems too much for you, then the servant will begin to think of the amount that way too—negligible to you and therefore not worth troubling about.

Servants will, especially in South India, establish a relationship of equality in some respects, and suddenly switch to a consciousness of caste, religion, age, and class status in others. Eating and drinking are the areas where caste and class taboos are strongest. The maidservant who will discuss with you intimate female problems, tell you how to treat your husband, and scold you when you get angry with the children, will not drink tea with you. She will take her own special cup and sit on the floor just outside the room you are in and continue to harangue you from there.

Servant to Servant

The servants will establish a hierarchical structure among themselves, with caste, age, sex and job status determining who can tell who what to do. This may not be the most efficient system. The brightest person, or the one who speaks the best English, may be your choice to relay messages to the cook; but if that person is also young, female and low-caste, your old male cook may not heed a word she says, and demand to have his orders directly from you.

Toilet-cleaning is an area of sensitivity for servants. Besides hiring a person to clean your house, you may have to hire someone who enters through a back door, never stays for tea, and does nothing but clean the toilets. This, the most degrading task, is reserved for the untouchable. Gandhiji made the cleaning of toilets an important tenet of his philosophy precisely because the taboo against it is so strong. But despite his teachings, most Indians haven't learned that lesson at all, and in some parts of India the stigma that attaches to the person who cleans the toilet is as strong as ever.

> This problem of hierarchy may be your most difficult when trying to manage your servants. Once it is sorted out, things can run smoothly. Whether you choose to honour their system, or fight to work out a more equitable system of your own, it is best to know the forces at work.

Hiring on References

In the old wealthy Indian joint families, the servants and their families were part of the whole structure. The children of the servants became the servants for the next generation. Even now, some Indian families have servants for their lifetime, and they are like members of the family. If the family's ancestral home is in Kashmir, then when a son or daughter moves to Delhi, a servant from home may accompany them. This is no longer so common, and even Indian families scramble around getting servants as best they can.

I have not yet come across a reliable agency through which you can hire your servants. One that I did approach seemed to be a front for some kind of escort service. The American Embassy women's organisations or clubs often have a registry of servants, through which you can contact some potential servant. And although the embassy is in Delhi, the other big cities have consulates. The Americans seem to provide the best help networks for their staff and families, and some of these services, such as the servant registry, are open to anyone who knows about them.

The servant's grapevine is the most common source for servants. Tell the servants of friends what you are looking for. The news that you need a cook, a gardener, a maid, will travel through their network, and applicants will show up at your doorstep with carefully preserved references from a previous job. The servant's references are treasures that are unwrapped and laid before you. These much folded and unfolded, old, tattered, brown-stained pieces of paper with the comments of previous employers are their credentials. My husband's cook, who worked with German families for more than 25 years showed me references from 1964. He had kept them all. You must read them, every single one; then you will realise that the person who stands before you is a paragon of every 'servantly' virtue. It can't be otherwise.

Hiring on Reference

When I met my husband in Delhi, he had an extremely well-run household with great servants. Shaukat, the old cook, and Jagdish, the man-of-all-work, lived with us. They were gracious, competent, and completely trustworthy. The *mali* (gardener) was rather fond of pruning, but he was such a beautiful old man and the plants seemed to love him. The *dhobi* (washerman), despite having only four teeth and the habit of talking to himself, was much better than any washing machine.

After my baby was born, I needed to hire an *ayah*, a woman especially to help with the care of children. She moved into my household and worked very well within it for two years. I did not hesitate to recommend her to a friend when we left the country. I was shocked when I discovered that my friend had had to fire her for pilfering. The other servants in my household had made it impossible for her to do anything like that while she was with me.

An Indian friend in Bombay with a large household and several servants suggested that you register your servants with the police, or at least say that you intend to do so. Then those with criminal intentions will decide this job is not quite what they were looking for. The Delhi Police website explains the procedure, and even provides a form. I have never done this, and even the woman who told me about it had never actually bothered, but just the mention of it was enough to sort out the riff-raff.

A perfect servant for someone else is not necessarily the perfect one for you. A friend's servant allowed the two small children (four and seven years old) in her care to walk to their friend's house, without knowing which friend, where the house was, or if the children knew where it was, while she watched TV. Her explanation was that the children wanted to go. That maid also had excellent references. It is possible that in her previous employment, she had never had complete care of children, or that there was some other, more intelligent servant in the house who had covered up her mistakes. What all this boils down to is that you should take references with a pinch of salt, and be careful how you word the ones you write yourself so that you don't unwittingly deceive the next person who reads them.

Because this relationship is perceived by the Indian to be more than between employer and employee, it is crucial to find men and women to work for you with whom you can establish some rapport. Suggest a trial period of a week or two, at a pre-established salary, before settling someone in your home.

Firing

At some point it may be your unhappy task to fire a servant. The reasons are usually petty theft, a personality clash with you or other servants, or negligence on the job. Servants have been known to take nips out of the whisky bottle, or say that they've boiled the water, and then just pour it straight into the filter from the tap.

A servant's refusal to discuss an accusation, or even to deny it will leave you in a fix if you are not sure of what you are saying. If you say, "I believe you stole my Cross pen," the gist of the response you get may well be, "If you dare think a thing like that about me, then I'm leaving." This is no indication of the rightness or wrongness of the accusation. If you are wrong, a servant may still feel hurt enough to leave. If you are right, this is a face-saving way to get out before being fired.

If you do have to fire a servant, it is not difficult if it is clear to the servant what exactly the problem was. If you are sure yourself what your reasons are, and that these are valid reasons, then the servant's desire to save face can work in your favour. You don't have to fire anyone; the servant will quit. For serious reasons like theft, you don't give notice or pay any money. Threaten to call the police if it doesn't go smoothly.

If your reasons are not seen to be valid, for example if the servant's personality grates on you but the servant has not actually done anything wrong, then you must give notice and a bonus of one month's salary for every year or part of a year the servant worked for you. You must also make up a convincing reason for your actions; for example, to the *dhobi* you could say that you have decided to get a washing machine. In these circumstances, you should write a letter of reference.

To Have Them or Do Without Them?

For various reasons, some people have trouble deciding whether to have servants. To every problem there is usually a solution—if you look hard enough for one.

Privacy

Despite all the advantages I see in having a servant, my foreign friends often complain about the lack of privacy. They say, "I can't walk around the house naked." That's very true, but it is hardly surprising that the concept of privacy has little meaning to someone whose whole family does all of its living, sleeping and eating in the same room. The servant who has not worked for foreigners before will not necessarily knock before entering, even if it's the bedroom.

Define your inviolable space and set the times when you are not to be disturbed. My husband had an arrangement that servants were not to come upstairs until he had buzzed for the water pump to go on. That worked reasonably well, although sometimes unexpected guests were required to hang around for hours and wonder goodness knows what about his activities, because, although the servant was not prepared to go up the stairs, he did not mind disclosing to these guests that *sahib* was in the bedroom, where he must never be disturbed!

If it is very important to you to be able to walk around the whole house naked, then consider some other arrangement. Part-time servants is one, and if you live in an apartment, then a maid who works elsewhere in the same building can also be hired to work for you. This is a common arrangement.

Sub-standard Work

Another complaint I've often heard is, "They just can't do the work up to my standards. I would rather do it myself." I hate housework so much that such an idea has never occurred to me. In fact, I can't even imagine how it could be done so badly I would rather do it myself. Let me put it this way: I would rather have someone come to the house and pretend to do it than do it myself. So you can see that this is a situation I am not well prepared to deal with.

Given their lifestyle, literacy and exposure to the world, are your demands reasonable? It is important to try to see the situation from their point of view. Take a simple thing like boiling the water: do they know about bacteria, the relationship between bacteria and diseases, and the fact that boiling and filtering destroy the bacteria? If they don't (and how should they if no one has ever told them), then the boiling and filtering of water seems like an arbitrary whim of the eccentric foreigner.

> In my house in Madras, there was no toilet-paper holder in the toilet, and so I just balanced the roll on the window ledge. The next day, I couldn't find the toilet paper anywhere in the bathroom. My maid had put it on my desk, 'with the rest of your papers'.

You can't take this kind of knowledge for granted. Every servant I have known has been ready and eager to try to understand my view and what I wanted from them. Sometimes, I could see by their expressions this did not always make much sense.

You can train your servants to some extent, and you may find that you have to keep repeating your corrections, but it is not because they are stupid or lazy. At a certain point you will just have to live with what they are capable of doing. Or you can do it yourself. Even in India, servants are losing ground to technology. The *dhobi* is being replaced by the washing machine; the driver is one person too many in the new small cars. Maybe this is a good thing. The children of servants are not becoming servants. There is upward mobility despite the caste system. My *dhobi* with no teeth has put his children through college. The daughter of my friend's cook is a well-known Kathak dancer who has performed all over the world. I saw her on TV in Singapore. India is changing.

SHOPPING

For more than a thousand years, people from all over the world have come to India just to go shopping. India offers up its splendours now as in the centuries before, not only the rare and wonderful and expensive, but the simple and necessary and everyday. Bazaars spill over with the abundance and variety of simply everything, including the kitchen sink.

The Supermarket

Posh neighbourhoods in the big cities have supermarkets, which certainly make the process of shopping much more efficient. The supermarket tries to have a good supply of all household necessities in one place. There are shopping carts and checkout counters with scanners; in the aisles, you will find frozen food, breakfast cereal, juice in cartons, cleaning products, dental products, almost anything you might need. At the end of your shopping your groceries will be packed into plastic bags for your convenience.

The Neighbourhood Market

Every neighbourhood has a market that supplies the essentials of life: fruit and vegetables, milk and rice, dry goods, hardware and stationery. The markets vary according to the people who live in the surrounding neighbourhoods, so that where South Indians live, you can find *kolam* powder, where Muslims live, you can find meat, and where foreigners live, you find very exotic vegetables like celery—with prices to match. Many Indians continue to shop at the neighbourhood markets even when there are supermarkets nearby, because of the quality and freshness of produce and the prices.

Foreigners can find even celery at a neighbourhood market in New Delhi.

A Market for Everything

There are also the specialist markets: different ones for flowers, fruit and vegetables, automotive parts, electrical wiring, export quality T-shirts, antiques and silver jewellery, and so on, for almost anything you can think of buying. If you can locate the right market that deals in what you are looking for, then you will find a cluster, or a block, or a whole street, devoted to shops selling nothing but that sort of thing. If one shop doesn't have just the right colour or size or shape, perhaps the next shop will.

Many market areas are arranged around a core, with each street leading off from it devoted to something different. The centre may have fruits and vegetables, and one street may have fabrics, another spices and provisions, another stainless steel, and so on. Others are more specific; everything to do with building, for example: wood on one street, plumbing fixtures on another, lighting and electrical supplies on another, and so on. Your neighbourhood market may have shops that supply all these things, but if you are looking for something specific, or for larger quantities, the variety and the prices are unbeatable at the appropriate specialist market.

Neighbourhood markets may well be open every day of the week, from early morning to late night, with no actual closing time; but for a few hours in the middle of the day, you can only get served by waking someone up. Still, if the baby needs milk, you know you can get it. Most regular stores open at 10:00 am, pull down their shutters from about 1:00–3:00 pm for lunch and siesta, and then stay open until between 7:00–10:00 pm.

The locations of such markets are well-known to Indians. The first time you go, it is helpful to have an Indian friend accompany you, as English may not be widely spoken. But even without a translator, you can manage, because many things are displayed and the shopkeepers know their subject of specialisation and will be eager to serve you.

Big markets usually close for one day a week, and this is not uniform throughout the city. In areas where many foreigners live, and where tourists shop, Sunday may be the holiday. In predominantly Muslim areas it will be Friday.

Some markets are closed on Mondays, others on Tuesdays. Find out before you drive across the city which day that market closes.

Door-to-door

You need not venture further than your own threshold to go shopping. In Indian middle-class neighbourhoods, fruits and vegetables, fish, kerosene for stoves, plastic buckets and stainless steel pots can be bought at the door. In neighbourhoods where foreigners live, cane furniture and baskets, carpets, embroidery, brass and other luxury items may also be available. Things will be balanced on the head, tied in complicated bundles on a bicycle, or pushed in a cart.

The man who buys old newspapers, bottles and tins comes door-to-door. So does the knife-sharpener, repairer of broken bamboo blinds, and the person who fluffs up and cleans the cotton stuffed in quilts. Snake-charmers and flute-makers, and men pushing tiny mobile merry-go-rounds and Ferris wheels also call out for customers.

Vendors announce their presence and their products with a distinctive call, some as melodious as a chant, that they sing

This man sells cane furnituire door to door.

out as they walk through the streets of the neighbourhood. Once you recognise each vendor's distinctive cry, you need only go to the door and shout or wave to get the person's attention. Then the goods will be unwrapped and displayed before you. Except for the luxury items like carpets and brass, it is not polite to call someone over 'just to look', with no intention to buy, as you might do at a shop. Once the street vendor brings down a load, he or she expects to make a sale. The prices are usually very good, but it is still necessary to bargain.

Bargaining

Bargaining is a way of establishing the best possible price for both parties involved in a transaction: the seller must feel that this is the maximum the buyer is willing to pay; and the buyer must feel that this is the minimum the seller is willing to accept. Then only will the process of bargaining have been successful.

Paying the first price short-circuits the whole process, leaving you overcharged, and the shopkeeper disgruntled. If you are incredulous, think about it. If you pay the first ludicrous price that's asked, the seller, rather than being pleased, will actually feel cheated—of the even more ludicrous amount you might have been willing to pay!

There are places where you just don't bargain. The provision store and bakery are not places to bargain, but the fruit and vegetable stalls are. All government-run emporia have fixed prices, so do the big department stores, and jewellery and *sari* shops. Smaller shops selling exactly the same thing usually don't fix prices. A store where the owner is also the salesman, or at least to be found somewhere keeping an eye on the premises, is likely to be a place to bargain, but if everyone in the store is an employee, then it's more likely that the prices are fixed. If the price is displayed, that's also a sign that the price really is fixed, although not in every case. Where a sign says 'Fixed Price' but no price tags are displayed on the items, it usually means the price was fixed when you walked in the door, and is subject to some friendly negotiation.

The big city shopping centre tries to recreate the Western mall.

For fruits and vegetables, and the day-to-day things, it may be easier to allow the servants to do the marketing; they'll get a better price. There is one price for the Indian housewife doing her own shopping, a higher one for the servant buying with someone else's money, and a yet higher one for the wealthy foreigner. (All foreigners are by definition wealthy—otherwise how did they come to India?)

Even so, the price difference will not be much, and it is not worth getting upset or throwing tantrums over what amounts to a few cents. Of course, it is not really the money; it is a matter of pride or principle, you say, to get a fair price. But it is better to pay the higher price if that means avoiding ill-will and arguments than to stick to your principles and cause unnecessary unpleasantness and inconvenience for yourself. As you stay on longer in a place, and get to know the language and people, and start to bargain with assurance, you will naturally get better prices. When you can get the same price as the Indian, you'll know you've really settled in.

For antiques or gemstones or carpets, a good deal of money may be involved, and it is well worth some effort to get the price down. The first step is to find out what the item you want should rightly cost. Ask at several shops, and learn to distinguish the variations in quality and workmanship. Try not to reveal the extent of your interest in a particular piece you want; ask the price of several items, including that one. The less interested you seem in a piece, the better your bargaining position. Remain patient and pleasant, and keep your sense of humour. It's a game of strategy. Don't put the seller into a position of losing face by accepting your price. Both sides have to move from their first offer, so never start with the price you're willing to pay. Start lower, and work your way up by small increments.

Bargaining for a luxury item takes time, even weeks, if you have the time, and if saving the money is worth the risk of losing the item to someone else. Drink tea, make small talk. Pretend to walk away. Come back another day and offer just a little more. Persistence will pay off. Once a seller has accepted your price, it is bad manners to try to bargain further, or to refuse to take the item. So don't start bargaining unless you are willing to buy for the price you offer.

One useful hint is that the first customer of the day has special status, and most sellers will be very anxious to make a sale to that person, even if it means selling at a reasonable rather than exorbitant price. So go early if you can.

The exchange rate between the rupee and the major currencies is so good that many things are a bargain at twice, thrice or ten times the price. It is not good for your bargaining position to translate from rupees into dollars, but should you ever wonder if you were overcharged, once you've bought the item, you can console yourself with the advantage given by the exchange rate.

WEATHER

The writer Nirad Chaudhuri, in his scathing book about India, *Continent of Circe*, says it is the climate that has made Indians fatalistic, robbed them of their ambition and turned them into swine, as Circe did the men who fell into her clutches. It

is certainly true that the heat and the rain are monumental forces that will shape your lives.

The blazing heat of summer, when the thermometer climbs to 42°C (108°F) in the shade, if there is any, is dry heat, which many people claim to prefer. At this time of the year, the desert cooler is a more natural and effective way to cool than an air-conditioner. It works on the same cooling principle as the human body—water evaporation. The desert cooler has a powerful fan that pulls air through a water-soaked pad of wood fibre and blows it through the house. It is a big, noisy machine, and the wood fibre pads must be changed regularly, but the cooling effect in this intense dry heat is so immediate and refreshing that the disadvantages are easily ignored.

Once humidity becomes a problem, the only way to effect any dramatic cooling is to resort to the air-conditioner. But then, the body must adjust daily to rapid and extreme changes in temperature: in moving from an air-conditioned house to the street, air-conditioned car to outdoor market, air-conditioned restaurant to outdoor pool, air-conditioned office to unprotected work site. Constant adjustment can take its toll. There is no perfect solution to the problems of heat.

In cities on the plains, like Delhi, where there is a marked difference between day and night temperatures, it is useful in the hot season to open the windows in the very early morning to allow cool air to enter the house, and then close all the windows and pull the drapes at midday, to keep the interior cool. In the dry heat, the marble floors can be damp-mopped in the afternoon to provide the cooling effect of water evaporation.

Delhi has a real winter. Temperatures at night can go down to 6°C (43°F). North Americans and Europeans may scoff, but when there is no central heating, the cold is deeply felt. Space heaters are the only recourse, although some houses may have a fireplace. The pleasure of winter is that during the day, the weather is clear and bright, with temperatures of about 18°C (64°F)—like a summer day in Canada. Now is the time to keep the windows closed all morning and open them when the sun has warmed the outside air, then close them again before the temperatures drop in the late afternoon.

When the monsoon hits, humidity comes close to saturation point. Bombay and Calcutta suffer the most. Low-lying areas can experience flooding, which affects traffic, power and telephone lines. No housing material is impervious to the effects of tropical weather—mud crumbles, bricks and cement sweat, and plaster takes on a blackish cast from mildew. Wood swells and doors and windows suddenly don't close. Clothes don't dry and need to be hung indoors under the fan, and only ironing will remove residual dampness. Then the air-conditioner is essential, not only to cool, but to dry the air. Shoes, leather belts, books, cassettes and video-tapes are all vulnerable to the effects of mould and fungus that flourish in a humid climate. Expensive equipment, such as computers, cameras, and stereos should be kept in a room that is constantly air-conditioned.

The monsoon brings the mosquitoes. Unfortunately, most houses in India do not have screens fitted on the doors and windows. Mosquito nets, mosquito coils, and various types of electric repellents can be found on the market and all have their advantages and disadvantages. In areas where the power goes off frequently, obviously the plug-in repellent will not be of much use. The mosquito coil, which burns very slowly throughout the night, like incense, sets off hay-fever symptoms in some people. The mosquito net is effective but inconvenient; still, there is nothing more satisfying than listening to the hungry whine of thousands of frustrated mosquitoes as you lie safe within your white tent.

Mosquitoes breed in shallow, stagnant water. Check your own garden, and even the neighbourhood, for places where water collects, such as empty flower pots and clogged drains. Many cities have a malaria control programme and may use fogging devices to disperse pesticides without any warning to residents. Be thankful that something is being done, but close the windows when you notice the characteristic hiss, the chemical smell and the white mist floating towards you.

HEALTH CARE

India has competent doctors and dentists, many of whom have been trained in Europe and America. Embassies and consulates in the big cities give out lists of doctors they recommend. But a doctor's merit cannot be ascertained by the number of degrees and certificates; personality, attitude and a manner that inspires trust are equally important. This is especially true of the paediatrician. Set out to find a doctor and establish a rapport with him or her before there is a medical problem. A personal relationship will insure care and treatment in emergencies. The best way to find a doctor is to talk to friends. The recommendation of someone who has already experienced the doctor's attitude and methods can save you some legwork.

Preventive Medicine

Many of the diseases peculiar to the tropics are spread by contaminated food and water—diarrhoea, dysentery and hepatitis are the most common, but the list includes worms, polio, typhoid and cholera. In the areas where most foreigners live, the unsanitary conditions that give rise to these diseases, such as open sewage and outdoor toilets, don't exist. So if you are careful, it is possible to avoid the really serious diseases, survive the occasional stomach upset and still have a good time in India.

Food and Water

Many of the illnesses you are likely to suffer in India, including the most prevalent and probably inescapable 'Delhi belly', centre around eating and drinking. Religiously using safe drinking water is the easiest and most important step you can take to avoid health problems. This sounds too easy, but since so many of the diseases are waterborne, it eliminates several potential problems in one simple step. Don't forget to use boiled or bottled water for brushing your teeth.

Make sure servants follow the correct procedure when they boil and filter drinking water, wash and prepare vegetables and meat, and store food. Food spoils very quickly in the tropics and should be eaten soon after it is cooked; in the interim, it should be protected from flies.

'Eat raw only foods that can be peeled' is a law for many foreigners in India, but sometimes the fresh salad greens that appear for a few weeks in winter, or the tiny, frosted pale green Hyderabad grapes seem worth taking some risks: soak these in a mild disinfectant solution, and then rinse thoroughly with safe water.

Some embassies even advise their staff to avoid fruits and vegetables that have a high water content, like cucumber and watermelon, because fields are often watered with untreated or 'raw' water. After being in India for some time, you will be better able to judge how careful you need to be. Give yourself time to develop immunities in India before tasting street food. Start off strict, and 'go native' slowly; it's wrong to assume that Indian people don't have the same problems with the food—they do. Diarrhoea is the number one killer of children in India.

Diarrhoea

That doesn't mean you must aggressively dose with antibiotics every stomach upset and attack of the runs. That's the first step on a treadmill of recurring stomach troubles because antibiotics wipe out not only the harmful, but also the beneficial bacteria, leaving the body less able to resist further attacks. The first course is to switch to mild and easily digestible foods, and drink plenty of water, soda or weak, unsweetened tea.

Even my kids know what BRAT food is—it's the acronym for the diarrhoea diet. Bananas, Rice, Apples (grated to be most effective), Tea and Toast. Diarrhoea makes you lose a lot of water, and in a hot climate, this can quickly lead to dehydration. The oral rehydration formula is a big pinch of sugar and a small pinch of salt in the glass of water. You can also buy more sophisticated formulas from the pharmacy. Drink as much as you can.

The kind of drugs that stop diarrhoea by slowing down your gut, or by solidifying the stool are counter-productive. Your body is trying to get rid of the evil germs as quickly as possible, and you're applying the brakes to that process. Still, if you're just about to get on a long flight, they can be useful. Antibiotics are a last resort. If you have diarrhoea that is accompanied by a fever, or with blood or pus in the stool, see a doctor. It may be some form of dysentery, and will need treatment with drugs.

Since there are vaccinations against cholera and typhoid, and gamma globulin injections against infectious hepatitis, some doctors in the West prefer to err on the side of caution and prescribe all of them. Remember, the shots against cholera and hepatitis do not guarantee total protection. Even after the shots, take care of what you eat and drink. The limited effectiveness of the shots only lasts about six months, so it may be more sensible to take them as the need arises—if an epidemic breaks out in your area, or before travelling, when it is more difficult to ensure absolute cleanliness.

Malaria

As with vaccinations, the prophylactic drugs against malaria are not perfect. Larium is now considered the drug of choice, as Indian mosquitoes are resistant to chloroquine. But Larium is known to cause serious side effects in a small minority of users, though some put the minority as high as one in five. In any case, Larium, Malarone and doxycycline give no protection at all from the other diseases that mosquitoes carry, like filariasis and dengue fever.

If you choose to take malaria prophylactics, make sure you take the right dose at the right time. It's dangerous to take too much; it's also dangerous to take too little. You must start a course of tablets before entering a malaria-prone area, and keep on taking them for some weeks after you leave.

Even if you take anti-malaria tablets, continue to use insecticide and mosquito nets whenever there are mosquitoes, and especially rigorously when there is a malaria epidemic in your area. Some strains of malaria are resistant to drugs. The huge swollen legs of some people that you see in India, sometimes called elephantiasis, is also spread by a mosquito. The malaria medicines offer no protection against that. Remember that the best protection is the one you take from the mosquito itself. Odomos is the most popular topical mosquito repellent

Heat

The Indian sun can be deceptive, because it often doesn't burn. Ironically, the dust and traffic pollution provide a protective haze. It can still cause sunstroke. Drink plenty of water because you get dehydrated very quickly. The Western tendency, when confronted by heat, is to remove clothing, the Eastern one is to cover up. Light cotton fabric cut to loosely cover the body will feel cooler than no clothes at all. Even small cuts and scratches get infected quickly in the tropical heat. They should be cleaned immediately with an antiseptic solution. Show your children and your servants how it should be done.

In the north, people stay up late, in the south, they get up early; either way, the day has to be stretched at one end to make up for the wasted hours in the middle, when whoever can, sleeps. A siesta in the hot afternoon is more necessity than indulgence, and a practice well worth cultivating.

Servants' Health

Do try to keep an eye on the health of your servants and their children. The basic health and nutrition advice you probably picked up in high school can come in handy. When my servant's third daughter started to walk I noticed she had slightly bowed legs. I sent her off to the doctor, and tests showed that she had rickets. The normal exposure to the sun in India should have made that most unlikely; but she had been kept indoors all the time because she was a sickly child. A regular dose of vitamin D and playing in the sunshine solved the problem and she now has lovely legs.

It is in your own best interests to have healthy servants. Jaundice, diarrhoea, lice, and numerous other problems can spread to you through them. Make sure they can get medical care at your expense so that they won't hesitate to go to a doctor when they need to. The best arrangement is for them to see the same doctor as you do, so that the doctor can report back to you if the problem is serious. Then you can check to make sure doctor's instructions are followed correctly. A servant in the presence of a doctor may hesitate to ask questions or admit to not understanding these instructions.

Rabies

India has the highest number of rabies deaths in the world—about 25,000 a year. Rabies can be transmitted not only by dogs, but by monkeys and rats, and not all animals exhibit the classic pattern of foaming at the mouth and acting mad. An animal suffering from dumb rabies, which is just as deadly, may not show these symptoms. Nor is it necessarily true that the rabid dog dies within ten days—they can survive as long as a year.

Given this state of affairs, it is important to teach children some rules. It is not safe to pet the numerous stray dogs, sometimes very cute ones, that wander the streets. Even the saliva of a rabid dog, if it comes into contact with cuts, scrapes or mucous membrane, is dangerous. In places where monkeys have gotten used to people (Rishikesh is a good example), they can be very aggressive if they see you have food. They are clever enough to know that it is easier to scare a cookie or banana away from a child than a grown-up. Teach your child to drop any food if an animal shows interest in it.

The rabies virus is easily killed, so the first step to be taken immediately after a bite is to thoroughly clean the wound with soap and water and then disinfect it with a cotton swab dipped in any common disinfectant such as Dettol or even alcohol. Then consult a doctor for an injection of an anti-rabies vaccine.

Several different types of vaccine are available in India. The ones that combine maximum effectiveness with minimum pain are human diploid cell vaccine, imported from France, and purified chick embryo cell vaccine, imported from Germany. The PCEC is now being manufactured in India and may be more readily available. They are very expensive, but can be taken in the arm instead of the stomach.

Presumably, any pet you bring to India will have been properly immunised. Should you acquire a dog in India, make sure it is inoculated with imported vaccine because, until the PCEC is widely available, the Indian one is simply not trustworthy.

Home Medical Kit

Keep the same things you would keep in any country. You may find it useful to bring bandages, individually packed antiseptic towelettes and insect repellent with you from your country. In the section on rural travel, I have recommended a book, *Where There Is No Doctor*. Buy a copy and keep it handy, even where there is a doctor. The English edition of the book, which is published by David Werner, is available at the Voluntary Health Association of India, at 40 Institutional Area, South of I.I.T., New Qutab Hotel, New Delhi-16.

HOSPITALISATION

If you take my advice and get to know a doctor before you ever need one, and if your case is not an emergency, then your doctor can make all the arrangements for your stay at a clinic or hospital. Very few questions will be asked if you are admitted to the clinic or private hospital where your doctor practises.

When my son had his head cut open and had to have stitches, the surgeon responded immediately. He left a golf game when he got my paediatrician's call and met us at his surgery. No questions were asked about money; only about my child.

There is no universal health insurance in India; if you look like you can afford to pay, then the paperwork will involve your health record rather than your financial one. Indians must have some way of sizing up the patient because I have been asked about money before a treatment only once; and in that case it was not a matter of life or death, but an expensive test I chose to have. That was the first time I was asked to pay in advance.

A good private clinic will be clean, and have friendly and helpful staff. You can usually have your choice of a private two-bed or four-bed room. Some places provide food, some don't. In the latter case, you must have someone bring in your meals. Someone might even have to go out to buy the medicine you need. When I had my baby, my husband had to drive over to the pharmacy to pick up the oxytocin needed to speed up my labour.

Private clinics are usually not equipped to handle emergencies. If you happen to have one, go to a hospital, where they will have all the complex and specialised equipment that may be needed. There are privately run hospitals, hospitals run by Christian missionaries and government hospitals. If you have a choice, opt for one of the first two, where you will find conditions comparable to any modern hospital in the world. In fact, India has world class hospitals where patients come from all over Europe, the Middle East and North America to have medical procedures that involve long waits or high cost in their home countries—hip replacements, liposuction, and so on. This has resulted in a new term: medical tourism.

I have heard horror stories of the treatment at some government hospitals. If for some reason you must go to one of these, the standard of treatment may be really bad, not by the doctors, who may be the same ones who also practise privately, but by the staff. These places are overfull and understaffed. You will need to have someone with you all day because the nurses may not be able to attend to you. Food must be brought in for your meals. You will see that each patient has an entourage of relatives who come in shifts and sleep on the floor if necessary.

Indian Medicine

Ayurveda is one popular system of Indian medicine that offers a holistic approach to illness and works with herbs and oils on a theory of balancing the body's humours—wind, phlegm and gall. The diagnosis is done not with expensive tests but by taking the pulse of the patients; the Ayurvedic doctor listens for many things other than the number of heartbeats per minute.

Treatment is with specially prepared pills made from the extracts of herbs. There are also special Ayurvedic massages with oils, and other kinds of treatments using powders or oils mixed with the sap of medicinal plants. The Ayurvedic doctor may recommend a special diet based on the qualities inherent in food, of being *sattvic* (pure), *rajasic* (stimulating) or *tamasic* (inducing languor). The benefit of Ayurveda lies in this: whether it does good or not, at least it does no harm, as strong allopathic drugs may do. It is supposed to work slowly but surely to treat not the symptom of a disease, but the disease itself.

There are fakes and charlatans as well as trained professionals practising Ayurveda. There have been stories of Ayurvedic medicines being adulterated with drugs like steroids. In 1991, 200 slum dwellers died in Delhi after drinking what they thought was Ayurvedic medicine. It is important to go only to respected practitioners of this ancient science. The Kottakal branch of Ayurveda, named after the village in Kerala from which it comes, is supposed to be very good.

Even those not sick can try Ayurvedic tonics and digestives. Herbal masks of sandalwood and almond paste and turmeric, hair oils to prevent greying and dandruff and hair loss, and drops to brighten eyes are more interesting than the Indian-produced Western-style cosmetics.

The risks to health come from three main sources: unclean drinking water, mosquitoes, improperly prepared food. Here are some shorts tips you should remember:

- Find a family doctor you can trust before you need one.
- Teach servants the principals of health that you expect them to adhere to: washing hands, using

boiled or bottled water, using protection against mosquitoes, etc.
- Go native slowly—Indians get diarrhoea too.
- Be wary of stray dogs.
- Slow down—the heat is seriously debilitating.

SCHOOLS

New Delhi and Bombay have international schools. The spacious, well-equipped American school in New Delhi has a swimming pool and all kinds of facilities. There are also smaller schools for the children of other nationalities: a German school, a British school, a French school and a Japanese school.

All the big cities have excellent Indian private schools offering an English-medium education, to which foreigners can admit their children. But one woman told me that there is a saying in Calcutta: 'Three things are hard to get in Calcutta: a job for your husband, a place to live, and hardest of all, a school for the children.' The Indian schools in the other cities seem equally hard to get into. People who had experience of this spoke of a basic difference in attitude: you need the school; the school doesn't need you. You can't check out the school to see whether you want to put your child there; the school will check you out to see whether they want your child.

It is not usually possible to see the classes, find out about the syllabus, get an idea of the teaching methods and philosophy from the principal and staff, so that you can make an informed decision. Rather, you are supposed to go with expressions of unquestioning admiration, and more or less beg the principal to admit your child.

One parent encountered a principal who seemed anti-foreigner; another met a principal who seemed to court foreigners. Many parents spoke of principals being concerned about their (the parents') position and status; diplomats therefore had an easier time. Someone else said that it is effective to just barge through the cultural barriers by playing the brash, ignorant foreigner to the hilt. An Indian woman with an American passport who had no recourse to either of these options was having a hard time. She complained of having to rely on hearsay from friends and acquaintances, and perhaps in the end be forced to accept whichever school would take her child.

For Indian schools, there may be long waiting lists and strict entrance requirements, with mathematics usually at a higher level for the age than in Western countries. Sometimes these are waived for foreign children. Once the child enters school, you have few rights as a parent to question teaching methods or homework, how the child is treated, etc. The school knows best, and you are not to interfere.

For younger children, there are numerous private playschools and kindergartens. Some of them are run according to the Montessori method, which emphasises playful, natural learning. For older children, boarding school may be one option to explore. There are some beautiful boarding schools in the mountains, both in north and south India. Some are run along traditional lines; some, like the Rishi Valley School, near Bangalore, are run according to a philosophy of education that encourages personal growth and development. For short periods, home tutoring is an option, as well-qualified Indian teachers can be found in the cities.

Ask around among Indian and expatriate acquaintances before settling on an Indian school. Since the notion of what constitutes a good school varies from person to person, and given the difficulties of getting information from the school itself, take the time to check thoroughly behind the scenes before approaching the school. Almost every parent whom I spoke to was first told 'no' and then talked into a 'yes'. Don't give up too easily on the school of your choice. Especially if you have older children, it is better to check out the availability of schools before leaving your home country, through your embassy or with company staff in India.

Culture Shock in Indian Schools
The international schools try to recreate the school environment in the home country, and therefore it will be

relatively easy for your children to fit in. But in an Indian school, the system will be different. Holidays will vary from city to city and even from school to school.

Your children may experience school culture shock. Suddenly, there will be a lot more homework (compared to Western schools). Even a 6-year-old child will have half an hour to an hour of homework a day. Uniforms may take getting used to. Girls may find Indian standards of dress and behaviour restrictive and inhibiting. Indian schools may not have as much hands-on work as Western schools. There may be much more theoretical work and rote learning.

One woman told me that her daughter was given 14 words to memorise for spelling, but the child did not know, and was not told, what the words meant. You may have to enrich your child's learning with experiments and practical work at home.

When your children are making friends, remember that foreign kids will probably leave at some point. That can lead to all kinds of heartbreak. Make the effort to find Indian friends for your children. You will likely have to make the first move. Get the phone numbers, invite the kids to your home, make friends with the parents so that your children have a stable circle of friends to shelter them from the trauma of comings and goings among their foreign friends.

TRANSPORTATION

The fact that there are roads and sidewalks in India, just like in any other country, does not have much bearing on the traffic. The sidewalks are for people to sleep, sell their wares, park their bicycles, have tea, listen to radio commentaries on cricket, do all manner of things that have nothing to do with walking from one place to the other. Pedestrians may attempt this obstacle course, or take their chances on the street with the buses, trucks, cars, autorickshaws, cycle rickshaws, bicycles, motorcycles, bullock carts, cows and the occasional camel or elephant.

Rules of Survival on the Road

Although it may seem chaotic, there are some rules, but they are rules of the jungle. At first glance, the rule that supersedes

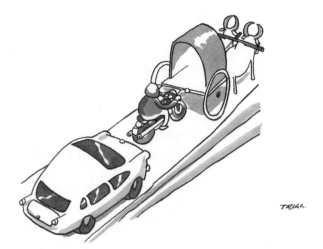

all others seems to be, 'The biggest on the road has the right of way.' The big Tata trucks, overloaded, garlanded, and painted with 'Horn Please', pay scant attention while barging into your lane, ignoring you as a lion might ignore a mouse.

The rule that takes precedence over the previous one is, 'The one who has least to lose has the right of way.' This is why the big imported Mercedes gives way before the battered old Ambassador, and the kamikaze autorickshaws give way to no one. The one rule above all others is, 'Cows always have the right of way.' Killing a cow is tantamount to killing one's own mother. All Indian drivers brake for cows. They don't always brake for pedestrians. Here are some quick tips for driving in India:

- Be ready for anything: all road rules are considered to be guidelines only.
- Use the horn.
- The cow always has the right of way.
- Don't expect warnings of roadwork, potholes, changes from four lanes to two lanes.
- Beware of buses—might is right.
- Traffic can include, but is not limited to, cars, buses, bicycles, autorickshaws, cycle rickshaws, bullock carts, hand carts, pedestrians, cows, goats, elephants, camels.

- Roads are considered useful for getting from one place to another, drying wheat, millet and rice, taking a nap, enjoying a long conversation with someone travelling in the opposite direction, changing a flat tire.

Cars

The most common car on the road is still the Ambassador, a copy of the old British Morris Oxford. The latest model looks not much different than the ones before, so the roads seem full of cars from the 1950s. The Ambassador is a sturdy, solid car that can cope with the roads in India, and can be patched together by every roadside mechanic, but it is hardly a status symbol.

The liberalised economy has led to new snazzy models and big SUVs like the Tata Sumo. These definitely signal the wealth and status of their owners. The latest small cars are more likely to be driven, carefully, by the owner, rather than by a driver.

Two-wheelers

Those who can't afford a car drive a two-wheeler—a scooter, motorcycle or bicycle. The two-wheeler is a great incentive for family planning, because the ideal family the

The Indian nuclear family, a product of urban life, fit on one motorcycle.

government promotes—two parents with two kids—is just what can be balanced on two wheels. Papa, the only one with a safety helmet, drives; one child sits just in front or just behind, Mama sits side-saddle, clinging with one hand to her husband, with the other to her second child, perched precariously on her sometimes very ample lap.

Using the Horn

It would be easier to drive in India without brakes than without a horn. In fact, Indian car manufacturers could save drivers a lot of trouble if they simply attached the horn to the accelerator. A horn, the louder the better, is an essential piece of equipment.

Perhaps it is because Indians have had an oral culture for so long, or believe so strongly in the mantra, the sound that has power far beyond any meaning. They need to hear you coming, even if they can see you coming perfectly well, before they take you seriously. Forget every bit of Western etiquette about the horn and start using it like the Indians—not just when you're about to run someone over, but a regular, short beep just to let everyone know you're coming.

Hand Gestures for the Road

Indian truck drivers have a repertoire of hand gestures that are used instead of indicator lights. A majestic turn of the wrist ending with the fingers pointing out the road ahead means, 'The road is clear, you may pass me.' An up-and-down flapping movement means, 'Slow down'. For a right turn, the driver, who sits on the right, sticks his hand out the window. For a left turn, the front passenger does it. If there is no front passenger, the left turn will not be indicated.

Buses

Buses in most big Indian cities are already so over-extended meeting the needs of Indians that they're not much use to foreigners. They are so crowded, they permanently tilt in the direction of the door from which the passengers hang, and

A busy street in India, with two-wheelers, autorickshaws and cars.

they slow down, rather than stop at bus stops, so only the athletic can get off or on.

The advantages are that they're dirt cheap and, being among the biggest things on the road, are safer than other forms of transportation. At off-peak hours, it is possible to find a seat. And no matter how crowded they are, Indians will always make room for one more.

Autorickshaws

Autorickshaws—often called 'autos' for short—are a pretty low life form in the traffic hierarchy, but they act as though they own the roads. What they lack in size, they make up for in numbers. They're noisy, uncomfortable, and polluting. Whenever autorickshaw drivers go on strike, traffic flows so smoothly, it hardly seems like India any more. Still, everybody is vastly relieved when they get back on the job, because the city cannot function without them.

They are black and yellow donkeys, three-wheeled beasts of burden on fast-forward, transporting people and things to places no other vehicle can reach. They can manoeuvre through narrow congested streets, sail over potholes, and weave through traffic jams with a minimum of damage to anyone willing to disregard their instinct for self-preservation long enough to make the journey. They are cheap, fast and almost always available.

All the black and yellow autos are fitted with meters, but if they are used at all, it is only to establish the base rate upon which the supplements and surcharges are added. If there has been a fare increase, and the meter has not been adjusted, one legitimate charge is a percentage of the meter rate, which will be calculated with a fare card that the driver is supposed to show you. The night charge for travel after 11:00 pm, 50 per cent over and above the normal fare, is also legitimate.

Several other charges have gained legitimacy through long habit. It is customary to fix a waiting charge if the auto is kept through a series of stopovers before reaching the final destination. Most autos also charge something when they take passengers to any destination that is out of the way, and from which they will have trouble getting a return fare. And if the distance is felt to be too short to bother with based on the meter fare, then a flat rate will be charged. These additional charges should be agreed upon before getting into the auto. They fluctuate according to what the market will bear. If it's raining you won't have much leverage for bargaining, but if there are six autos and you're the only fare in sight, then it's a buyer's market and you have the advantage. At the end of the journey there is no need to tip.

Autorickshaw drivers have an inbuilt radar that detects newcomers to the city, and they will take advantage of the situation. This is unavoidable at the beginning, and you'll be driven around in circles and then overcharged for the privilege. It happens to Indians too, and everyone complains about unscrupulous drivers while lamenting the lack of alternatives. You can try to find out what the fare should be, and some street on the route, so that you can say, "Take me via Ring Road." But most drivers will be able to confuse you if you're just faking it. Once you know your way around, and can dictate the route and the fare with a voice full of the authority that only comes from experience, the unwanted sightseeing tours will cease.

Taxis

The metered taxis are black and yellow. They are usually Ambassadors in Delhi, Calcutta and Bombay, and Fiats or 'Padminis' in Bombay. They do not drive around looking for passengers. Instead, they wait at taxi stands at strategic points throughout the city: shopping areas, railway and bus stations, airports, big hotels, tourist attractions and the posh neighbourhoods. They can be summoned by a phone call, if the phone works.

Taxis cost considerably more than autorickshaws, and have the same supplements and surcharges over and above the fare that the meter shows. At least for the first trip, the visitor can avoid haggling as well as being overcharged, since the major airports, and even some railway stations, have introduced the very pleasant, convenient and hassle-free pre-paid taxi service. There is a counter at the airport or railway station where you fill in a form with your name and destination. You pay a fixed amount according to the distance, get a receipt, and go out to the taxi queue. A taxi will be assigned to take you, and its licence number will be recorded in the book at the counter. When you arrive at your destination, you hand over the receipt to the driver. You pay nothing further to the driver unless there is some change in the route, for example, if the hotel you intended to go to is fully booked, or if you wish to give a tip.

Often, a man who appears to know the driver will climb in and sit next to him. This may be just for company, or to get a driving lesson on the way back, or because he happens to live in that direction. If you are a woman travelling alone, or if for any reason this makes you uncomfortable, it is well within your rights to demand that the co-driver get out.

If you regularly use the same neighbourhood taxi stand, you can trust the drivers and the prices. In strange parts of the city, you may be overcharged, but it is unlikely that you will encounter any other unpleasantness from a taxi driver, such as theft or assault.

The black and yellow metered taxis are usually pretty old and look battered. 'Tourist taxis' are ordinary looking Ambassadors in much better condition, and even air-conditioned if you wish it. They can be hired for 5 hours, 10 hours, or by the week. There is a fixed rate that includes the car, the driver, the petrol and a certain number of kilometres. You pay over and above that for any additional kilometres or hours. This is the most convenient and pleasant way to handle a morning of shopping, a full day of sightseeing, or any short trips to places outside the city. The cost is comparable to taking taxis over the same distance, but without the waiting charges and the hassle of finding one at each spot.

There are many 'tourist taxi' companies in the big cities. The ones outside the five-star hotels may charge more, but usually the rates are pretty similar. Everything is done very professionally, and although you may bargain a little to get the best rate—2.00 rupees for each additional kilometre instead of 2.20 rupees, for example—after that there is no need to discuss money. The driver enters the time and the mileage from the meter when the journey commences (it should be predetermined whether this is when he leaves the garage or when he starts off with you in the backseat); he does the same thing at the end. Then you calculate how much is owed and pay it to him directly, or have the office send you a bill if it's a long-term arrangement.

It is customary to give the 'tourist taxi' driver a small amount for meals and tea at the appropriate times, and a tip at the end of the day if his service has been satisfactory. The driver's share of the amount you pay for the car hire is very small, and he depends on the tips.

How to Get Where You're Going

Ask a taxi-driver in Madras to take you to Anna Salai, and you'll probably get a puzzled look. Ask a Bombay taxi-driver for L.D. Ruparel Marg, or Bhau Sahab Hire Marg, and you will really confuse him. For all intents and purposes, Anna Salai is Mount Road. And for many people, L.D. Ruparel Marg is still Nepean Sea Road, and Bhau Sahab Hire Marg is Mount Pleasant Road.

Most Indian cities are huge and sprawling, and although there may be maps of the city core, there are no up-to-date street maps for the maze of streets in residential neighbourhoods, often called colonies. A map will show you where Anand Niketan is, but it won't help you very much to find E-16 Anand Niketan, which is the complete address for a house in New Delhi, except for the postal code.

A friend whom I talked to recently is still trying to remember the present name for Clive Road in Madras. The fervour of nationalism resulted in the British names for roads being changed to names of famous Indians, but the old names pass out of usage very slowly.

The neighbourhoods seem to grow like banyan trees: the whole configuration has a sense of organic, unstructured growth, rather than a logical street plan. The colonies are named like movies—each one seems to have a sequel. In Delhi, you have Greater Kailash Part One, and Greater Kailash Part Two, which were so popular that they had to create East of Kailash and Kailash Colony.

Once you arrive at the neighbourhood you are looking for, it becomes a game to find the specific address. Let's take the theoretical E-16 Anand Niketan in New Delhi. 'E' refers to a whole section of the neighbourhood, where all the houses are in the E block. That's easy, you think to yourself: simply pass A block, B block, C block, and D block, and then you come to E block. Wrong! That may have been the original idea, but it seems to have been abandoned long ago. There is some systematic arrangement, but that varies from colony to colony, and will only come clear from an aerial view.

So if you drive through a colony along one street, you come to A, B and C, just as you expected. But don't get complacent, because now you leap suddenly to G, H and I. The blocks D, E and F are on the street parallel to the one you're on. You are just as likely to have found A, D, M, P—in that order.

Now, let's say that by driving around aimlessly for half an hour, you do manage to find the block you are looking for. Now it's simple, right? All you have to do is follow the numbers, E1, E2, E3, and so on, until you reach E16. Unfortunately, not always. Imagine that the houses were built and numbered like that. Then after they were all finished, some people came along and built new houses in between some of the old houses. If the E block had 50 houses altogether at the

Guide map for a posh neighbourhood in New Delhi.

beginning, then the new one built in between E26 and E27 may be E51. Sometimes, when it gets too confusing, the authorities just go along and number all the houses again. Then you have an old number and a new number to track down. Some houses on the street have the old number, and some have the new number.

In New Delhi, the neighbourhoods display maps. All you have to do is check the map, right? Wrong again. The maps were painted by sadists who purposely left out the very helpful marker 'You Are Here'. So first you have to try and figure out where you are on the maze in front of you, without the benefit of street signs on the roads around you. Only then can you try to locate your destination. Good luck.

The best thing is to ask for directions, not once but several times. The best people to ask, I've found, are teenage boys on bicycles. They are the only ones who seem to really know the neighbourhoods. The mobile ironing men, the delivery boys at the small neighbourhood provision stores, and autorickshaw or taxi-drivers at a neighbourhood stand are also good bets. The last desperate measure is to check the location with the neighbourhood post office. They have a kind of street directory of their postal district, and they can help you.

Remember that directions hardly come as 'Go straight for two blocks and turn right on to G.N. Chetty Street.' You will be more likely to get street directions that are aligned to the magnetic pull of the neighbourhood landmarks: the cinemas, the hospitals, the temples. For example, 'Go towards Revathi cinema, and take the second turn after the Ganesha temple; there you'll find it.' Don't be taken in by the expression of absolute authority on the faces of those giving directions; even those who haven't understood your question can sound very sure of themselves. People don't like to admit they don't know where a place is, or else they think you must be asking about a different place, because that's the place all the other foreigners ask about.

In Madras, I remember how difficult it was to find the Sanskrit College, because everybody kept directing me to Motilal Banarsidass, a small obscure bookshop that the whole neighbourhood knew because so many foreigners came to look for Indian books. The rule is to ask at least three people, and then take the majority decision.

BEGGARS

Adjusting to the constant haunting spectre of poverty is difficult without benefit of the theories of *karma* and reincarnation to make it more palatable. The homeless live in makeshift shelters at the roadside, beggars stick their deformed and leprous limbs into car windows at the red light, poor children lick discarded wrappers picked up from the pavement near the ice-cream stall.

Handing out money is no solution: it makes begging a viable way of earning a living, and therefore perpetuates the whole vicious circle. Anyway, a few coins only attract more hands demanding more coins and it will not stop. The only two possibilities seem to be to remain sensitive and be constantly assaulted by these images, or to become insensitive, to the point where the poor and their problems cease to exist.

There are ways to have an easier conscience without either reaching for your change purse or hardening your heart.

First, donate your money or services to any of the numerous volunteer organisations working in the city. These groups address such problems at the roots, and your contribution there will be effective in a way that a few coins here and there can never be. It will also be easier to turn away without feeling overcome with guilt or helplessness the next time a beggar appeals to those emotions.

Sometimes the need to do something immediately is overpowering. Small children, often so full of life and energy despite a lifetime of dirt and malnutrition, can be hard to

A flute seller shows off his wares in the street.

resist. Bear in mind that money given into their hands goes into the pockets of the adult who put them out on the street to beg; it brings no benefit to the child. If you keep a supply of sweets or fruit in your bag for such children, you will be rewarded with expressions of absolute delight, for these end up where they belong. You could also observe who the poor give to, and give to that person. Those with very little money are remarkably generous; but they have a well-developed sense for who deserves the generosity and who does not.

Finally, buy the flowers, balloons and trinkets that people sell to avoid the final degradation of begging. This is not advice for you to respond to the emotional blackmail of every person who approaches you with some piece of useless junk or tourist kitsch. But all over India, there are craftspeople who make a living selling simple and beautiful things—bamboo flutes, painted clay figures, woven baskets—for what amounts to a few cents. Support those who are still trying to make an honest living on the street.

Whenever and whatever you give, always do it as you leave a place, otherwise after your first gesture of kindness you will be besieged by demands for more. Hand out the sweets as the light turns green and the car pulls away, buy the balloon as you get into the taxi, leave a few coins on your way out of the temple.

EMOTIONAL HEALTH
Your Children
So many factors influence how well a child adjusts to India that the matter is unpredictable. The child's age, sex, mother-tongue and innate personality make up one set of factors; the part of India, the school, the neighbourhood and the perceived charms of the place left behind make up the other set of factors. The combinations and permutations are sure to yield some surprises.

The restrictions that Indian society places on contact between the sexes may be very frustrating to teenagers, but will not have much effect on smaller children. Again, in big cities such as New Delhi or Bombay, among certain strata of society, Western standards are fast becoming the norm, so this may not be an issue. Other restrictions on freedom of movement, not being able to hop on a bike or skateboard to go to a friend's house, for example, may cause problems.

Indians love children. Indian children of any but the poorest parents are given almost unlimited freedom up to the age of five or six: infants are breastfed on demand until two or three, or even older. They are not diapered and are carried and indulged in everything. Your small children will enjoy the same carefree life. Any attempt to discipline them will have to come from you, and it will be viewed by your servants and Indian friends as most inhumane. Indian discipline, such as it is, consists of bribes and bogeymen, haphazardly applied.

The advantage of this system is that you can take children with you anywhere, including to performances, restaurants and parties; there is no social activity from which children are excluded. Even classical dance and music performances are regularly accompanied by the cries and whines of small children, who, without any embarrassment or anger, are carried out of the theatre, and brought back when they have quieted down.

After the age of six, boys are still allowed a lot of freedom, but girls are increasingly expected to comply with a standard of behaviour considered appropriate for girls. They must care for younger siblings, help with the household chores, and fetch and carry for their fathers and brothers. Your daughters will not be expected to do those things, but they may be prevented by social opinion from doing some other activity, such as riding a bicycle or playing soccer.

Children will adjust to some things much faster than you do; the weather, for example, may not be an issue at all after a short time. Other apparently trivial things may be a constant source of irritation: they may want cold milk for their cereal, and once it has been boiled, the cook forgets

Indian children tend to address all grown-ups as 'aunty' or 'uncle'; your children may be expected to do the same. Using the person's surname is considered too formal, but using the first name would show a lack of respect; if your children don't like the English terms applied to strangers, you could teach them the Indian terms.

to cool it in time for their breakfast. You can help sort out some difficulties, but others you may just have to live with. The cheese, the cornflakes and the peanut butter will never taste the same as back home.

I've often noticed that foreigners may avail themselves of every opportunity to get to know the country better, but rarely pass on these opportunities to their children. They may attempt to learn the language, but not arrange classes for their children. They have parties to get to know all kinds of people, but don't make the same arrangements for the children. They see performances and visit museums, but don't take the kids along. Their children don't know simple terms, don't understand basic Indian etiquette, don't have Indian friends or see the best of India. It takes an effort, but the children who have benefited from such an effort will stand out from the crowd of foreign children in India, for their sense of security and ease in their surroundings.

The Stay-at-home Spouse

Forgive me for the sexist assumption that this is the woman. In all the cases I have encountered, this has been the case. The woman in India with servants may feel completely superfluous, and almost like a child herself. The fact of having servants creates a sense of dependency where none existed before. You used to do everything yourself, and all of a sudden somebody else is handling it.

But soon enough, you will get used to it, and you will be able to enjoy your free time without guilt. In Chapter Seven, you will find some suggestions that may spark your interest. If you choose to, and can find a job, you are allowed to work. Or you can take up volunteer work. This achieves many things. You have a chance to make a meaningful contribution when the spectre of poverty haunts you. You can use your skills, if you have expertise in some field. You get a chance to meet people, perhaps practise the local language. You can make use of your contacts in the expatriate community—to collect toys for a children's centre, for example.

There are many social work organisations in all the big cities, and many of them are run by women. Some are run by religious missions. Some work mainly with women, or express a strong feminist perspective. Some are oriented towards education, teaching skills and improving literacy. There are also environmental groups and research. Some are involved with raising money, others work directly with the people concerned. Before you react with enthusiasm, be warned that such organisations welcome volunteers in theory, but sometimes have practical problems. Most of them arise out of a simple discrepancy—what the foreign volunteer in India wants to do may not be what the Indian welfare organisation feels she is most useful doing.

You may prefer field work, for example working in the slums. But unless you have skills suited for that work (medical skills are the ones most often required), putting a foreigner out in a strange environment, with unfamiliar conditions and an unknown language, creates more problems than it solves. Your greatest asset as a volunteer may be the ability to raise money, or collect other kinds of contributions from among your expatriate friends. That is a valuable and even crucial contribution, which cannot be underestimated.

Check out the organisations before you get deeply involved, so that you know if their ethical stance is in line with your own. Talk to someone there frankly about your skills; knitting, photography, writing, teaching English as a second language and design are things I have done as a volunteer.

FOOD &
ENTERTAINING

CHAPTER 6

'And there were soft delicacies, all manner of drink,
and every sort of food, along with various kinds of
condiments: sour, salty, and pungent.'
—*Ramayana*, quoted by Robert P. Goldman
in the essay, 'Ravana's Kitchen'

To an Indian, social interaction is as necessary as air. Judith Kroll, an American poet intimately connected with India, once wrote, 'I can't imagine anyone there saying, 'I'm very busy—but let's have lunch in a couple of weeks.'' Family and friends are highly valued and the demands of these relationships set the pace of life.

Hospitality and graciousness are the mark of a good Indian host or hostess. The guest is something akin to a god, and must be welcomed as such. In your role as a guest, any mistakes or faux pas will be overlooked, and never mentioned. Sadly, this leaves you unenlightened, and likely to make the same mistake again. When it is your turn to host Indians, the tables are turned, and you may well be unpleasantly surprised by the demands of that role. Again, nothing will be said, but the attendance figures at your next party will tell their own story. This chapter prepares you for some possible pitfalls.

INSTANT FRIENDS

The foreigner to India is likely to be overwhelmed by invitations. Chance acquaintances and total strangers will want you to attend their son's wedding, stay in their homes, go along with them to a dinner party, come to tea whenever you feel like it. Many visitors to India find this instant friendliness and sociability threatening; others come to love it as the best of India, the quality that makes up for the material inadequacies, and the one that they miss most when they leave.

Instant Friends

Once, when my small son and I stayed in Jodhpur, Rajasthan, at the state-run hotel, the young man at the reception, Ashok, invited us to his home for dinner. I believe it was because I mentioned that my brother's name was also Ashok. I went and met his parents, sister, niece, widowed aunt, and new bride. He even called over his best friend to meet me.

They cooked a Rajasthani feast for us, which, as a mark of our friendship, we all ate off the same huge plate. His whole family was friendly and outgoing. They asked me questions, played with my baby, draped me in Rajasthani clothes, and enjoyed my company and my strangeness. I have a photograph of his two sisters, one on each side of me in my borrowed finery, all of us grinning, to remind me of that day. They even came to the train station to see us off the next day.

My journal is full of happy encounters with perfect strangers, and I've heard many similar stories from others who have travelled around India. This is a special quality of Indians, wanting to know you and welcome you into their homes.

Although I have never felt uneasy or unsafe in these encounters, you should be warned that there are clever Indian con men who use the natural friendliness of Indians as a cover for their own tricks. Newspaper stories tell us that tourists have been robbed by young men who struck up conversations in just the way so many Indians do. For example, if the line for buying train tickets is very long, the person behind you may make casual conversation, and then offer to get you train tickets quickly through someone he knows while you have a cup of tea. All you have to do is give him the money and he will do the rest. Any situation where money passes hands between you and a stranger is suspicious.

In the situation I have described, no one had anything to gain from me. Also, I knew something about the person I was trusting. I knew that the young man had a responsible job, and that I was going to dinner, not with him alone, but with his whole family.

In big cities and tourist centres, it doesn't hurt to be wary of instant friends who offer you something that sounds too good to be true. It probably is. But don't be so cynical that you pass up opportunities to enjoy Indian hospitality, make friends, and get to know the country better. Ashok the hotel receptionist told me about the best place for cold coffee in the whole of India; and I met his aunt, a woman outside my experience. She married at six and was a widow at nine, subsequently living for more than 60 years in the prison of her widowhood.

Generous to a Fault

When I was walking in the hills of the Eastern Ghats, I got lost and stopped at a small mud hut to ask the way. The lady of the house poured out a glass of fresh buttermilk, spiced with cumin and chillies, and cooled in a mud pot. I was so thirsty, I could not restrain myself from gulping it down. She immediately poured out another glass, and another. I'm sure the family went without buttermilk that day because of me. Yet, when I offered her money, she refused, smilingly but with a touch of scorn. It's true—I would have had to give her something more than a few rupees to match the generosity of her gesture.

Sometimes the difficulty is to extricate yourself from such situations without hurting anyone's feelings. When I was on holiday in Puri, Orissa, an old couple invited me to accompany them to Calcutta. They felt I should see Calcutta, and I agreed it was something I intended to do. Before I knew it, the train reservations were being made, and I had to explain carefully that the plans I had made long ago could not be changed. But I wrote down their phone number and address, and when I go to Calcutta, I will give them a call.

The offering may be tea, bananas, a handful of roasted peanuts, fresh peas in season. Generosity may be limited by circumstances, but the graciousness of Indians seldom is. This graciousness is one aspect of their culture that transcends the barriers of social, economic and physical distance; it is found among the poor and the rich, rural and urban, North Indians and South Indians.

Vague Invitations

You may meet with the invitation to 'drop by anytime'. In E M Forster's *A Passage to India*, Mrs Moore meets with a situation where she tries to pin down a specific day and time with a Mrs Bhattacharya, who is gracious but vague. In the end Mrs Moore settles with her on the coming Thursday, only to find out that the Bhattacharyas are leaving for Calcutta the following morning, so won't even be in town on Thursday. Mrs Moore is bewildered by this exchange, but one Indian friend to whom I read the passage understood the situation perfectly. She said, "The guest is blessing you, doing you a great honour by visiting you. How can you be so rude as to try to restrict them to a certain time?"

'Drop in anytime' really does mean that they would like to see you again. But it is definitely better to phone and check before turning up on the doorstep of people you've just met. Not that you will ever be turned away. But as the honoured guest who is doing the host a favour, it is your responsibility to try not to cause inconveniences.

The Guest is Always Right

A chance acquaintance invited me to dinner one day soon after I arrived in New Delhi. I had not found an *ayah*, so I asked whether I could bring my three-year-old son along with me. "Of course," was the enthusiastic reply.

I presumed dinner was to be with just the family, since my son could also come. It turned out to be a very fancy party, with a lot of people, a lot of drinking, a lot of sophisticated conversation—and no other children. Food wasn't served until 11:00 pm. They had made arrangements for my son: a simple dinner he could eat earlier, and a bedroom where he could sleep. But it was a strange place; he wouldn't eat or sleep, and we both had a miserable time.

An Indian host would not like to deny the requests of a guest: if you ask whether you can bring your children, your pets, your house guests, your aged parents, you will not be refused. Use your ingenuity, ask indirect questions, ask a mutual friend—but try to discover whether your request is appropriate.

EATING IN AN INDIAN HOME

The proper table etiquette in an Indian home varies according to the kind of home. There may not be a table or cutlery; you may be eating with others or you may be eating all by yourself while everyone in the family watches you. In Ashok's house, the whole family and I ate off the same huge plate. This had never happened to me before or since. In India, you have to be prepared for anything.

Three Encounters

If you were to come with me to my cousin's house in the Madras suburbs, your meal would progress quite differently from a dinner in a Delhi home, or one in a Gujarat village. You are likely to encounter something similar to one of these during your stay in India, and if you travel around, you may come across even more variations.

An Indian-style kitchen.

Christian, Middle-class, Madras

In this middle-class home of a schoolteacher and a lawyer, you would be invited to lunch rather than dinner, for that is the most important meal of the day. You are served first, with the men of the family, while the women wait on you.

First, you are offered a small towel and shown a sink, which stands on its own just outside the dining room, where you are expected to wash your hands before the meal. This is a *thali* meal. A big heap of rice on a stainless steel plate with a rim is set before you on the table. All around it are placed small servings of different vegetables. There is one meat serving because this is a Christian family, and your presence makes it a special meal. Even meat-eating families in India do not have meat every day. The liquid dishes, the *sambhar* and *rasam*, essential parts of a South Indian lunch, are served in small stainless steel bowls beside your plate.

With only the fingers of your right hand, you mix a bit of one of the vegetables with a portion of rice sufficient for a mouthful. You then scoop up the whole mixture into your mouth. And so you continue, making different combinations until you are done. It's a messy affair, and you need some

A *thali* meal comes with everything, and so does the *dosai*, and this is the cutlery you can expect.

dexterity to get the wetter morsels into your mouth. If you seem to be having trouble with any part of this procedure, my grandmother or cousin or niece would notice, and hunt for a spoon and a fork and offer them to you. They would not be part of a matching set.

After the meal, you would again be offered the towel and the sink, to wash your hands and rinse out your mouth. In my cousin's home, the strongest drink you are likely to be served is coffee, South Indian style: strong, milky and sweet. Now the ladies of the house will sit down to eat, while you and the men retire with your coffee to sit in the sitting room and chat.

Muslim, Upper-class, Delhi

In a traditional Muslim home, alcohol is taboo, but in Delhi, in some elegant, upper-class Muslim homes, liquor is served and drunk without inhibition. In cosmopolitan New Delhi, you can choose from a bar well stocked with everything from Scotch whisky and Russian vodka to Indian rum. The custom is to drink a lot before dinner.

Dinner starts at 10:30 or 11:00 pm. The table is laid with the appropriate tablecloth, napkins and cutlery. Food is served Western-style, in courses, starting with soup if it's winter, and ending with fruit for dessert. The main course is Indian food, rice, *dhal* (lentil stew), vegetables, meat, yogurt, and various pickles. The meat (never pork, which is prohibited by Islam) is *halal*, or ritually slaughtered. Since it is North India, there is also unleavened bread—thin, piping hot *chapathis* brought in fresh from the kitchen one or two at a time, and served to whoever needs them by a watchful servant. These are eaten with the hand. Break off pieces with your right hand and use a piece to fold around the vegetables and meat. This can be done very neatly, with the *chapathi* serving as your eating utensil. At the end of the meal, servants will bring around a finger bowl with warm water for you to wash your hands.

Hindu, Peasant

In a rural home in Gujarat, say a village in Vyara district, the first thing served to you as soon as you enter is a glass of water. The water has been cooled in clay pots, which give it an earthy fragrance; sometimes a few cardamom seeds are added for their sharp perfume. Water never tasted so good!

When it is time to eat, a member of the family pours water from a small jug for you to wash your hands. You are expected to have your own clean handkerchief to dry them. There is no separate dining room. You are seated on the mud floor of the kitchen and a brass plate is set on the floor in front of you. (The plate may be of stainless steel, or a leaf.) The staple is thick wholewheat *chapathi*, very different from the refined version served to you in the Delhi home. There is one vegetable, *dhal* and some raw chillies. If the family could have afforded it, meat would have been served.

In the evening, when it is cool, the rural meal may be served outdoors, with you and the male members of the family seated on string cots. Even if you are a woman, you may eat with the men; you are foreign and fall outside the boundary of rules that bind the community. In rural Gujarat, you may be offered local homemade brews, such as a country liquor called arrack or toddy. These are strong, pungent and ruthless drinks that may knock you out quickly. Be warned.

> You may eat all by yourself while the whole family watches you. They will eat only after you have finished. But don't feel you have to rush. It is polite to eat with relish, and accept, with a show of reluctance, a small second serving.

Eating with the Hand

My grandmother says that eating with a fork and knife is like having a shower with a raincoat on. Much of the sensual pleasure associated with eating is tactile, and cutlery just gets in the way. Eating with your fingers prevents burned tongues and saves on dishwashing soap. You don't have to remember which fork goes with the fish. The advantages are numerous, but the pleasure it gives is much more basic, something that the child in every grown-up can appreciate.

In all classes of society, both urban and rural, food is only taken to the mouth with the right hand. This is the most important part of the etiquette of eating in India. Once you have started eating, and have your right hand covered with gravy, it is all right to serve yourself, using the serving spoon, with the left hand. When you watch Indians eat, you will see that they keep their left hand on their lap, out of harm's way. South Indians plunge in with their whole hand; Northerners are more restrained, using only the fingertips up to the second knuckle.

This prejudice about the left hand can be easily understood in the light of its use to clean oneself after defecating. That doesn't make it any easier for a left-hander like my left-handed son. The older he got, the more his eating with his left hand upset some people around him. By the time he was seven, he ate with his right hand, though he did everything else with his left, and I had never said a word to him about it. A left-handed adult should be aware that there is a very strong cultural bias against putting food into the mouth with the left hand. A left-handed friend who travels often in India makes a point of using her right hand when she eats with very traditional people.

Table Settings

Some Indian friends told me the story of their dinner at the house of an important Indian diplomat. The table was beautifully set with the best silver and the food was exquisite. The dinner started formally, but as the evening progressed, the two couples found they had much in common and it began to seem more a meeting of old friends. The diplomat's wife said, gesturing to the glittering array of forks and knifes, "If I had known you would be so nice, I wouldn't have bothered to bring out the heavy artillery."

That comment sums up one common Indian attitude towards cutlery: weapons to impress the enemy, but not necessary between friends. Indian food is not meant to be eaten with knife and fork, as anyone who tries it will quickly learn. Indian friends who come to your home may not be adept at wielding your weaponry, and may not know which knife goes with the fish. On the other hand, you will also meet Indians who handle their knives and forks with precision, and find American table manners appalling. A new generation of

Westernised Indians who never eat with their hands makes any kind of generalisation difficult.

Dinner Gifts

Bringing a gift when you are invited to dinner is not mandatory. After all, you are the honoured guest. Until recently, it would have been almost insulting to bring sweets or a bottle of wine; it would have been tantamount to saying that you felt your hosts couldn't provide these things. This is no longer true. Nowadays it is a custom that has become very popular. Fruit, flowers or a box of sweets are perfect gifts on such occasions, and will offend no one.

STAYING IN AN INDIAN HOME

If you stay in an Indian home, bring something from your home country as a gift. It would be much appreciated. But I must add this proviso: know the social status and religion of your hosts. A bottle of foreign whisky would be the perfect gift for some, and not at all appropriate for others. If you know you are staying with someone, it is a good idea to ask them what they would like. It used to be that many things were not available in India. Now since the economy has opened up, almost everything that Indians used to covet from the West is easily available here.

> You will have to use your imagination to think of something—maple syrup, the best quality chocolate and cheese, exotic liqueurs, a unique CD or book are all things I have been asked by friends to bring.

In an Indian home, you may not always have your own room. The private bedroom is something known only to the very rich. In most middle-class homes, the bedroom is wherever the bedding is rolled out. In many cases, the room for bathing and the toilet are separate, and toilet paper will not be found. When you stay in a house with servants, and the servants have had extra work on your behalf, it is a kind gesture to give them some money as a gift when you leave. But always check with your host or hostess. Let them help you decide on a suitable amount. Giving too much, in relation to their monthly pay, may set a precedent that your host won't appreciate.

PARTY ETIQUETTE

As in most aspects of Indian life, there is no single standard of behaviour that applies everywhere you go. This is not to suggest there are no rules for parties in India. There most definitely are, but they vary from place to place, according to the religion, the age, and how conservative or traditional the people are. You will encounter a wide range of patterns. Following is only a rough guide.

In Mumbai

Mumbai has a relaxed, informal style, where anything goes. You are likely to meet up-and-coming actresses, advertising executives and business people out to have a good time after a hard day's work. Dress is casual chic, and in these circles, Western standards of modesty are quite sufficient. A friend told me that a gathering of friends after work may even choose 'pot luck'—everyone brings a dish, something I'd never heard of in India. The club is a popular place for entertaining.

In Delhi

In Delhi you are more likely to attend official parties. Strict protocol is the rule, and government officials and diplomats are concerned with appearances even after office hours. Official parties start on time—that is, about 30 minutes late. Unofficial parties start late, after the official parties are over presumably, and it is quite done to attend several parties in a night.

Diplomatic parties can be staid affairs. The Indians who are invited seem to be selected on the basis of their ability to turn up on time, and they turn up like bad pennies at every single party. But every once in a while there will appear a diplomatic couple with flair, and their invitations will be coveted by a more interesting crowd.

Delhi parties can involve a lot of drinking and talk about politics, and the trendy 'farmhouse' parties, in beautiful gardens outside of town, boast the latest designer drugs, as well as fashions. When food is served, it signals the end of the party. You eat and leave. The best survival tactic for the rigours of party-going in Delhi is to eat something before you go, then pace your drinking carefully so that you can make it until the food comes.

In Chennai

Chennai parties used to be quieter affairs, for even the South Indian movie stars are more conservative than those in Bombay. But over the last ten years, Chennai has evolved a party culture, and now smoking and drinking are as common here as anywhere in India. One quality I have observed though is the inter-generational quality of even big parties—kids, twenty-somethings, their parents and even grand-parents may well be attending the same party.

Dressing
Women

In India, as in any other country, there are parties where anything goes: see-through blouses, leather hot pants, thigh-high boots, or whatever the latest fashion dictates. In urban India, revealing clothing and big designer names are worn with aplomb in certain circles. Another group of people, though, will be completely oblivious to your Armani or Dior.

Legs are normally kept well covered in India, so when they are revealed they get a lot of attention, which is something you may not want. Pants are quite acceptable, if they are dressy for dressy occasions.

Some women visiting India wear *saris* to parties. Regretfully, it is a common complaint among Indians that foreign women, with the rare exception, look hideous in a sari. While the *sari* does cover a multitude of figure flaws, it seems to accentuate the worst points in a Western figure. It needs practice to walk in one gracefully and with confidence, and there are subtle rules for the correct placement of the loose end that goes over the shoulder to serve modesty.

I attended one such ceremony in the company of an American woman who wore, with her stylish dress and hat, blue stockings. A guest not used to such sophistication said to me, in Hindi, "Poor woman. Does she have wooden legs?"

If you do wear a *sari*, make sure that it is one appropriate to the occasion. And whatever you do, don't boast about how cheaply you bought it at that outdoor bazaar. Indian women take great pride in their *saris* and wear different kinds in the different seasons: crisp cool cottons in the summer, rich heavy silks in the winter; modern chiffons for a dinner party, traditional handlooms for a wedding.

They can tell, just by looking, what your *sari* costs. Not that price is the point. An Indian woman might also wear a very inexpensive *sari* to a fancy party, but her *sari* is very likely to be unique and beautiful—perhaps a tribal *sari* from Orissa, worn with heavy tribal jewellery, and bought for Rs 50 before it became fashionable and was sold in every Delhi *sari* shop for ten times the price.

Your servants will invite you to weddings and naming ceremonies and so on. This is a situation in which a *sari* would be appropriate. They will take it as a gesture of goodwill and equality with them if you were to take the trouble to wear an Indian outfit. Your servants may be used to your Western clothes, but all their guests may not.

Another common Indian costume is much easier for the foreign woman to wear—the loose pants and long over-blouse

Your bazaar find which turns out to be common in Delhi may still be put to use. When you return to your home country, you have an elegant and unusual outfit that is also a conversation piece. No one will notice if the folds are not just so, and you can even boast about how cheap it was.

that is sometimes referred to as a Punjabi suit. The pants are called *salwar* when they are loose and flowing, and *churidar* when they are tight from knee down, and overly long, so that they bunch up over the ankle. The over-blouse is called a *kameez* or *kurta*. They are usually sold as a set, and the styles come and go out of fashion just as styles in the West. They can also be made to order to your own design.

Men

The once ubiquitous 'safari suit', a short-sleeved shirt-jacket and matching pants is almost extinct, except among government officials. The Indian fashion houses are creating well fitting, elegant yet comfortable clothes for men. Shirt and tie, Indian style *kurta* pyjama or fitted jacket and pants, and suits are all worn by men at parties, and they are becoming just as fashion conscious as women. In cold Delhi winters or if you are sure that the venue is air-conditioned, a suit with tie is appropriate. In Bombay during the monsoon, just a shirt with tie is much more comfortable. If the party is at a club, some clever men take clean shirts and shower and change right there, so as to be absolutely fresh for dinner.

GIVING PARTIES

Successful parties, as I discovered from a diplomat's wife who was famous for hers, require hard work and imagination. At the time when power cuts were an inevitable part of every evening, and other hostesses were suffering, she had a power-cut party lit only with candles and oil lamps. Her own warm and open personality was certainly a good part of her success, but equally important were these simple rules that anyone can follow.

- Don't make the mistake of cultivating 'token' Indians, just so you can have some brown faces at your parties. Not every Indian you meet can be your friend. The passage from acquaintance to friend can be instantaneous, or it may never happen. The concept of friendship is taken very seriously, and once you have crossed that line towards closeness, you may ask for anything from your Indian friends. The beginning of that process is to make all your guests feel that you have invited them for what they are rather than for what they do.

- Every guest that you really want to come should be contacted personally by phone, even when there is a printed invitation. Invitations should be sent out early, and phone calls should come closer to the party day. Guests do not always 'RSVP', nor do all guests who say they are definitely coming actually turn up. And some guests bring their own guests.

- Alexander Frater, in his book *Chasing the Monsoon*, recounts how he was brought along to a monsoon party in Goa, by strangers he happened to be seated with in a crowded restaurant. It was taken for granted that the host, being Indian, would welcome even a total stranger to his party. A gracious Indian hostess said to me, when I was the total stranger brought along to a party, "What is a stranger, except a friend you haven't met?" This is the same poise and equanimity Indians expect when they arrive with people you weren't expecting. If guests are late, or come with friends (or aged relatives or strangers picked up off the street), or don't come at all, your warm and gracious manner must not change.

- If a guest felt it was necessary to ask before bringing along a friend, that formality is an indication of social distance. If guests feel that you have been disturbed—by the lateness or the unexpected friends and relatives—they will simply not come to your next party (without informing you, of course) so as not to disturb you again. The informality of Indians in your presence is a compliment, and you must take it that way, rather than as a sign of lack of etiquette.

- Guests are invariably late. Sometimes it's because they have come to your party from another one. During the party season in Delhi, some guests may be dropping in on three parties in an evening. It's a compliment if yours is the last party they attend, so you should be pleased if they are very late. Since it is so hard to predict when guests will arrive, and how many of them there will be, a proper sit-down dinner for Indians just doesn't work. Save that for your expatriate friends. A buffet with places set at a table is the perfect compromise. It is easy to add or subtract place settings as the need arises. It also accommodates the variations in your guests' dietary restrictions.

What to Serve
Food

The latest anthropological survey of India found that only 20 per cent of the 4,636 religious and ethnic communities consider themselves to be strictly vegetarian. That is still a lot of people, and in India, it is necessary to take them into account. Always serve a separate vegetable dish. Strict Muslims do not eat pork, and all other meat should be *halal*. Many Hindus eat meat, but not beef. Lamb, chicken and fish are the meats eaten by all Indian meat-eaters. The food at the buffet table should be clearly labelled so everyone finds it easy to decide what they can eat. Never skimp on vegetarian dishes; make sure that these are also something special, and in keeping with the meal, not just an afterthought.

Good food is an absolutely essential element of a good party. Indian guests love to try something special from your own country, and that is what you will be able to do best. You may not be able to judge whether your cook's Indian dishes are up to the standards of Indians used to excellent home cooking, so it is better to stick with what you know. And when you find

If you don't want the hassle of cooking, catering services are available. Some restaurants and hotels also cater, or you can even have big parties on their grounds. There are smaller, more personalised caterers who work to achieve the same quality of taste and presentation as the home-cooked meal.

something that your guests love, always serve it, as they will ask for it every time they visit.

Drinks

The same anthropological survey found that alcohol is consumed in well over half the 4,636 communities, and the use of tobacco is even more widespread. By the same token, almost half the communities in India don't consume alcohol, and many don't use tobacco. Islam forbids drinking, and the Sikh religion forbids drinking and smoking, but not everyone is strict in these observances. Traditional Indian women,

Offer drinks in a general way, so that no one can take offence, or become inhibited: "What would you like to drink?" rather than "Would you like a beer?" Even those who normally drink may not drink on certain occasions, religious festivals, for example, or if there is an older, much respected relative present. Always have juice and soft drinks on hand for the non-drinkers.

whatever their religion, don't smoke or drink, but Indian women of a certain social strata are almost as likely to smoke and drink as the men.

The hard liquors are well appreciated in India, especially whisky, which should be imported (Black Label, if possible, to cater to the greatest snob appeal). Indian whisky falls under the label of IMFL (Indian Made Foreign Liquor) and just doesn't have the same status. Some of the many brands of Indian beer are good: Kingfisher and Black Label are recommended by my German husband, who knows his beer. Indian wines are getting more drinkable, and more Indians are drinking them.

CONVERSATION

If you are ever stuck for a conversational gambit in India, talk about families. Yours and theirs will provide the raw material for endless small talk. If a test match is going on, then just start on cricket. But once you get to know a person better, any topic is acceptable.

Indians love to talk about politics and religion. They enjoy opinionated discussions and don't necessarily want to hear only polite platitudes from a foreign guest. As long as you know what you are talking about, you can air your radical opinions freely. Otherwise, it is better to stay silent, especially if the subject is India. Indians don't like to hear half-baked theories about India and its problems.

Conversation is an art form here; people take the time to really talk. It is not necessary to bare your soul. I have had long discussions about mangoes, dance performances, famous people, different ways of cooking okra. Almost anything under the sun merits attention.

FOOD FOR THOUGHT
Regional variations in India are expressed vividly through the food. What a person eats does provide some insight into what a person is. Religious and caste restrictions make their way into the diet. The weather and the geography influence what's available to cook. The history of foreign invasions shows in the mixing of cuisines.

Hindus believe 'you are what you eat' as much as 'you eat according to what you are'. The hierarchies of caste show up again in the ordering of food; a three-tier system describes qualities inherent in all matters. *Tamas*—the lowest quality—is associated with the lowest castes. It means inertia, heaviness, darkness. *Tamasic* foods include alcohol, decaying meat (also smoked or preserved meats), and mushrooms and fungi. *Rajas*—the quality of passion, energy and raw strength—is associated with the warrior and merchant castes. *Rajasic* foods are red meat, hot spices and strong tastes like garlic and onions. *Sattvic*—the highest quality—means purity, spirit, lightness. It is associated with the Brahmin caste. *Sattvic* foods are milk and yogurt, nuts and seeds, fruits, vegetables and grains.

Food is also judged to be 'heating' or 'cooling'. Mangoes are heating, so if you eat a lot of mangoes, you are advised to also eat yogurt, which is cooling; otherwise you might get prickly heat. If you have a cold, don't take rice, cucumber and radish, which are cooling. Indians make a delicious drink that is supposed to prevent sunstroke during the hot season. Roast or boil a whole raw mango, then mix the flesh with a paste of mint leaves, roasted and ground cumin seeds, black salt, pepper and sugar. Dilute with water and drink it before venturing out in the sun. You will get many versions of this kind of advice, which Indians take very seriously.

THE SPICES
Curry is not an Indian, but a British, concept. Curry powder is not only not sold in the shops, no one even knows what

it is. Curry is not available in Indian restaurants, only in the ones catering to foreigners. The word may have come from the South Indian *kari podi*, a blend of ground spices, or from *karhi*, a yogurt-based sauce thickened with chickpea flour. Somehow the word has come to be a catchall term for almost any meat or vegetable cooked with a spicy gravy that originates in India.

In India, the dishes commonly lumped together by the foreigner as 'curry' all have specific names according to the way it is cooked and the region from which it originates: *bhartha* is a kind of vegetable puree, *kuttu* is a combination of vegetables from Tamil Nadu, *shukta* is a Bengali bitter vegetable stew, *korma* is a dryish braised preparation from the north that can be either meat or vegetable, *vindaloo* is usually pork or prawns cooked in a paste of chillies, garlic and cumin and has its origin in Goa.

The equivalents to 'curry powder' are the blends of spices called *masala*. Most Indian cooks make the mixture fresh, in a combination suited to the meat or vegetable being prepared, but some popular combinations can be bought readymade. These include *chaat masala*, *sambhar masala* or *garam masala*, and they contain from five to 12 or even more different spices, roasted and ground together.

A good cook stocks perhaps 22 different spices and herbs. The most popular are *jeera* (cumin seeds), *haldi* (turmeric), *dhania* (coriander leaves and seeds), *laung* (cloves), cardamom, *rai* (black mustard seeds), *hing* (asafoetida powder) and dried red chilli.

FOOD VARIETIES
The best of Indian cuisines is not to be savoured in fine restaurants, but in the homes of ordinary Indians. That is why those who have tasted only restaurant Indian food may come away with the impression that it is hot, too spicy, too rich, or that 'everything tastes the same'.

The delicacy and simplicity of home-cooked Indian regional cuisines is not to be found on any menu. There are very few restaurants that offer the specialities of Kerala, where I was born. No menu I have seen lists the tiny sardine-like freshwater fish that my grandmother used to clean and cook whole, in a dry mixture of grated coconut and spices, or the preparation of green papaya, or the dish she prepared using jackfruit seeds.

A Priceless Meal
Not one of the very expensive five-star hotel restaurants I have eaten at matches the meal prepared at the home of a wealthy devotee for a visiting holy man, which I was lucky enough to attend. Every dish was marked not by extravagance, but by extreme simplicity. No onions, no garlic, no red chillies, and of course, no meat. This was *sattvic* food at its best: the freshest vegetables in season cooked with delicate spices to tender perfection. I spent the night there, and next morning, I found beside my bed a glass of mango pulp thinned with a little cream, and sprinkled with slices of tender green almonds.

The thick, heavy, greenish millet bread that is peasant fare in Gujarat and Rajasthan is not featured in the restaurants there. I tasted it for the first time when I went into the kitchen of a small restaurant in Jaisalmer, and found the cook's children eating these healthy wholemeal flatbreads, smeared with sweet homemade butter, instead of the insipid 'Corn Flecks' and 'Tost' that were offered on the menu.

I could go on and on about the wonderful dishes cooked by my friends and relatives—Simi's lotus root Kashmiri style, Prabha's mango ginger *chutney*, Meena's mother's green gram, coconut and brown sugar dessert—but that would serve no other purpose than to make your mouth water. The key to getting to know the best of Indian cuisines requires getting to know Indians. Restaurants offer only the most basic fare; once you've tasted all they have to offer, you'll be ready to venture further. With an adventurous palate, and some initiative, you will be able to discover a cuisine as rich and varied as India itself.

Regional Specialities of the North
Breads
The bread/rice divide is the culinary line that separates the north and south of India. Although rice is an important staple even in the north, it is the variety of unleavened breads

there—the different kinds of *roti*—that provides the basic sustenance. Wheat, corn and millet are used separately or in combination to create pan-fried and baked breads.

The simplest of ingredients, just wheat flour and water kneaded together, makes *chapathi*. In the hands of a skilled cook, the *chapathi* is rolled perfectly round and swells up when heated on a cast-iron griddle. When made with freshly ground flour, and served piping hot with a little butter, the *chapathi* becomes far more than the sum of its ingredients.

Other types of bread use the same basic ingredients differently: *roomali roti* is the white flour rolled as thin as a handkerchief; *paratha* is cooked with ghee; *puri* is deep-fried; *phulka* puffs up like a balloon. Or the ingredients can vary, but the form stays the same: *makki ki roti* is made of cornflour, *bajre ki roti* is made of a kind of millet, *mooli ke paratha* is stuffed with radish.

Heating Foods

The winter chill is still fought in the body with the 'heating' foods: the greens called *methi* are cooked with potatoes or used as the stuffing for *paratha*. Watch out, it is also supposed to be a potent aphrodisiac. *Ghee*, wholewheat and *urad dhal* are also supposed to raise the body temperature. A special winter treat is *khichri*, a mixture of rice and *dhal* cooked together. *Gajjar ki halwa* is the winter dessert prepared from the wonderful red carrots found in the north, cooked with lots of *ghee*, thickened milk, sugar, raisins and nuts.

Meat Dishes

In the cold regions of the north, such as Himachal Pradesh and Kashmir, even the Hindus eat meat, including the Brahmins, who avoid only beef. Kashmir once had a Hindu *maharaja* (Indian prince) who, in deference to both the major religions of his kingdom, outlawed pork and beef, so the Muslims of Kashmir don't eat beef either. Lamb and mutton are very popular, and there are a variety of ways of cooking these meats. *Rojan do piaza* is lamb cooked with onions and *shahi korma* is a richer dish with almonds and yogurt.

Moghul Cuisine

The Moghul-influenced cuisine of North India has a rich tradition developed and nurtured in the imperial courts. It uses cream, yogurt, nuts, raisins and *saffron* to create lavish dishes like *navaratna* or so-called nine-jewelled *korma* and the golden *biryani*, suited to the cold climate, and fit for kings.

Tandoor Foods

When the invaders from the West crossed through the mountain passes into what is now Pakistan, they brought with them their robust, flavourful dishes, cooked in the traditional clay oven called a *tandoor*. The diet includes a lot of meat and oven-baked bread instead of rice. The meats are marinated in yogurt and spices before being baked in the *tandoor* over a wood fire. *Tandoori* chicken, leg of lamb and the various kebab and *tikka* (skewered meats) are popular.

Naan and *roti* are two of the many varieties of bread; *naan* is made of white flour and raised with yeast, and *roti* is unleavened and made from wholewheat flour. They are broken into pieces with only the right hand, and used to sop up the delicious gravies that enhance some of the meat dishes.

Most *tandoori* kitchens are open, so you can also watch your meal being prepared. With the meats, there is not much to see, as they have been marinated and now simply go into the oven on their skewers. But the making of the various breads is fascinating to watch, as the cook shapes the balls of dough and, using a wet cloth, slaps them on the side of the clay oven, where they stick until they are done. At the precise moment that they are ready, the cook reaches in and catches them as they peel off from the side, a split second before they fall.

Adventurous visitors are encouraged to try their hand at *naan*-making, which looks easy, but somehow the cook's naan clings perfectly, while the amateur attempt ends up more often than not as a soggy blob in the hot coals.

Drinks

Tea is the most popular drink in the north. Called *chai*, it is tea leaves boiled with milk and sugar, a far cry from the English version of the drink. Sometimes cloves and cardamoms are added to give a distinctively Indian flavour. It is drunk throughout the day at every opportunity, and is the appropriate end to any meal.

North India Specialities

- *Chapathi*: unleavened wholewheat griddle fried bread
- *Paratha*: unleavened wholewheat and *ghee* griddle fried bread
- *Roti*: unleavened wholewheat oven baked bread
- *Naan*: leavened white flour oven baked bread
- *Biryaani*: rice cooked with spices and meat
- *Dhal*: generic name for any of a number of soupy lentil or bean preparations
- *Tikka*: marinated and skewered meat baked in a *tandoor* oven
- *Raita*: yoghurt, vegetable and spice preparation
- *Chaat*: hot or cold mixtures of fruit, vegetables, potatoes with spices and spicy sauces
- *Samosa*: vegetables or meat in a thin wheat wrapper, deep-fried
- *Kulfi*: Indian ice cream
- *Halva*: a sweet made by cooking wheat, fruit, even carrots with *ghee*
- *Burfi*: sweet made with milk solids
- *Chai*: tea leaves boiled with milk and sugar, and sometimes spices

---

Regional Specialities of the South
Rice

Here in the south, no meal is conceivable without rice. When I travelled around Italy with South Indian musicians, I had to listen to their constant complaint—no rice. Pasta, potatoes, pizza—nothing could satisfy them. And the risotto was cooked al dente, not soft and slightly sticky as they liked it. They were relieved to come home to rice for breakfast, rice for lunch and rice for dinner.

There are many varieties of rice, and each region has its favourite. Some varieties are suited to one preparation, but not another. In Kerala, there are purple and red varieties, which are ground into flour for the steamed breakfast rolls called *puttu*. This was the breakfast of my childhood, the fat purple rolls bordered with white, freshly ground coconut, mashed and kneaded with milk, sugar and tiny bananas.

A good cook chooses rice by its look, feel and smell. A shop may offer as many as 30 different varieties and qualities. In the south and east, the more glutinous short-grain rice varieties, such as Nellore, are popular. Northerners prefer the long-grain varieties, which hold their shape and remain fluffy and separate when properly cooked. When the rice has been parboiled, it is called *sela chawal* in Hindi. Parboiling is a process applied to the unhusked paddy, which forces the nutrients from the husk into the grain. But Indians prefer the raw rice, or *kacha chawal*, which is more costly, and is supposed to have a better flavour when cooked.

Basmati rice, whether Patna *basmati* or Dehra Dun *basmati*, is especially appealing. *Basmati* rice gives off a delicate and distinctive nutty aroma while cooking, and is the most expensive. The other varieties of long-grain rice are suitable for everyday use. There are special varieties suitable for soaking and grinding for the traditional South Indian answer to crepes, the *dosai*.

Rice turns up in many shapes in South India. Rice and lentils soaked together, ground to a thick batter, and allowed to ferment slightly is the basic ingredient in a number of favourite South Indian dishes. When this batter is poured on a griddle and fried, it is called *dosai*. When the *dosai* is rolled around a spicy potato onion mixture, it is called *masala dosai*. When the *dosai* is spread very thin and fried crispy, it is called paper *dosai*.

When the same mixture is steamed in rounds, it is called *idli*. When the mixture is pressed in a doughnut shape and deep-fried, it is a *vadai*. When the *vadai* is soaked in a yogurt-spice mixture, it is *tayir vadai*. Just as with the northern varieties of *roti*, there are variations of *dosai*, *vadai* and *idli*. For example, *rava dosai* and *rava idli* are made with wheat. The latest trend in South Indian restaurants is to offer *dosai* in different combinations and with exotic fillings, popularly termed 'designer *dosai*'.

Thali

The *thali* is actually a rimmed circular tray made of metal, usually stainless steel, but sometimes brass or silver, or even gold. Arranged on it are the *katori*, small bowls of the same metal. A *thali* meal is everything served at once on such a plate, rice or breads in the middle and a fragrant, rainbow assortment of side dishes around this staple in individual *katori*. Each meal should contain the *shat rasas*, the six critical essences: sweet, sour, salty, pungent, astringent and bitter.

The *thali* meal in a restaurant includes a sweet of some kind, which Indians often eat, or at least taste, first. The other *katori* will hold yogurt, the vegetable of the day cooked without a gravy, another vegetable with a gravy, a *pachadi* or raw vegetable salad, and a *dhal* preparation, which could be a thick lentil stew called *sambhar* or a thin lentil broth called *rasam*.

South Indian Specialities

- *Dosa*: thin pancake made with rice and *urad dhal* soaked together, ground into a paste, and fermented slightly
- *Masala Dosa*: *dosa* fried especially thin and wrapped around a potato-onion mixture
- *Oothapam*: same mixture, in a thicker pancake
- *Idly*: the same mixture, steamed in little round cakes
- *Sambhar*: a watery *dhal* and vegetable stew served with all of the above
- *Chutney*: name for any of the numerous intensely flavoured side dishes prepared with ground coconut, chilli, herbs and spices. Also served with all of the above lentil and rice based dishes.
- *Pongal*: rice and *dhal* cooked together; it can be sweet or savoury
- *Uppuma*: cream of wheat made into a savoury dish with diced vegetables and spices
- *Payasam*: creamy desert with thin rice noodles, raisins, cashews, and spices
- Coffee: in South India, it's pronounced *kapi*, and served with milk and sugar already added

The *thali* meal is essentially a vegetarian experience. It is especially popular in South India, but there are regional variations, as in Gujarat, where the savoury yogurt stew, called *khaddi*, has a distinctive sweet taste.

In South India, the whole array is sometimes served on a banana leaf, with the rice heaped in the middle, and the side dishes in luscious globs and puddles all around it. Since food is eaten with the hand, after the meal there are no dishes or cutlery to wash, and no garbage either, because the cows will recycle the plates. The *thali* or banana leaf meal at restaurants is usually an all-you-can-eat affair; vigilant waiters quick on the draw with their ladles will refill the *katori* and rebuild the mountain of rice with swift passes before you can burp, which is the polite way to end a good meal.

MASTERING THE HEAT

When someone in India asks whether the food is hot, they are not referring to the temperature. Indian food is cooked with an assortment of spices, but sometimes, especially when you first arrive, hot red chilli seems to dominate. Your tongue feels like it is burning, your eyes water, and you break out into a sweat. Yes, the food is hot.

You don't have to go in for any heroics. There is no shame in admitting that the food is too hot. You won't perspire so much if you avoid the chillies. Your intestines will be grateful, because the pepper burns on the way in and the way out. And last, you will be able to taste the rest of the food.

Don't try to put out the fire with water, beer, wine, or soft drinks; they only increase the burning sensation; reach for yogurt, which soothes the tongue and tempers the heat, or banana, plain rice and grated coconut. By the end of your stay in India, you'll be surprised at how little you need this advice.

COMPOSING AN INDIAN MEAL

When you are invited to an Indian friend's house, you will see that the special meals prepared have as many as 20 different dishes. All the food is served at once except for the sweet and the *paan*, which are served separately at the end. These elaborate feasts are only for special occasions. But even the simpler meals are built up the same way.

The bare bones of the meal are the staples—the rice or the bread, or, as is most popular, both rice and bread. The feast may have both *chapathi* and *puri*, as well as plain rice, coconut rice, and a *biryani*; a simple meal would have rice, plain or fancy, and/or bread, plain or fancy. Around this foundation the meal is assembled.

The *dhal* is the next important ingredient. A thick stew made with any dried bean, pea or lentil is called *dhal*. The varieties of *dhal* seem endless, and it is said that there are as many different ways of making *dhal* as there are households in India. *Dhal* is nutritionally rich, and when combined with whole grains, or other proteins, it supplies the body with a complete protein that is as nourishing as meat, so it is very important to vegetarians. *Dhal* and rice or *dhal* and unleavened wheat bread are the poor Indian's breakfast, lunch and dinner.

A variety of vegetables cooked together or separately is next in importance. Vegetable markets are laden with a large assortment, arranged in neat piles. Many will look familiar to you, but there are many vegetables that I have seen only in Indian markets. The reptile-like bitter gourd, the drumsticks, the fenugreek leaves and the snake gourd are some of the more unusual ones you will find. A good meal should have at least two different vegetable preparations, one cooked dry and the other with a gravy. Vegetables should be chosen and cooked according to the season: *sarson* (mustard leaves) and radishes in winter, for example.

Meat is equally important for those who do eat meat. Religion, caste, and social status will determine what place it has in a meal. Whether for religious or financial reasons, even regular meat-eaters in India are not likely to eat meat every day. Chicken, lamb and fish are the meats that do not offend meat-eaters with special meat taboos. Yogurt is also an essential ingredient in a good Indian meal. It is often served plain at the end of the meal, to cool and refresh the palate, or with the meal, plain or flavoured or mixed with raw vegetables. The vegetable-yogurt salad is called *raita*.

The meal will be complete only with a few *chutneys* or pickles. These can range from fiery hot to almost sweet.

They enliven the meal and tease the palate. For some dishes, pickles and *chutneys* are essential elements: *tayir sadam*, a South Indian preparation of rice and yogurt and spices, begs for a lemon pickle, and *samosa*, a triangular stuffed and deep-fried pastry, calls for a dip of fresh mint *chutney* to be complete.

Paan

The traditional end of the meal is *paan*, not a sweet, although Indians love sweets and eat them on many occasions. The little green parcel of betel nut leaf wrapped around sauces and spices is meant to be chewed slowly to release the flavours and aid in digesting the meal.

There are many varieties of *paan*, some of which are addictive and pack quite a punch, but a *paan* once in a while will not do any harm. *Paan* stains your lips a sexy red; at the end, you spit it out rather than swallow it, except for the *mithai* or sweet *paan*, which are delicate and safe to swallow.

At the end of the meal, you may be offered, instead of *paan*, a tray of spices and rock sugar to freshen your breath and leave your mouth with a sweet taste. The licorice-flavoured fennel seeds, called *saunf*, are commonly offered, dry-roasted, and sometimes sugar-coated or combined with melon seeds, almost like an after-dinner mint.

Sweets

The making of Indian sweets is an art form, and even the best cook may buy her rich puddings, fudges and candies from a famous sweet stall. Many of the sweets are made from milk that is cooked until it thickens, or curdled and strained; others are thick fudges made from nuts and fruit. The finest varieties are dressed up with silver and gold leaf for a spectacular effect.

Many Indian sweets tend to be overly heavy and sweet to the Western palate. But some, like *sandesh* from Bengal, and r*as malai*, can be very delicate. The rice and the vermicelli noodle puddings—*payasam* and *kheer*—which are more likely to be homemade, can be addictive. If you have a sweet tooth, then it pays to experiment. Try *kulfi*, the Indian version of

The *paan wallah* makes *paan* to your taste just outside a restaurant.

ice cream, in North India, and Mysore *pak*, a chickpea flour fudge of an irresistible consistency, in South India. Calcutta is famous for its milk sweets like *rasgolla* and *sandesh*, and Calcuttans all over the country get their sweets shipped from home.

RESTAURANT FOOD

Dosai and *idli* and the other 'tiffin' or snack items on the menu of a South Indian restaurant come with the condiments that traditionally go with them: coconut *chutney* and the lentil stew called *sambhar*. These are considered breakfast, teatime or 'tiffin' foods, and are usually available round the clock as an anytime snack or light meal.

The *thali* meal, which is also complete in itself, and includes the sweet and sometimes even the *paan*, is a main meal. *Thali* meals are available only at lunch and dinner times. *Tandoori* food is most appropriate for dinner. In *tandoori* restaurants, the best way to get a delicious meal is to go with several people and order several kinds of bread, several kinds of meat (with and without gravy), the traditional black *gram dhal*, one or two vegetable dishes, and the *raita*.

Then everyone shares. Order the breads as you need them, so that they come to you fresh and hot from the oven.

STREET FOOD

The street vendors do brisk business in India. I swear I won't, but always do, indulge in the delights offered on the pavement. I simply cannot resist freshly squeezed sugarcane juice. Most of the machines are manual, and when you make your order, one man shoves in the purple-green stalks of cane while the other turns the handles that work the press.

If you wish, half a lemon and fresh ginger root are also pushed between the stalks. The juice gushes out and is strained and poured over the strictly taboo (unhygienic) ice. The resulting beverage is nectar. I turn a blind eye to the fact that the glasses are rinsed in a bucket of greyish water. So far I've never been sick from my indulgence. But you are advised not to adopt such a casual attitude to health.

If you do try street food, try to stick to food that is freshly cooked. Look for the street vendors to be found wherever the well off shop; for even the rich get the urge for a spicy snack, but they have a nose for scenting out the shops with the best foods.

Bhelpuri

Bombayites can't live without their addictively delicious *bhelpuri*. It is a personalised concoction of thin, crispy lentil flour noodles, puffed rice, and wheat crackers stirred up with diced boiled potatoes, chopped raw onion and coriander, then jazzed up with the *chutneys*, red-hot, tart and sweet.

Both the making and the eating of the different preparations require skill, finesse and raw courage. The *bhelpuri* vendor sits like a greasy wizard among his wares, ready to whip up magic potions with the golden egg-sized puffs called *puri*, the puffed rice, the piles of thin golden noodles called *sev*, the peas cooking in their spicy gravy, the boiled potatoes, the *dahi vadas*—soft, spongy dumplings soaked in yogurt, and the *chutneys*, red, green, and velvety brown. He uses his bare hands to concoct from these ingredients the fiery delights for which he is famous, and his sweat is probably the elusive missing ingredient that makes any safe homemade preparation pale in comparison.

Pani Puri

Pani puri is best eaten with the assistance of an expert. The vendor breaks a hole in the top of the crisp, puffed *puri*, stuffs it with *moong dhal*, quickly fills it with spiced water and hands it around to his customer, who must without a moment's hesitation thrust the whole thing into the mouth. If not, the precious spiced water comes squirting, dripping or oozing out of the *puri* all over the front of shirt or *sari*.

Once the *puri* is in the mouth, there still remains the problem of chewing and swallowing it without choking. Only by dropping all inhibitions and contorting the facial muscles grotesquely can this be effected. To aficionados, it's worth every ridiculous grimace.

Chaat

In New Delhi, rich and poor stand side by side to attack the little leaf dishes in which the *chaat-wallah* mixes up the spicy-sweet, flavourful combinations of *chaat*. Cold *chaat* is a fruit or vegetable salad flavoured with the secret combination of spices that keeps customers addicted to one particular *chaat* stall. Hot *chaat* is based on potatoes fried up dry on a griddle, mixed with spices and lavished with fresh green mint or coriander.

The street vendor is very much a part of the street scene in India.

ENJOYING INDIA

CHAPTER 7

'India is no place to say "I know exactly what I want to do"
—something always intervenes and mocks that resolution.
I travelled light, but still the greater part of my baggage
was mental—my mind brought England along with me,
and saw it shattered, sometimes with awe,
and sometimes with dismay.'
—Brian Thompson, *Great Train Journeys of the World*

FESTIVALS

Baro mase tero parban means '12 months, 13 celebrations'. In India, this is an understatement. Given the regional and religious diversity, it will come as no surprise that there are all kinds of excuses for festive exuberance.

Some places are more famous for their festivals than anything else. The peaceful village of Pushkar is buried alive in pilgrims and cattle at full moon in November–December, when the desert tribes and camel caravans come to trade. Thiruvaiyaru is just a dot on the map marking the final resting place of the great Carnatic composer Thyagaraja, until it is deluged by musicians and music-lovers attending the festival that marks his birthday. Some festivals, although celebrated elsewhere in India, are known for the special fervour of their celebration in a particular place. Republic Day, for example, has to be seen in Delhi to be fully appreciated; the spectacle of the camel regiments in front of the pink sandstone Rashtrapati Bhavan at sunset during the 'Beating the Retreat' is soul-stirring.

There is no single festival that can claim to be celebrated all over India with equal importance: Diwali is popular in parts of the north, but hardly causes a stir in the south. There is no pan-Indian festival: a festival celebrated by the Hindus may not be celebrated by the Muslims, and vice versa. Even a festival celebrated on the same day may be significant for different reasons in different parts of the country: Ram Lila in North India celebrates the victory of Rama over Ravana; in the south that day is called Dusshera, and it celebrates the victory of the goddess Chamundeshwari over the demon Mahishasura.

The Hindu calendar is different from the Western one, and Indians move between the two, using the Western one for the day-to-day of work and school, but shifting to the Indian one for festivals and life-cycle celebrations—for example, birthdays calculated according to Hindu calendar fall on different days every year according to the Western calender. The Hindu calendar tries to reconcile both lunar and solar cycles, so that one year is the time the earth takes to complete its orbit around the sun, but each month is a lunar one, the time the moon takes to orbit the earth. Some complicated calculations are needed: the lunar day, called a *tithi*, is calculated using the difference in the longitudinal angle between the position of sun and moon, and a month is added every two and a half years to make this all work out. Dates for most religious festivals are fixed according to this calendar and are not set until the end of the previous year, so check dates for public holidays, travel, banking, etc. Some of the more colourful festivals are described below.

January

New Year's Eve doesn't receive much attention because there are so many other possible beginnings to the year: the Hindu New Year is actually celebrated in April, the Parsi New Year in March, and the fiscal New Year on the first day of Diwali, in October. But January does have the harvest festival of Pongal, celebrated in Tamil Nadu on the 14th or 15th.

On the first day, evil spirits are driven out of the home and burned on huge bonfires, and the home is completely cleaned, whitewashed, painted and re-thatched. The next day, family members put on new clothes and cook—in new pots—a special dish with the newly harvested rice, raw sugar, *moong dhal*, cashew nuts and raisins. Everyone carries home the long purple stalks of sugarcane; the stalks are peeled, and the fibre chewed to release the sweet juice, then spat out. The third day is for the cattle: the cows and bullocks are

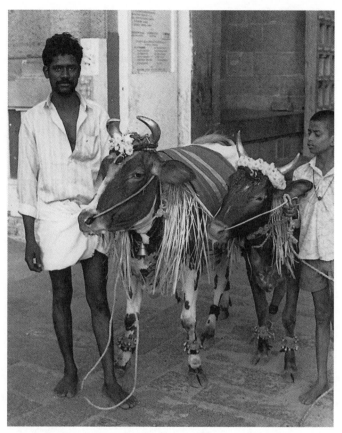

Cows decorated and taken to the temple during Pongal.

washed, anointed with *kumkum* and turmeric, decorated and fed, and even taken to the temple.

January 26 is Republic Day. It is celebrated in all the state capitals, but with most pomp and ceremony in New Delhi. Tickets are available for seats on benches especially set up on Raj Path to view the early morning parade. It is cold in Delhi at that time of the year, and the smell of mothballs from all the shawls and sweaters perfumes the air, but nothing can detract from the pageantry of the event, which may end with a shower of flower petals from helicopters and a fly-past. The rule that no food is allowed at the parade is enforced so that birds will not be attracted and endanger the planes during the low-flying, precise formations.

February–March

According to the Hindu calendar, this is the arrival of spring, Vasant, and the people of North India, and especially Rajasthan and Gujarat, celebrate the end of winter by playing Holi. Normal rules of behaviour are suspended: women pretend to battle with men, *bhang* (hashish) is added to milk and drunk, and anyone is a fair target for the coloured powders and water that are traditionally thrown.

This is one festival that can get a little out of hand, and it is best to go to a Holi party, rather than join the street celebration, especially in the cities. The men can get quite intoxicated and rowdy. If you do go out on the streets, wear old clothes and be prepared to become every colour of the rainbow, and soaking wet into the bargain. If you are invited to a Holi party, wear spotless white, the perfect canvas for the brilliant pink, red and yellow powders with which you will be painted.

March–April

The birthday of the Jain saint Mahavira, the birth of the Hindu god Rama and Christian Good Friday are all public holidays, and celebrated by the communities concerned.

Designs at the threshold of a house are more complex for festive days.

April–May

The Hindu solar New Year begins in the month of Baisakh, and is celebrated all across North India and in Tamil Nadu. In Trichur, Kerala, the magnificent temple festival of Pooram is celebrated with appropriate grandeur. The most magnificent elephants in Kerala are splendidly decorated to take part in a day-long procession accompanied by music and hypnotic drumming. The festival ends with a fireworks display that heralds the dawn.

May–June

Buddha Purnima is celebrated on the full moon in the Hindu month Jeth, and it commemorates his birth, enlightenment and death.

June–July

The Rath Yatra is a festival that marks the journey Krishna took from his childhood home with the cowherds of Gokula to the city of Mathura, where he killed his evil uncle. The images of Krishna and his brother and sister are dragged through the streets of Puri, Orissa on massive *raths* (chariots) that require 4,000 people to pull them. The special form of the deity is called Jagannath, from which the English word juggernaut is derived.

July–August

The coming of the monsoon is an event in itself, and marked with special 'monsoon parties' in Goa. The deserted city of Mandu, in Madhya Pradesh, is especially beautiful at monsoon time, as are the desert cities of Rajasthan, where the festival of Teej is celebrated with singing and dancing, and swings are hung from trees.

Raksha Bandhan is celebrated all over North India, by sisters tying the *rakhi*, a protective thread—simply cotton dyed with turmeric, or fancy silk and glitter—around the wrists of their brothers. Brothers offer their sisters gifts in return. It is not necessarily a blood relationship that is so marked; a girl can tie *rakhi* for a close male friend, placing their relationship on the level of brother and sister. It is a mark

An elaborate festival celebration in India involving the participation of many.

of special affection, and along with all the other relatives, Indians often have 'rakhi brothers' and 'rakhi sisters'.

August 15 is the anniversary of India's Independence, marking the actual transfer of power from Britain, represented by the last viceroy, Lord Mountbatten, to India's first prime minister, Pandit Jawaharlal Nehru. Traditionally, the prime minister gives a speech from the ramparts of the Red Fort in Old Delhi.

August–September

The popular blue-skinned god Krishna exists partly in myth and partly in history. His birthday, Krishna Janmashtami, is a public holiday celebrated all over India, but especially in the places related to the historical figure: Mathura, where he was born, Brindavan and Gokula, where he played his childhood pranks and flirted with the *gopis* (milkmaids), and Dvaraka, where he eventually moved his capital. Songs, dances such as the *ras*, where he multiplied himself to be able to dance with all the milkmaids who loved him, and plays re-enacting his most famous exploits are special features of the celebration.

The chubby elephant-headed god Ganesha, remover of obstacles, has his birthday celebrations on the full moon in September. Now is the time to savour the *modak*, a rice-flour ball stuffed with sweetened coconut that sweet-toothed Ganesha, with good reason, particularly relishes.

In Mumbai (Bombay) especially, Ganesh Chaturthi is preceded by ten days of rituals and *puja* (prayer), and preparation of the idols. Painted a gaudy pink, the potbellied god is set in *mandals*, street shrines erected all over the city with funds canvassed from neighbourhoods. The shrines are simple or 'kitsched' up with disco lights, depending on the area. Every night, the family outing is a sightseeing tour of the various *mandals*. The festival ends with a half-day procession of the 250 or more Ganesha idols on floats, accompanied by frenetic dancers worked up to fever pitch by the hard-driving drumbeats, down to the Arabian Sea to be immersed. Pink powder is thrown everywhere.

September–October

The same ten days during this lunar month are celebrated all over the country, but in different ways, commemorating different mythological events.

In the north, the period is called Ram Lila, and it celebrates Rama's victory over the demon Ravana. Episodes from the *Ramayana* are enacted, in folk-theatre styles in street performances and in classical styles in concert halls. On the last day, gigantic effigies (stuffed with firecrackers) of the demon Ravana and his evil cohorts are set on fire. Delhi and Varanasi have the most spectacular productions of Ram Lila.

In the south, the festival is called Dusshera, and this celebrates the victory of the goddess Chamundeshwari over the buffalo-headed demon Mahishasura (Nowaddi). Each day is sacred to one or other of the goddesses, but the last three days are especially devoted to the goddess of learning, Saraswati. Students make offerings to their teachers and worship their books. Musicians worship their instruments, and craftspeople and artisans, their tools.

In Calcutta, the same festival is called Durga Puja, as Durga is another name for the goddess Chamundeshwari.

Months on the Indian Calendar

- Chaitra — March–April
- Vaisakh — April–May
- Jyaistha — May–June
- Ashadh — June–July
- Shravan — July–August
- Bhadrapad — August–September
- Ashvin — September–October
- Karthik — October–November
- Margashirsha — November–December
- Pousa — December–January
- Magh — January–February
- Phalgun — February–March

October–November

Diwali, or Deepavali, the festival of lights, follows Ram Lila, and marks Rama's triumphant return to the throne after his long exile. Little clay oil lamps are lit outside each house to guide him home, and to welcome Lakshmi, the goddess of wealth. Like Christmas now in the West, Diwali is associated more with the trappings than with the original event that inspired them.

List of Festivals

- **January**
New Year	1 January
Kite Festival and Pongal	14–16 January
Republic Day	26 January
Id-ul-Fittr	
Vasant Panchami	

- **February**

  Mahashivaratri

- **March**

  Holi

  Id-ul-Zuha

  Mahavir Jayanthi

- **April**

  Easter

  Baisakhi

  Muharram

  Buddha Purnima

- **May**
Labour Day	1 May
Birthday of Rabindranath Tagore	8 May

- **July**

  Rath Yatra

  Guru Purnima

- **August**
Indian Independence Day	15 August
Rakshabandhan	
Janamashtami	

Parsi New Year

Ganesh Chaturthi

- **September**

Onam

- **October**

Birthday of Mahatma Gandhi   2 October

Durga Puja

Navaratri

Dusshera

- **November**

Birthday of Guru Nanak

Guru Tej Bahadur's Martyrdom Day

- **December**

Christmas   25 December

TRAVEL

Whether beckoned by the temptations of another temple, another beach, another breathtaking view, or driven by the relentless heat, the monsoon, the noise and dust of the cities, the traveller in India can find infinite reasons to travel. While in other countries you may take the train to go from point A to point B; in India, you go from point A to point B in order to take the train. The good traveller embarks as if on a journey of exploration into unknown territory; for that is what India is. Expect the unexpected and get ready to enjoy the trip, because it may be very, very long.

Trains

If you want to experience the 'real' India, all it costs is the price of a second class unreserved ticket on a passenger train. It doesn't matter where it's going. You will be one among the nine million passengers that travel each day, somewhere on the 65,673 km (40,807.3 miles) of track of the second largest railway system in the world, probably wishing you were somewhere else. 'Real' Indians will be crammed into every available centimetre of space on all sides, and the smell, the dust, the noise and the spectacle will envelop you in an experience you may be hard put to like, but you will certainly never forget.

Of course, if you don't want to get quite that real, there is second class reserved, three-tier sleeper, two-tier sleeper, second class AC (air-conditioned) sleeper, AC chair car, first class sleeper, or first class AC sleeper, moving up from the broad base of the pyramid, through successive layers of caste and class, right up to the rarefied top.

If your concern is with reaching your destination rather than the experience of getting there, then take note of categories such as broad gauge, narrow gauge and metre gauge, mail, express and super-fast express, which will determine the speed of the journey. But given that 8,999,999 other people are also travelling on any particular day, it should come as no surprise that your decisions will be based as much on what's available as on what you can afford or what you're willing to put up with.

Second Class

'Second class unreserved' means that no seat will be assigned to you, and whoever has a ticket is entitled to climb on the train and find a space to stand, sit, lie or squat anywhere within the compartment. This is how the majority of Indians travel.

For a journey during the day of not more than a few hours, without children or luggage, the fascination of watching village India at very close quarters may make up for the discomfort. When I travelled from Madras to Madurai, I had to stand for eight hours and never once could use the toilet. Still, all these years later, that journey hasn't melted into every other trip from point A to B, and it makes a good story, especially the part about how, when I finally got a seat, the baby sleeping on the luggage rack above me peed on my head. An old woman present assured me it was as good as holy water. If you have no option but to travel this way, then get the help of a porter to secure a seat.

Reservations are only issued for sleepers, with some exceptions. Your reservation entitles you to a seat during the day and a berth to sleep on at night. The three-tier sleeper used to be called third class, and some padding may have been added to the wooden seats to justify the name change. The best berths to get are the upper ones, or the ones along the side, if there are two of you travelling together; here, you will not be at the mercy of the other passengers as to when you can sleep. During the day, passengers from the intermediate stations may be allotted seats for some parts of the journey on some trains. Adjustments are expected to be made, but as a foreigner, you may wish to exert your prerogative to be somewhat eccentric in this regard, and not let people crowd you.

Second class AC is offered on some routes and can be very comfortable on a long journey. There is usually a careful watch kept to make sure that people who are not supposed to, don't get on. You travel protected from dust and heat and beggars. The disadvantage is that the splendours of India unravelling before you are filtered through murky double layers of glass. You'll miss the tender green of young rice shoots in the paddy fields, which is surely the most beautiful colour in the world.

Second class, but not second class AC, offers a ladies' compartment. A woman travelling alone is often automatically assigned a berth in the ladies' compartment unless she specifies otherwise. When travelling without a reservation, it's worthwhile to check if here you might find more room; sometimes you might have to chuck some men out first. It is well within your rights to do so, and no one will make any serious objection to your claim. Because the compartment is closed off from the rest of the carriage, if it's full, and if each woman has the usual assortment of tin trunks, duffel bags, baskets and bedding rolls, the effect can be claustrophobic.

In second class AC compartments, and in first class as well for that matter, the Indian-style squat toilets are always cleaner than the Western-style pedestal kind. The Indian-style toilets are gleaming stainless steel, while Western-style ones are scratched and stained plastic. On the other

Cleanliness is not necessarily better in second class AC than in plain old second class. Passengers at both levels are equally inclined to litter and spit, so that even if the first starts out being cleaner, it'll be just as dirty as the other in no time.

hand, the squat toilet is harder to use in a shaking, rattling train, with the hole so close and open to the track underneath, but there is a handle to hold on to. No toilet paper is supplied, but there is a tap for water. Bring your own toilet paper or plastic mug with you.

First Class

The first class compartments seat and sleep four or two passengers. They offer a degree of comfort and privacy with greater access to the world you're rattling through, because the glass on the windows can be raised. It's just the right combination for a long journey. First class and second class AC cost about the same over the same stretch.

If you need bedding, it should be ordered at the station before you leave. A railway attendant will then bring you a roll with a thin mattress, sheets, blanket and pillow at bedtime. Someone will also come around to take orders for bed-tea, breakfast, lunch, tiffin and dinner at the appropriate times; your order will be telegraphed ahead to the next station, and the food will be loaded on stainless steel trays, steaming hot and very appetising. Though various Western-style options will be offered, the Indian meals are better quality. First class AC is also available on some routes, and they are very clean and comfortable, but almost as expensive as flying. First class seats are more readily available than second class AC.

For couples travelling first class, one romantic alternative is to book the coupé, the compartment that has only two berths. It is possible to request it when making your reservations, and as long as it's available, you'll get it. There aren't that many on each train, and honeymooners book them months in advance. But since not many Indian couples go on honeymoons, there's always a chance.

Reservations

The reservations counters in the big cities have been computerised. As long as the electricity is working, and the systems are not down, the process of getting a reservation is much faster than it was a few years ago. Computerisation also allows you to make onward and return reservations more easily, at least from the big cities. If you plan your trips in advance, a travel agent can make your train reservations. The more in advance the better. The closer to your date of travel, the fewer your options, as the well-travelled routes are booked out quickly.

New Delhi and Madras have special tourist booking offices. All tourists holding a foreign passport are eligible for the foreign tourist quota, which is available at most stations on the tourist trail. This means that on each train, there are a specific number of seats reserved for foreigners, which will not be given out to other passengers until the last minute.

You must have your passport with you, and the passports of all the passengers travelling, in case one person is taking care of the bookings for friends or family. You may also be asked to pay in foreign currency, or at least produce an encashment certificate to show that you changed that much foreign currency. The staff is very knowledgeable and helpful about routes, connections and times and can explain the options to you in detail.

The fastest train is the super-fast express, which is faster because it doesn't make as many stops. The express and mail services are next, and passenger trains are the slowest, stopping at every little station. These are the categories to look out for when making your reservation if speed and convenience are your priorities.

There are still some routes where the trains are pulled by steam locomotives; for an aficionado of trains, India can be paradise. One of the most spectacular steam journeys is on the Darjeeling Himalayan Railway from Siliguri to Darjeeling. You have only until the year 2013 to enjoy the old steam locomotives, which are found more on the metre gauge routes, because the government intends to replace them all with diesel and electric-powered engines by that time.

No Seats Available

If there is no tourist quota or if it has already been filled, and you are told at the counter there are no berths available, go straight to the stationmaster. It is important, when told there is absolutely no way you can get a seat, to be patient and persistent till that answer changes.

Once you get the ear of a sympathetic stationmaster, apply persuasion rather than force; a woman travelling alone or with children can always appeal to his protective instincts, a man can have a flight to catch, or a meeting it is imperative for him to attend. Explain your problem in personal terms, always remembering that although it may be within his power to help you, he is under no obligation to do so. Nevertheless, there exists a VIP quota, a stationmaster's quota and an emergency quota. Even if his quota is completely gone, if you make an impression on him, he may phone the next station and get you a seat from that stationmaster's quota.

Beyond the Call of Duty

In Puri, Orissa, because of a misunderstanding with the hotel peon who made my reservation for the return journey to Madras, I ended up on the waiting list. I went to the station several hours before my train was due and contacted the stationmaster. He was busy and hardly seemed to listen. I waited patiently in his office while he did different things. Half an hour later, he looked up as if surprised to see me there. I explained my problem again, stressing that I was alone and had two children with me. He said, rightly, that I should have made my reservation earlier, and started to leave his office. I followed him, explaining the misunderstanding with the hotel staff. I was not the only one, by the way; there were several other people in the same predicament. I walked with the stationmaster as he went up and down the platform going about his duties.

I told him I was on holiday in Puri, this was my first time here, we had stayed at the Great South Eastern Railway Hotel, including various other details that had nothing to do with train reservations. Before long, we were chatting like friends. He went back to his desk, checked my waiting list status and found that I did not have a seat. Then he did something above and beyond the call of duty. He phoned another stationmaster at one of the stops ahead, and after some pleasantries, got me two seats on his quota. Then he sold me four unreserved seat tickets—for myself, my two children, and the maid.

When the train arrived, he contacted the ticket collector, explained my situation to him, and made sure I was allowed to board the second class AC compartment and sit there despite not having proper tickets until I reached the next station. Even then, the ticket collector had to find two more seats for us, and finally, in the middle of the night, we had our berths. I paid no bribe, nor was any kind of payment for these services even hinted at.

Planes

Every day, Indian Airlines, the national carrier, takes 36,000 people on 90 flights to 117 destinations—with a fleet of only 52 aircraft. Everyone who has had occasion to travel by Indian Airlines has horror stories to tell about bad service, bad food, delays, flights being cancelled and so on.

The problem arises from the simple fact that tight scheduling to meet the heavy demand means that all the aircraft are flying every day from dawn to dusk, with servicing done at night. Indian Airlines cannot afford the luxury of keeping planes on standby in case of technical difficulties. If a fault does come up, there is no alternative but to take as long as it takes to set it right before the flight takes off.

The weather—monsoon, cyclones and fog—closes certain airports regularly and there is not a thing anyone can do. The political situation—including Punjabi terrorists and Tamil terrorists and Kashmiri terrorists—means that every threat of bombs, hijacking or sabotage must be treated as real. Every day, there's a call, which usually turns out to be a hoax, but must nevertheless be taken seriously. The bomb threat drill takes four hours. And as part of the routine check-in, baggage, passengers and staff are carefully screened. Despite all these factors, Indian Airlines claims that flights are on time at least 85 per cent of the time.

International surveys have put Indian Airlines close to the bottom of the scale for service, efficiency and safety standards. But now, travellers have some alternatives, with the entry of new private domestic carriers such as Air Sahara and Jet Airways. This may well force Indian Airlines to improve to keep up with the competition.

Reservations

The system of reservations and confirmations has been fully computerised, so the process of getting a ticket is faster. But Indian Airlines is unable to meet the demand for flights, and on the high density, or 'trunk' routes, it is often necessary to book a week in advance to get a confirmed seat. On less travelled routes, two days in advance should get you on the plane.

If you don't get a confirmed seat, you will be wait-listed and given a number that shows your position on the list. You'll be automatically moved up if there are cancellations. If you do get a confirmed seat, and then change your plans, there is a cancellation fee, and the amount you pay depends on when you cancel.

Buses

In India, buses always 'ply'. Indian buses ply the same routes as trains, sometimes faster, sometimes slower; they also ply the routes that the trains don't, so sometimes a bus is the only way to go. On well-travelled routes there may even be air-conditioned 'video' coaches that show Hindi movies en route. But the local state-run buses are usually crowded and painfully slow. The 55 km (34.2 miles) from Agra to Bharatpur took four hours on a local bus.

Bus travel is easier if you can manage a few words in a local language. It will be even less confusing if you can, however slowly, read the script. On most buses, the signs are not written in English and in small towns and villages, it may not be easy to find someone from whom to get instructions and directions. At the very least, learn to pronounce the name of your destination correctly: Delhi is pronounced 'Dilli', with the 'd' sounding more like 'th' in 'this'; Kolkatta, which

foreigners usually pronounce with the stress on the second syllable, actually has the stress on the first and it's not 'cal' as in 'California', but as in 'cul-de-sac'; Agra doesn't begin with 'a' as in 'apple', but with a lengthened 'ah' as in 'ugly'.

Toilet facilities during a bus journey may mean that men go on one side of the road and women on the other. The long skirts and *saris* that most Indian village women wear, without underpants, make it possible for them to squat and relieve themselves without any loss of modesty. Squirming out of a pair of jeans is a lot more embarrassing, so dress appropriately.

Cars

A car with a driver is the luxurious way to hit the road. The driver will know the way (or at least know how to ask), stop whenever you want him to, and not when you don't. It is possible to find cars for hire at railway stations in the smaller towns, and if your destination is a popular one, the taxi may pick up a full load of passengers who will split the fare between them. It is worthwhile to bargain over the fare.

In big cities, agencies offering 'tourist taxis' are to be found near the hotels. For out-of-town trips, you can negotiate a round sum that works out cheaper than the daily rate. There is usually no need to arrange accommodation for the driver; it is understood that he will sleep in his car. The exceptions are the luxury hotels, which often have hostel-style accommodation for drivers, at an extra charge. You pay that, of course. Otherwise, just give the driver money for meals whenever you take yours. In some places, it may be convenient if you all eat at the same place, but don't be surprised or offended if your driver chooses to sit at a different table.

Very recently, drive-yourself car rental agencies started in India. Given the hardships and inconveniences of driving in India, and the dirt-cheap, excellent drivers, it hardly seems a step forward. But for those who love driving and want adventure, the possibility now exists. This is a facility that is currently available only in the big cities, and through the five-star hotels. It may be available elsewhere soon. You must be at least 25 years old, have had a driving license for at least two years without any major convictions, and hold a valid international driving license. You must also make an insurance deposit of 10,000.00 rupees, which is refundable.

Driving at night is to be avoided if at all possible. Few roads are lit and few vehicles have working headlights. You can play a game:

- one headlight coming towards you—a motorcycle, or a truck with one broken headlight
- two headlights—two motorcycles, or a car passing a truck, each with one headlight broken
- three headlights—one truck, passing a car, or two trucks and one motorcycle
- no headlights—any of the above.

Get the picture?

RURAL INDIA

Rural India is not just City India without electricity and running water. It is a whole other experience. You may be the first white person the village ever encountered. Or you may be the second, the ones before having sunbathed in the nude on the schoolhouse roof, and been only interested in smoking illegal substances.

The villages of India far off the beaten track are another world, in another time. Theoretically, 70 per cent of villages have television, but what that means is that there is one TV set in the village and everyone gathers around it. The signs of the 20th century stand out like anachronisms: the Rajasthani cowherd with shocking pink turban, embroidered high-waisted, pleated shirt, narrow trousers and brocaded leather slippers delivers his milk from a motorcycle; the crowd around the TV set, segregated according to caste and sex, are watching *I Love Lucy*.

Village India does not understand the concept of purposeless travel. Visiting relatives, attending important ritual celebrations, going to market and making pilgrimages for religious reasons are legitimate reasons to travel. Simply to see the world is not. It's an activity outside the village context. This does not mean you can't go to a village and find

Rural girls dancing in Gujarat.

a place to stay. But you will be the object of curiosity. If you are a woman travelling alone, you are especially vulnerable because you stand outside the cultural context to which the rules of correct behaviour apply. You may encounter curiosity, and it may be expressed in ways that make you feel uncomfortable: open staring by people who come very close, touch your things and make comments and laugh in a language you cannot understand.

React with openness and smiles. Don't hand out money to the children; think about the message of such an action—that wealth is to be found in the cities, where there are more wealthy foreigners like you. The villages where foreigners have passed through are the ones where you are likely to encounter children begging. It's a behaviour they have learned from your predecessors.

Accommodation

Small towns near the main road have some form of accommodation, like a *dak* bungalow or circuit house. These are small buildings kept for the use of government officers (forest officials, for example) but if they are not in use, it is quite legitimate for the person in charge of them to rent them out. Unfortunately, the person in charge usually sits in an office in the nearest big town, so you have to plan a little in advance to use these facilities.

They are usually clean and adequate, and sometimes they are real finds—little colonial cottages that look like they were left by the British. It is worth trying the *dak* bungalow or circuit house even if you have not made reservations in advance, because the man on the spot may be able and willing to accommodate you.

A place to sleep is called a 'lodge' and restaurants, if they have names, are called 'hotels' in some parts of India. In the remote villages—the ones that you have to get to by taking a bus from the train station, a bullock cart from the last bus stop and walking 5 km—there is unlikely to be anything in the nature of a hotel or restaurant. In such a case, approach a person of the same sex to point out the head of the village. Present your request to him. Once you make your problem clear, you may depend on the hospitality of the villager. A

The open field is the classroom of a rural literarcy programme.

place will be found for you to sleep, and you will be given food to eat.

In places where there is no alternative, you may be accommodated with a family, perhaps that of the village head, or with the local schoolteacher who may speak English. Accommodation may be a mat on the floor among the rest of the sleeping family, or a woven string bed out in the courtyard under the stars. Food will be a meal shared with the family. The food can be very spicy.

Ask questions about toilets, bathing, and other such details of someone of the same sex. Be prepared for toilet facilities to be quite primitive. The bathroom may be the river, or an area enclosed with thatch, and a bucket. The toilet is very likely the open field. Ask a person of the same sex for directions, for it is common for women to go to one place, and men somewhere else. Take your plastic mug filled with water to clean yourself afterwards. The time to go is early in the morning before the sun rises, or in the evening after the sun sets. Thus everyone's modesty is protected. Water is a precious commodity when it has to be carried from the nearest well. Use it with great discretion.

It is difficult to generalise about what is correct behaviour; each situation will call for something different. You must be sensitive to non-verbal cues.

Cultural Sensitivities

A friend who works in a rural area told me about a visitor she invited to a folk performance in a village in Tamil Nadu. He watched the performance intently, smoking almost throughout. The folk performance on this occasion had religious and ritual significance (rural performances very often do), and so it was not proper to smoke in that area. If he had looked around him, he would have seen that men regularly left the performance area for a smoke. Nobody, including my friend, ever told him how insulting he was being, and probably to this day he doesn't realise it. My friend expected him to be more sensitive, which was why she had taken him to see the performance in the first place.

Villagers will never offend a guest who has honoured them with his presence by telling him what to do. It is up to you, the visitor, to be conscious of the behaviour and feelings of the people around you. It is not even possible to make a generalisation like, 'Observe what others do, and then do the same.' In another situation, you may have to do just the opposite. For example, all the women may eat together after the men have eaten, but a foreign woman may be served with the men. A foreign woman travelling alone stands outside the context of village rules. This gives her more freedom: dress codes are more relaxed for her, and she may do certain things, like smoke or drink, that village women are prohibited from doing. But it also means that she may not be entitled to the same protection and consideration that the village women get. A man who would never molest one of his village women might molest a foreign woman.

Payment

One difficulty will be to repay the generosity of your host. A refusal of money may be just the first step towards accepting it, or it may be a genuine expression that this is not something to be repaid with money. Be ready with other means of payment. Pens, lighters and disposable razors make good gifts to carry to villages. Most Indians like having their pictures taken; if you are carrying a Polaroid camera, you will always have the perfect gift—the magic square that turns into the picture of your host family. It is important to ask before taking photographs. If you take photographs, it will be much appreciated if you mail back copies.

Getting Lost

When travelling extensively in rural areas, it is best to carry a good map of the region. If you do get lost, look out for someone who speaks English. Even in the remotest village, there is usually someone who does—the teacher, the doctor, the bank clerk. Be sure to ask at least three people for directions, and ask more if you can't come up with a majority decision.

It is unlikely that you will encounter hostility, unless you have wandered into a political situation and your presence is misunderstood. This is a rare and exceptional circumstance.

Even then, someone will likely take you in hand and get you out safely. In the normal course of events, you can expect to be received with friendly curiosity and simple hospitality according to the means of your host.

The best way to experience Village India is with a friend. Many Indians living in the big city have ancestral homes in small villages, and return there regularly for visits or holidays. They may be surprised by your interest, but will usually be proud to show you around.

Health Care in Rural Parts

In India, there is only one doctor for more than 2,000 people, according to the latest statistics. Taking into account the number of doctors in the urban areas, the number of persons per doctor in the rural areas is much, much higher. This is a fact to take into consideration when you travel off the beaten track. Be prepared to be your own doctor. *Where There Is No Doctor* is an excellent practical book that you should read and memorise before setting off. It gives absolutely no-nonsense direct advice for when you truly have to take responsibility for your own health. There is advice on how to deal with emergencies like snake bites and broken limbs.

Be prepared for minor medical problems with your own medical kit, which should include disinfectant, bandages, paracetamol for fever, and so on. Take enough of any medication that you are on so that you don't have to look for nonexistent pharmacies. If there is a serious medical problem, get back to the nearest town.

TRAVELLING WITH CHILDREN

Indians love children; this makes some aspects of travelling with children in India easier, and other aspects more difficult. You don't have to try to stop your children from making noise, running around, climbing all over things— basically behaving like children. The people you encounter, men as well as women, will play with, carry and amuse your small baby or toddler, and if the child is friendly, he or she will be taken off your hands for hours at a time. You can even take your children to dance and music performances or the cinema without fearing that they will disturb the audience.

Unfortunately, the almost universal affection that children generate may manifest itself as touching, pinching and teasing of a kind that your children may not like. You can explain the situation to older children, but the little ones, who are subject to most of the handling, will only understand that they are being hurt by total strangers. You can tell people politely and with a smile to leave the children alone, and, if possible, take them a little distance away. There is no point trying to explain unless the person speaks English, and such a person is unlikely to be pinching your child.

On trains there is always food available, but it may be too spicy for your children. In airports, there is not always a restaurant, or it may not be open at the time when delays and cancellations have left the children desperately hungry. Even on the plane, the food that is served may be very spicy. It is better to carry something with you—bread and a jar of peanut butter, or some hard-boiled eggs.

Bottled water is available almost everywhere; you can find the plastic bottles at tea stalls and soft drink stands. Only in the most remote places will you have to find alternatives. At hotels and restaurants, ask specifically for bottled water, for which you will be charged. The prohibition against drinking water from the tap also includes the water you use to brush your teeth, and ice.

While travelling, stick to fruits that can be peeled and food that is cooked. Milk is usually boiled automatically in India, and yogurt is always made with boiled milk, so these are safe. Ice cream is usually not, except all over the state of Gujarat, where there is a large and modern dairy industry, and from the state-run milk booths in other places.

Train journeys can be very long: 36 hours from Madras to Delhi, 18 from Madras to Trivandrum, and 35 from Bombay to Calcutta. Delays at the airport can run to several hours at a stretch. Children get

Here is a good game for trains: make a list of things you are likely to see out the window, common and uncommon, and fix a value to each. For example, 10 paise for white birds, goats and cows, 50 paise for windmills and temples, 1 rupee for oxen pulling the plough, 5 rupees for an elephant. Then let them sit at the window and accumulate money. Add it all up and pay them when you arrive at your destination.

bored easily. Bring along books and travel versions of popular games for older children, and encourage them to find other children on the train or in the airport to play with. There always are other children.

Fun for All

Children have different concerns when travelling, and it is important to allow them the freedom to focus on these. I was reminded of this when I visited the exquisitely beautiful Jain temples at Mount Abu in Rajasthan. The carved white marble is breathtakingly intricate, and the designs on the ceilings are cosmic in their conception. My three-year-old son spent the whole time there throwing a feather down from some stairs, watching it float down, and then running to pick it up and do the whole thing again. My nine-year-old sat at the entrance watching everyone divesting themselves of leather belts, wallets, handbags, binocular cases and watches with leather straps. We all had a great time.

Squat toilets need practice before the journey starts. On the train, with all the shaking and rattling, it can be difficult to keep one's balance and that can be frightening. Dress the children in clothes that make it easy for them to relieve themselves at roadsides, if the bus depot toilet is just too filthy, for example. Disposable diapers are just now making an appearance, but only in the big cities.

In India, mothers never allow their children to cry. As soon as a baby starts to wail, it will be picked up and put to the breast, or jiggled and distracted in some way. Toddlers are immediately given what they want at the first sign of tears. If you allow your child to cry, people around you will become visibly upset, and may even try to intervene, by offering sweets to the child, for example. If your child is at the age of temper tantrums, you will have to endure the censure of the crowd to effect any discipline. By Indian standards, you are being a bad parent. Indian children, except those of the Westernised rich, never seem to need disciplining, in spite of being spoilt rotten as babies.

Children quickly pick up the attitudes of their parents. When faced with the frustrations and difficulties of travel, it is all too easy to talk rudely to or about 'them', as if dividing the world into them and us. They are the ones with the funny customs, and we are the normal ones. Making disparaging or sarcastic comments in your own language may relieve your stress, but it will also affect your children's perceptions of the society they see around them. They will not feel or show respect for it if you don't. It is important to teach your children that, as visitors, your norms are no one's concern but your own. The onus is on you, and not on the Indians, to make the necessary adjustments.

CULTURE

There are both exotic and familiar ways to occupy your leisure hours in India. You can amuse yourself with polo, which came to India from Persia. You can find elephant polo, camel polo and bicycle polo in Jaipur, the common variety in Delhi and Calcutta, or polo at a height of 3,505 m (2.2 miles) in Leh. If polo is too hectic, then you can take up an exotic musical instrument. There's a whole variety to choose from: the *shehnai* that makes a sound like the noise of crickets, a sound that seems to enter your head; the *ghatam*, a clay pot that you invert on your bare belly and play like a drum; or the *sarod*, which has 19 strings. If you can play a Western musical instrument well, you can apply to join a symphony orchestra.

Eat your way through the variety of Indian foods. Learn to drape a *sari*. Have massages with oils and herbs. Take a course in Ayurvedic medicine. Your Indian friends will be pleased to help you get in touch with the right people if you wish to learn anything or participate in any activity. Here are some of the more popular ways of passing time in India.

CINEMA

Popular Indian cinema, or 'Bollywood', churning out about 800 movies a year is badly maligned by the intelligentsia but despite the intellectuals and the feminists, these crowd pleasers sell about a 100 million movie tickets each week.

'Movie' is an inadequate term for the Indian film. Something like Marathon Entertainment, Education and Escapism Package would better describe three satisfying hours of complete freedom from the rigours of the real world. Petty concerns like logic and continuity are not allowed to spoil your fun. If you can ask, "How did he get across the river without getting wet?" or "Wasn't she wearing a different sari in the last shot?" then you have not settled into the right frame of mind for the Indian cinema experience.

Everything is suggested—there is no overt nudity or sex (kissing has only been allowed in Indian movies since the end of the 1980s) and even the violence is patently phoney. Granted, some of the gyrating in the dance sequences is pretty raunchy, and the lyrics for the songs are full of sexual double entendres, but Indian movies are meant to be entertainment for the whole family, and they are usually suitable for even children.

The movie I saw had the usual cast of stock characters and scenes: the evil brother-in-law, the best-friends-who-become-enemies-through-a-misunderstanding, the wet-sari-sequence and the dream-dance-sequence. Of course, the hero and heroine don't die at the end. But a Hindi movie aficionado would have known that right from the start, because their names matched: Radha and Vasu. (Vasu is another name for Krishna, and the Radha-Krishna connection is explained in *Chapter 2: An Overview* on pages 31–32.))

Who cares if small liberties were taken with reality? Why shouldn't a village in the mountains in North India have a constant supply of big red, yellow and green helium-filled balloons so that the lovers can send messages to each other? It's just a modern update of the parrots that were supposed to take messages between lovers in classical literature and dance, and no more unlikely. Besides, the typical Indian cinema-goer gets a heavy dose of reality outside the cinema hall; what's needed is an escape from all that.

Leave your critical faculties at home, and go to see Indian movies to understand the Indian ethos. They are not subtitled, but it's a good way to familiarise yourself with the local language, and you don't really need to understand the dialogue to know what's going on. When the good guy says to his enemy, "There can only be one deal between us, and that deal is death!" his stance, facial expression and tone of voice express fully his heroic defiance.

The actors' stylised emotions may look like overacting, but it is faithful to the tradition of all the Indian theatre forms. The villainy of the villain, the hurt of the betrayed wife, the heroism of the hero, are portrayed with the same mannerisms and heavy-handedness in the acclaimed theatre and dance forms such as Kathakali and Bharata Natyam. I find it ironic that the same people who revile the acting in Indian popular cinema admire that stylised portrayal of 'types' when it appears in some ancient traditional theatre form.

The movies are rich anthropological source material. Where in reality corruption abounds, in the movie the incorruptible hero prevails. But no explanation is offered to account for the palatial house of the incorruptible police officer who is managing on his meagre salary. In a country of arranged marriages, romantic love flowers again and again on the big screen. But the lovers who successfully marry are always as ideally suited for each other as if a master matchmaker had picked them out. If they were not, if one was of the wrong caste or the wrong religion, it would never work out in the end. The girl would die tragically, leaving the boy free to marry the girl appropriate to him.

Again and again, the hero is an underdog, a poor hardworking man, a rickshaw puller or a railway porter, the best-fed rickshaw puller or porter ever seen in India. They fight all odds, stand up against the injustices meted out to them and their compatriots by the rich and corrupt, to win the girl—living out on the screen the hopeless fantasies of the poor who spend their money to watch them.

Cinema-goers identify so closely with their heroes that it is no wonder the actors can then go on to glorious political careers with the masses behind them, recreating in real life the fervour they portrayed before the cameras. It's worked particularly well in South India, where the cine-hero MGR went on to become Tamil Nadu's chief minister, replacing another show business personality, only to be succeeded after his death by one of his most popular on-screen as well as off-screen heroines, Jayalalitha.

Art Movies

The Indian so-called 'art' cinema caters to a more Westernised taste, and some of the movies are excellent by world standards—those by Satyajit Ray, the most famous of Indian directors, for example. The director Aparna Sen has created movies with strong and interesting female characters. Other famous directors are Shyam Benegal, Adoor Gopalakrishnan and Mrinal Sen.

Unfortunately, the alternative Indian cinema, while winning awards around the world, doesn't get much exposure in India itself. Cultural centres and film societies are the places to look for screenings of art movies. Their plots—heavily dosed with intellectual argument and not song and dance—are meant for an urban elite who are well-educated, refined and fastidious, and have a somewhat Westernised outlook. Taxi-drivers and women hawking fish won't spend their hard-earned money to see them.

English Movies

Several cinema halls show English language movies, but these are usually American box office hits. If you are a movie buff, watch out for the morning shows, which sometimes have good movies. The cultural centres of some countries represented in India offer screenings of movie shows, festivals or retrospectives of work from their home countries. India also has a film festival every year; it takes place in Delhi on alternate years, and in a state capital every other year.

Video parlours make up for the lack of variety in the cinema halls. They offer pirated copies of the latest English-language movies and are to be found in every neighbourhood shopping centre. Even a serious movie buff should find enough of interest in India. But you'll know you've been here too long when you start finding the art movies a little bleak and tedious, and wishing there were some song-and-dance sequences in *Rambo*.

TELEVISION

Doordarshan is the national TV network formed by Indira Gandhi when she was the information minister. Her idea was to reach even the remotest village with news and information of relevance to the rural audience. It began in black and white, for just a few hours a day, with a news bulletin, a movie to attract the masses, and then information for farmers. At the time, the government policy was to impose Hindi across the land, and so all broadcasts were in that language. Eventually, the hopelessness of making India Hindi-speaking was recognised, and regional language studios were set up.

Everyone criticised Doordashan, but there was nothing else. With advertising, the network made money and updated all the facilities so that, technologically at least, it is competitive. But both Doordarshan and its radio counterpart, All India Radio, continue to be government-controlled, subtle and sometimes not so subtle propaganda machines for the ruling Congress party.

As soon as VCRs became available, Doordarshan faced its first serious competition. The news magazine *India Today* came out with a weekly video news magazine which is now very popular. Sometimes the weekly video is more up-to-date with current issues than the daily news on Doordarshan. Now there is also Star TV, which beams BBC, and Zee TV, MTV, the Sports Channel, CNN, all of which are available by cable from enterprising neighbourhood satellite dish owners, for 24 hours a day or as long as the power is on—the best and worst in television from around the world.

Government control of the news can be a blessing in volatile political situations. After Indira Gandhi's assassination, Doordarshan and All India Radio suppressed information about the tragedy until the new prime minister was confirmed and troops were in place around the country. Thus rioting was kept under control. Now, that kind of censorship is no longer possible. During the riots in Ayodhya, fuelled by the Hindu-Muslim conflicts over the building of a temple on the site of a mosque (which was supposedly built on the site of a temple), BBC broadcasted every incendiary picture they could get all over the country.

Doordarshan is doing all it can to regain the ground lost to VCR, satellite dishes and neighbourhood cable. They have increased the number of channels, with different kinds of programming. A new batch of talented young producers is creating Indian versions of popular TV formats—the sitcom, the soap, the talk show. Then, the only snag would be that the additional channels can only be reached with a dish antenna positioned away from the AsiaSat which beams Star TV. Viewers will have to choose between foreign-made or home-grown; or get two TV sets.

Doordarshan provides a little something for everyone: classical music and dance for highbrows, and *Chitrahaar*, a selection of song-and-dance sequences from the movies for the rest of us. For your servants, the Sunday feature film is a must; never require them to work at that time. Doordarshan also has live broadcasts of important sporting events, like Wimbledon, the French Open, the World Cup, major cricket test matches, but no baseball or American football.

THEATRE

Bombay is famous for its English-language theatre scene—Indian actors and actresses doing Neil Simon and Bernard Shaw, that kind of thing. There is also a vibrant regional language theatre in Hindi and Marathi. The main theatres are the Prithvi in Juhu, and the National Centre for the Performing Arts, which has four theatres and is building a fifth.

Delhi is well represented by contemporary Hindi theatre. The National School of Drama is located there, and they do adaptations of Bertolt Brecht into various regional theatre forms, offering an exciting cross-cultural experience. Delhi also has performances and festivals of traditional and contemporary theatre from all over the country, to see some of which you would otherwise have to go to some remote village in Assam or Kerala. The theatres in Delhi are located in the Mandi House area, where Doordarshan has its offices. Triveni Kala Sangam, on Tan Sen Marg, in the same area, offers interesting lectures, art courses and performances, and has art galleries and a bookshop, as well as a little café serving tea, coffee and basic food to the arty crowd.

Madras has only one professional Tamil repertory company, Koothupattarai. This offers contemporary theatre with a social consciousness, and often takes its message to the streets. There are some amateur theatre companies doing both English and Tamil theatre, but it is hard to talk about a theatre scene in this city that does not have even one well-equipped theatre for drama. The Museum Theatre used to be the best, but it is now no longer easily available except for government-sponsored events. Now, the Music Academy is the best that Madras has to offer.

Calcutta nurtured the beginnings of Modern Indian Theatre in the late 18th century. Theatre plays adapted from novels, and including interludes of mime, songs and dances, as well as revolutionary folk theatre with a strong communist message, and street theatre attract the audiences here. One of the oldest traditional theatres in Calcutta is the Star, which has a revolving stage. Others include the Rabindra Sadan, which stages a performance most evenings, and the Birla Academy. You can ask about performances at the information centre opposite the Calcutta Club on Acharya J.C. Bose Road.

THE ARTS

All the traditional art forms in India are intimately linked with religion. Architecture and sculpture came together in the building of temples and the carving of deities; music and dance are part of the ceremonies of worship. The art of theatre itself was sacred, and the act of watching a play involved actor and audience in a shared aesthetic experience.

Classical Dance and Music

The folk dance and theatre forms are not purely entertainment. They are a part of the lives of Indian people. The traditional castes of performers still perform their traditional art forms on the traditional ceremonial occasions before an audience that is steeped in the same religious and social context.

The classical forms, on the other hand, have been torn out of an ancient context and thrust onto the modern secular concert stage. Sometimes, the art form can nonetheless transcend the great barriers that exist between the performer and the audience, as in the case of Ravi Shankar, who moved even Western audiences that had little idea of what he was doing. Sometimes the art form loses its impact, as in Chakkiar Koottu, a theatre form from Kerala, where the minute facial movements and subtleties are lost on the modern audience. When that happens, the form starts to die out. Sometimes the art form transforms itself to reach out to the modern audience, as in the choreography of Birju Maharaj. He has taken Kathak, a North Indian dance form, from an intimate, solo court setting into group patterns of spectacular turns and complex footwork that thrill even across the distance of the relatively remote modern stage.

A child learning the traditional art forms starts young.

Dance Forms

Indian folk and classical dance performances provide glimpses into another space and time. There are several classical Indian dance forms, but I have chosen four to describe here: Bharata Natyam, Kathak, Odissi and Kathakali. They are well represented by excellent artists in all the big cities. They originated in different parts of India, but all rely, in varying degrees, on rhythm, facial expression, hand gestures and storytelling. The costumes, music, and dance techniques are very different.

- Bharata Natyam evolved out of temple ritual in South India and used to be performed exclusively by girls dedicated to the temple from childhood, or born into that community, called *devadasis*. The precise and chiselled movements seem to be the natural play of the geometry of the human body. At its best, it sparkles. Crisp footwork and graceful arm movements illumine the rhythms, and eloquent eyes and face and mobile fingers bring the stories to life.

- Kathak came from the caste of storytellers, and evolved in the Moghul courts. It is full of virtuosic turns and intricate rhythms brought out by the feet, the ankles circled by a hundred bells. The dancers in their exquisite costumes look as if they have just stepped out of a Moghul miniature painting.

- Kathakali is more theatre than dance. The faces of the male dancers are elaborately painted to symbolise their nature (green faces belong to the good guys), and they dramatise stories from the *Ramayana* and *Mahabharata*, or, in modern versions, Western plays like Macbeth and Faust. Kathakali is one theatre form that maintains its original audience in the villages of Kerala, where it is part of religious ceremonies, and also reaches a highbrow audience among the cultured of the city, where it is art.

- Odissi is curved and graceful, with the dancer taking the position called *tribhanga* (three bends), where the body curves like an 's'. It was first performed by young boys as part of religious ritual in the temples of Orissa. Nowadays, it is performed more often by women. It has a sculpturesque quality, as if an ancient stone frieze of dancers had been

The author, in traditional Bharata Natyam costume.

put in motion. One part of the dance repertoire uses the *Gita Govinda*, medieval poems in Sanskrit on episodes in the love life of Krishna and his beloved Radha.

Appreciating Indian Dance

In all the styles, both the pure dance sequences (which are decorative and full of complexities of rhythm, graceful poses and delicate hand gestures) and the expressional dance (which sets out to tell a story or create a mood) move in a circular, spiralling way, rather than in a straight line from the beginning to the end. In the pure dance sequences, the dancer breaks up the eight beats of the time cycle into different rhythmic patterns, always ending each sequence on the sam, the first beat of the next cycle.

The expressional dances do not tell the story by starting at the beginning and going to the end, but by elaborating, say, the beauty of the lover, his face like the moon, his eyes, his lips, before going on to his rejection, by turning away, by pulling away his hand, by not coming to the secret meeting place, returning again and again to his beauty, before ending with the nuance of the heroine's despair.

Many dance and theatre forms take their stories from the *Ramayana* and *Mahabharata*, and their love lyrics from the many songs and poems about the love between Krishna when he lived in the cowherd community, and Radha, the beautiful *gopi*, or cowherd girl. Most of the audience knows the stories well. Just as a Westerner might look at three little boys dressed in bed sheets, and recognise the Three Magi of Christ's birth and experience an emotion that was partly dependent on the special significance of that story, the Indian audience goes halfway to meet the performer with its emotional involvement in these stories.

The performances do not set out to create dramatic tension, but to bring the audience to the experience which is distilled from emotion, or *rasa* (literally, 'juice'). The audience that is prepared to participate with the artist in the experience as real as taste are rasikas. The techniques for creating *rasa* are elaborately spelt out in the ancient Sanskrit text on the science of theatre, the *Natya Shastra*.

I have been studying Indian dance for more than 30 years now. In my encounters with foreigners who watch Indian dance, I have often noticed a reluctance to just look at it and enjoy it. There is a sense that there must be something more that they're missing. They are afraid to say that they just don't like it, that they find it boring and overly long and repetitive. The truth is, much of the dance they see is just that. One of the reasons is that foreigners end up going to see the wrong shows. Either they see a show called 'Dances of India' over dinner, or go to some prestigious event featuring a 'legend'. Neither of these kinds of performances are likely to show Indian dance at its best.

Don't see Indian dance for the first time at the shows arranged by hotels as part of a package that includes food. Good Indian dancers and musicians will not perform while food is being eaten. This would be disrespectful to the art form. A dinner-and-show package is likely to feature second- or third- or fourth-rate performers. This is not always true; once in a while they do get good artistes and make arrangements so that their art is not compromised, but you'll never know that until you learn to recognise the difference between a first-rate and a fourth-rate performance.

The legendary dancers tend to be monumental in girth as well as reputation. Anyway, someone in the audience will make a point of telling you that this performance of hers is nothing, and you should have seen her ten or 20 years ago, when she was really good. And so you should have. Many of us who love Indian dance go to see a dancer past her prime to remind ourselves of how sublime she once was. There are some exceptions to this rule, men and women who transcend age and weight and girth in their performances, but these are rarer than the press reviews would have you believe. In 20 years of watching Indian dance, I can count them on one hand.

Look for a performance, in a theatre or cultural centre, of one of the top young dancers rather than one of the 'legendary' dancers. It's much more fun to see a slim, lithe, lively dancer doing interpretations of erotic love poetry. It is not necessary to know the stories; if the dancer is good, you feel these stories. Still, if you can read up a little about the exploits of Krishna and Rama and Shiva, some of the hand gestures will start to be intelligible. You will appreciate the once-in-a-lifetime performances much more if you have already learned to tune in to the subtleties of the dance in this easier way.

Dance performances of the different styles are often held in the four major cities. There are also regular dance festivals, like the one at Khajuraho, the famous temple complex in Madhya Pradesh, where top artists perform. But in their place of origin, the dances can be found in their most authentic representation.

Kathakali is still danced in the temple compound, in all-night performances lit only by oil or kerosene lamps, in Kerala. Bharata Natyam is performed on the concert stage instead of the temple even in Tamil Nadu; but the Madras audiences can recognise and appreciate subtle nuances, thus bringing out the best in the dancer. Odissi in Orissa doesn't have the gloss of the big city performances, but it is closer to the original form, and Kathak in the villages of Uttar Pradesh still tells the traditional stories.

MUSIC

E.M. Forster likened Indian music to Western music reflected in trembling water. But the difference is much greater. The closest that Western music comes to Indian music is in jazz. Both Hindustani music of the north and Carnatic music of the south have developed as if harmony simply didn't exist, concentrating exclusively on two basic elements, the *tala* (time cycle) and *raga* (melody). Both also give great importance to ornamentation with vibrato and quarter-tones that someone once said are 'the jewellery that the melody wears'.

North Indian Music

A performance of Hindustani music may be on one of the stringed instruments like the *sitar* or the *sarod*, or a wind instrument such as the oboe-like *shehnai* or the bamboo flute, or simply the human voice. It is accompanied by the double drum, the *tabla*.

The recital begins with the *alaap*, the slow, detailed delineation of the *raga* or melodic scale, without any rhythm. The next stage is when the musician incorporates rhythm into the melody. After that, the *tabla* is added, the tempo increases, and the composition begins. About 5 per cent is previously set, and 95 per cent is improvised. The classification of *ragas* in the North Indian system is interesting. Some *ragas* are specified as being suitable for certain times of the day, certain seasons and certain moods. The great musician Tansen supposedly had the ability to start fire by singing the appropriate *raga*.

The correct response to the overwhelming emotion that a beautiful phrase or subtle nuance the musician has created is to exclaim, "Wah, wah." Don't make the mistake of 'wah-wahing' while the musicians are tuning their instruments. Tuning takes a long time at the beginning, and can happen again right in the middle of a piece. A distinctive swaying movement of the head also expresses profound appreciation,

Young Indian musicians try fusion—with guitars and *tablas*.

and no 'wah wah' would be complete without that. You can observe many examples of this movement during your first concert, and then practise in front of a mirror until you get it right for the next one you attend.

South Indian Music

Carnatic music is played on instruments like the *veena*, the violin and the flute, accompanied by the double-headed drum, the *mridangam*, and perhaps also the *ghatam*, or clay pot. The recital always begins with a song in praise of Ganesha, the god with the elephant head who is worshipped at the beginning of any important undertaking. Only the bare skeleton of the pieces in the recital will be learned; the rest is improvised, according to very strict rules.

Carnatic music also has pieces where the musician takes time to carefully carve out and define the details of a *raga* before launching into a composition. But in Carnatic music, the rhythm and the time cycle are important elements, and before long, it is full speed into the complicated repeating drum patterns that make this music so exciting.

If you attend a Carnatic music concert among South Indians, you will notice that a large part of the audience

In order to show your expertise in Carnatic music, you must learn to keep *tala*. Then you should do so as ostentatiously as possible, through every difficult passage. Fake it whenever you lose the beat by sneaking glances at the people around you, and don't forget to mark the return to *sam* with an especially grand flourish. That's what I do.

is 'keeping or putting *tala*'. That means they are marking the time cycle with a specific pattern of hand and finger counts. This is one pleasure unique to Carnatic music—to keep time and thus keep track of how the musician, whether violinist or singer or drummer, makes all those intricate mathematical patterns end up just right so as to land smack on the *sam*, the first note of the next cycle.

MUSEUMS AND HISTORICAL SITES

Each big city has its museums and art galleries. Historical sites, temples, palaces and monuments of great beauty are also to be found around almost every corner. Every tour guide and tourist information booklet lists them. But there are places even the tourist guidebooks don't mention, and the only way to find out about them is to do a little research or talk to some old India hands—the kind who've travelled the country on bicycle.

I know some places myself: a Shiva temple in the mountains, an old colonial hotel on the beach, a National Award winning sculptor who carves exquisite Ganeshas. I share these rare finds with only a few, for if too many learn about them, they may become just another stop on the tourist circuit. If you show an interest and do some searching yourself, you too will discover your own secret places; wheedle some out of seasoned travellers by displaying well-informed interest and curiosity about their travels. All there is to see of India certainly does not yet appear in any guidebook.

The Archaeological Survey of India has publications on well-known and not so well-known historical sites. Its central office in Delhi is well worth visiting as some of its publications are superb. Relevant booklets are also available in the National and State Museum bookshops.

Children watch a traditional craftsman decorate a pot.

CLUBS

'The Club' is a hallowed vestige of the British Raj. Each big city has its clubs, and these are more or less anglicised. You get culture shock stepping out of India into one of these: the ladies playing bridge, the men drinking whisky, everyone talking plummy Queen's English while being served bad food by obsequious waiters. It's like entering a time warp, except all the faces are brown.

The Gymkhana Clubs, Cricket Clubs, Polo Clubs and Golf Clubs often have temporary memberships for foreigners. Some require that your name be proposed by a member. Besides the sports facilities that they provide, which are often excellent, they are an invaluable way of establishing contacts, keeping up with the workings of the upper echelons of power in politics and commerce, and just making friends.

If your company or institution does not provide membership to a club, you may write to its secretary, asking about membership requirements. If your job requires that you wine and dine Indians regularly, a club membership will save you endless headaches. Remember, though, that some clubs have strict dress codes, at least for certain areas, and it may not include traditional Indian wear for men, like *kurta*-pyjama, or *dhoti*, the long draped lower garment popular especially in South India. A jacket and tie may be de rigeur. For women, traditional clothes are acceptable, but very casual Western dress may not be. It is a curious fact that everyone firmly believes their own club is the most exclusive.

HEALTH CLUBS

Many of the five-star hotels allow foreigners living in India to use the hotel pool, tennis courts, sauna and gym by paying an annual or semi-annual membership fee. This is just a cash transaction and requires no sponsorship, so it is an easy and convenient way to gain access to Western-style fitness facilities. Standards vary considerably, so check thoroughly before signing up.

Some hotel health clubs even offer aerobic classes. An added benefit is that after all your sweating and straining, you can go to the hotel beauty parlour and get a massage.

CRICKET

The loss of productivity that besets India during a five-day test series attests to the obsessive interest Indians take in the game of cricket. It's one game where India still has a world standing. When India is playing against its arch rival Pakistan, work grinds to a halt as workers huddle around the man with the radio. Managers shoo them back to their jobs self-righteously, then phone home to get the score from their wives. Shopkeepers all seem to be nursing earaches; no, it's just the transistor held over their ear so as not to miss a moment. Customers get scant attention. Roads are blocked with traffic as every single person who can get tickets tries to get to the stadium. All the people who reported sick are stuck somewhere in the traffic jam.

Bombay is the worst. Even street urchins get in on the action by marking the score on blackboards at street corners, so the motorist without a radio never needs to go for long without all the details. Days are focused on keeping track of the score, and nights are spent at gala events for wining and dining cricketers. Fans idolise some players as much, if not more than they do movie stars. Even movie stars idolise cricket players. I have included a brief translation of cricket terminology so that you will not be completely left out when all the guests at your next party start talking this strange language.

As one sports writer said, cricket is 'polite baseball', a 'delightfully desultory, ingratiatingly indolent' sport. It is played on a 22-yard pitch. At each end is the crease, the 'home' for the batsman. Just behind each batsman are the wickets or stumps—three slender sticks stuck into the ground with two smaller sticks or gulleys, balanced so that the slightest movement will knock them off.

The team consist of 11 players each. The batting team sends out two batsmen, one to each wicket. One batsman stands in the crease, with a 28-inch flat bat, ready to receive the ball. The other, called the runner, stands at the other wicket. The fielding team sends all 11 players to different positions on the field. The slips or field positions are evocatively named—first slip, second slip, silly mid, point, long on, square leg, and so on.

The other team captain chooses a bowler, who stands well back of the far wicket, takes a running start and throws the ball in one continuous overhand motion, completing his throw before his rear foot passes his wicket. If there is any break in the movement of throwing, it is called a no ball. An over is six throws, no balls not counted. The bowler is not required to bounce the ball in front of the batsman, but he usually does, because that's when he can put spin on the ball and bowl hooks.

The batsman's job is to prevent the ball from hitting the wicket, and at the same time to score runs. When the batsman hits the ball he has to decide whether it's safe to run—then he and the other batsman race back and forth between the two wickets, scoring a run each time they exchange wickets. A batter is clean-bowled if the ball hits the wicket, he's caught if he hits the ball but the fielder catches it before it hits the ground, he's LBW—leg before wicket—if the ball hits his legs and the umpire feels it would have hit the wicket if his legs had not been in the way, he's run out when he's running between wickets and the fieldsman throws the ball and hits the wicket before he makes his ground, and he's stumped when he's moved out of his crease while batting, and the wicket-keeper tags the wicket.

Bowling a maiden over is nothing more romantic than throwing a run-less sequence of six balls. India has not produced any really good fast bowlers, but has a lot of spin bowlers, who bowl slow with a crafty spin. The Maharajajamsahib of Nawanagar, better known as Prince Ranjitsinghi, or just Ranji, was a slick 'bat' who made two double centuries in a single match on a single day, and 3,000 runs a season for him was a common occurrence. The Ranji Trophy, named after him, is the most important national event, and is played by the state teams, from which the national team is selected. Other cricket playing countries are Pakistan, Sri Lanka, Australia, New Zealand, West Indies, Britain, South Africa, and Zimbabwe.

The traditional test match lasts five days, and requires each team to play two innings with each day's play lasting five or six hours, with breaks for tea; but half the matches end in draws, with perhaps only three of the four innings finished. It's possible to watch games of three days, 322 runs not out, or also watch one bowler take all ten wickets. The new version is much more exciting. Introduced less than ten years ago, one-day cricket limits the number of overs to 50, and as many runs as possible must be scored within that limit.

When India plays against Pakistan, which it did until recently only in a third country, all kinds of rivalries are at work; pockets of Muslims in India may support Pakistan and then riots break out. But just recently, India played against Pakistan in Pakistan, and then the Pakistani team came and played in India, signalling a more cordial relationship between the two countries.

Most educated people in India have a more than ordinary interest, so that talking cricket when a match is on is almost inevitable. Although cricket is extremely popular throughout India, Bombay is the most rabidly enthusiastic, and many of the best Indian cricketers are from Bombay or at least the state of Maharashtra.

TRACKING THE TIGER

India has some of the most beautiful game sanctuaries in the world. Not only tigers, but elephants, rhinos, lions, and various species of deer and monkeys can be seen in these reserves. Each geographical and climatic region of India offers a different wildlife experience.

There are 55 national parks and 247 sanctuaries in India. They are being promoted by each state as tourist destinations, so train and bus connections are usually easily available from the big cities. Some of these parks are only hours away: Bharatpur from Delhi, for example, is only 3 hours on the train, and Vedanthangal is only 80 km (49.7 miles) away from Madras. They offer a delightful excuse to pack a picnic and head out in a jeep with some friends.

The game sanctuaries in each state give an idea of what the whole region must have looked like at one time. Tropical forest reserves are a refuge for a profusion of plant and animal species, and a lure for foreign tourists intent on catching a glimpse of some rare animal or bird. Some endangered species must now pin their hopes for survival on India: the one-horned rhino, the great Indian bustard, and the gharial, for example. An abundance of wildlife is there for those who are interested in something other than seeing a tiger at any cost.

But the animal with the most mystique is the tiger. Seeing a gharial just doesn't have the same appeal. In the 1960s and 1970s, people realised, just before it was too late, that the Indian tiger was on the verge of extinction. An estimated 40,000 tigers roamed India at the beginning of the 19th century; in 1972, there were fewer than 2,000. Just in time to halt this decimation, Project Tiger was launched. It gave the impetus to a conservation effort all over India, covering 12 per cent of the total area under forest cover, and by 1986, the all-India tiger census counted more than 4,000 tigers.

There are parks in all parts of India that are part of Project Tiger, but probably the most famous, and one of the oldest (founded in 1936) is Corbett National Park. It was given this name in 1957, after the late Jim Corbett, the hunter-naturalist who wrote about his true-life adventures in the pursuit of the tiger. The *Man-eaters of Kumaon* still thrills readers all over the world.

In Corbett, you can go out to look for tigers on elephant-back, and that is an adventure in itself, believe me. It is amazing what precarious narrow paths a massive beast like the elephant can negotiate, putting one giant foot in front of the other. The trackers are kind enough to arrange that the elephant stops under a mulberry tree, so that the sweet purple berries temper disappointment if one fails to see the magnificent beast. For it is not easy to see a tiger, since, unlike the lion, it relies on forest cover to get close to its dinner. It is a solitary animal, and except for a brief mating period, it is only the mother and young cubs that hang around together.

Tigers, being at the apex of the food chain, cannot survive unless the animals they feed on are present in sufficient number. Unfortunately, cattle compete for the same grazing land as the black buck, the sambhar, and other wild ungulates on which the tiger preys. Tigers cannot be protected unless the whole forest in which it hunts is protected.

Despite the Indian government's policy of conservation, the rate at which forest cover is being depleted is frightening.

It has gone from 40 per cent forest cover less than a hundred years ago to around 7 or 8 percent in 1987. Part of the reason is that the needs of human beings always supersede the needs of animals in a country like India. For example, elephants need about 200 kg of green fodder a day; the vast ranges that provide such fodder get turned into plantations and hydroelectric projects.

For the Love of Nature and Animals

In Ranthambhor, a Project Tiger game reserve, I experienced firsthand what happens when the people living on the periphery of these reserves feel that their livelihoods are threatened by measures taken to protect wildlife and their habitat. The field director at the time was Fateh Singh, a charismatic, enlightened and somewhat eccentric Rajput, who embodied all the fiery energy of that fighting race.

He took a few of us out in a jeep at dusk to look for tigers. When he stopped the jeep to check out some cows that were grazing inside the reserve, he was surrounded by herdsmen and beaten with thick bamboo staves. He said to them, "I am Rajput, you can hit me as you want." Badly hurt and bleeding, and with a broken kneecap, he managed to walk back to the jeep. We could do nothing but watch in horror. He survived. Some park rangers have been killed in similar situations.

Demographic pressure is only one side of the picture. Misguided policies are the other. There is no national fuel wood policy, even though the forests are so depleted that some rural women must walk several kilometres a day to gather cooking fuel. A smokeless *chula* (cooking stove) has been developed that is cheap and would reduce fuel consumption by as much as 30 per cent. Why doesn't every wood-burning household in India have one? Even in some cities, half the domestic cooking is done using wood.

Even the foreign tourists are doing their little bit to further degrade the environment. Popular trekking areas like the Valley of Flowers in the Himalayas have suffered more from tourism than any other single cause.

Valuable efforts are made by government and non-governmental agencies and individuals to preserve the habitat and wildlife of India, and wildlife conservationists have realised that the success of these reserves is dependent on the human beings who live just outside. Their needs must be taken into consideration, along with the needs of the tiger and the tourist. That is the sad paradox that confronts the wildlife enthusiast in India.

GETTING THE MESSAGE

CHAPTER 8

'*Is* there an Indian way of thinking?
Is there *an* Indian way of thinking?
Is there an *Indian* way of thinking?
Is there an Indian way of *thinking*?'
—A. K. Ramanujan, from the essay
'Is There an Indian Way of Thinking?'

FOR MOST OF ITS HISTORY, India has had an oral rather than a visual culture. The four Vedas, which took about a thousand years to compose, were memorised and passed on from teacher to disciple. They were not written down until centuries later. Moreover, the very sound of the word is considered to have magical power. Perhaps this accounts for the Indian love of conversation, discussion, and speech making, where words are used as an incantation, as much for their music as for their meaning.

ENGLISH IN INDIA

During more than two hundred years of British domination, English was the language of power and influence; this is no less true today. It exerts as much influence on those who don't speak it as on those who do. English is the language of upward mobility, jobs, and prestige. No Indian language holds out the same promises or opens the same doors. About 28 million people speak it, or like to think they do. Government policy has recognised its role and function by listing English as one of the official languages in the Constitution.

Although there are several hundred languages spoken in India, English in its many varieties is the language the foreigner will most often encounter. No other language in India can be used in so many diverse social situations, across such cultural barriers, and over India's immense distances. You will meet several forms, some of which are given below.

Impeccable English

'Regularly at five in the morning Jagan got up from bed, broke a twig from a margosa tree in the backyard, chewed its tip, and brushed his teeth. He was opposed to the use of a toothbrush. "The bristles are made of the hair from the pig's tail," he declared. "It's unthinkable that anyone should bite a pig's tail first thing in the morning."'
—from *The Vendor of Sweets* by R K Narayan

Many Indians speak and write English with the ease and fluency of native speakers. The urban professional elite that has existed in India for more than a hundred years was educated at the best schools in India or abroad and has a command of English that is accepted wherever English is spoken. Journalists, poets and novelists have created an impressive body of work in their second language. Whether writing about a small town in South India (R K Narayan), a west coast fishing village (Anita Desai), or Indian children born at midnight on Independence Day (Salman Rushdie), Indian writers have given a world audience a uniquely Indian vision—and been accepted.

Almost English

'First people die. White colour the man, red colour the woman. People bring the body in burning place near the river. He wash the body in the Ganges. After body will keep and people go in government office. He write the name which person to death. Then government know how many persons to death…After come there make five rounds and then start fire. After three hours body will finish and less piece of body throw in Ganges water.'
—Boatman guide on the Ganges River, quoted by Dr Mehrotra

Taxi-drivers, guides, servants, shopkeepers, street vendors in the tourist centres—all the semi-literate or illiterate professionals who make their living through contact with foreign visitors to India—need English to survive. When both speaker and listener are equally intent on communication, a limited vocabulary, unconventional grammar and approximate pronunciation will get the message across.

Indian English

'While the parents get ready to receive the costly gifts, both in cash and kind, and the relatives, friends and all near and dear ones, get renovated for participating in the marriage party (a festive reception coupled with dainty dishes, both hot and cold), the boy and the girl are left to tend for themselves.'
—S K Vinayaka, 'How to Choose a Wife'

Between the two extremes is the English of popular parody. It is spoken with an accent very heavily influenced by the mother tongue, and abounds in clichés, misused idioms and archaic literary flourishes. Like many other non-standard varieties of English, such as Australian English, Indian English has developed characteristics of pronunciation, grammar and usage that make it almost a foreign language to the Standard English user.

Most Indian speakers of English use it not to talk to foreigners, but to each other. It is a pan-India link language for university students and professors, doctors and other professionals, railway and airline officials and staff, clerical workers in banks and post offices, hotel and restaurant staff. It is the language of business, science and the media.

Newspapers and journals use a variety of English full of Indianism; so do the national television and radio stations. Business letters are also written in Indian English. For most, it is a second language used, just as Sanskrit and Persian were in ancient times, for a different purpose than the intimate, emotive mother tongue.

Spoken English

Spoken English is flavoured by the regional languages, with colourful results. You will be asked, "Ju bant room

saarbees?" in Punjab, and "You yate yenup yeggs?" in Tamil Nadu. In some parts of India, you will be confronted with pronunciations like 'estrait', 'espin' and 'eskool'; in other parts of India the same words become 'satarait', 'sapin' and 'sakool'. The cadence and rhythm of the mother tongue lend a distinctive singsong quality to English speech. (For those who cannot figure out the words or phrases in this section, I have included a translation at the end of this chapter.)

Very often, English is learned in school from a teacher who also learned it in school, rather than acquired through the process and pressures of life. Archaic, literary forms are preferred to the simple statement: sad demise rather than death; the fair sex rather than women; felicitate rather than congratulate. Native Indian languages have elaborate systems of honorifics and terms of respectful address. Thus English used in speeches or letters is ornate and flowery, formal and excessively polite.

Grammatical anomalies—as in the formulating of sentences by intonation alone, as in "What he wants?"

You may be asked to kindly do the needful and to grace the auspicious occasion with your august presence and then offered salutations and prostrations by your obedient servant who will end by thanking you or even profusely thanking you, whether there is anything to be thankful for or not.

and "Where he is going?" or in the use of since instead of for, as in "I am working here since four years"—rarely affect comprehension. More confusing are the English words used to express a different meaning. For example, in South India, a military hotel is actually a non-vegetarian restaurant. Matrimonial ads in the newspapers provide many examples: the requirement homely and fair doesn't call for the person to be plain and impartial, but to have homemaking skills and a light or wheatish complexion; a good face-cut is not an accident while shaving, but nice features; and a teacheress is a female teacher. No matter what the age, the prospective bride and bridegroom are always the girl and the boy.

English doesn't have enough terms for the intricate network of family relationships, so new ones have to be devised. Cousin-brother expresses the intimacy an Indian feels towards the father's brother's children. A co-brother-in-law is the husband of the wife's sister, to distinguish him from one's own sister's husband, who is felt to be more closely related.

Other typically Indian situations require their own vocabulary. Money that is the declared charge for a thing or service is paid in white; the amount charged over and above that, undeclared, is black money. The practice of calculating payments in black and white, so prevalent in business as to be taken for granted, and even extending to more mundane transactions such as paying the rent, makes the extraordinary perfectly banal. Well-used Indian words from the various Indian languages are simply appropriated. A mild *lathi* charge is conducted by the police with their long, iron-bound bamboo sticks. A *pucca* house is made of cement, bricks and tiles instead of mud and thatch. A full *bandh* is a total strike, where the whole city grinds to a halt.

Some Indian words are used with English grammatical endings, and when the speakers get carried away, it's hard

Many so-called hotels are actually restaurants.

to say if they're still speaking English. Take this description of a politician's schedule: "First, there is mass contact at a *padayatra*, then to the *jhuggi-jhopdis*, a jeep *yatra*, and going on to attend two Divali *melas* as evening closes in." But since the same thing happens the other way around, Hindi sometimes becomes easy to understand: "*Jab aadmi ka* personal life *kumzor ho*, he should be careful. Because the *samnewale* will grab the first chance to hit back."

When an Indian tells you, "Give your passport" or "Stand there in line," without the usual courtesy words, he or she does not intend to be rude. Most Indian languages have no specific word for please; it is expressed in the verb itself when using the polite form of address. This sometimes gets lost in the English translation. While business letters very often end with the meaningless formula, 'Thanking you', in day-to-day speech 'Thank you' may be more conspicuous by its absence. First, the culture does not instil the need to acknowledge every transaction with an expression of gratitude; since people are only acting in accordance with their duties, special mention is not required. Even in the giving of gifts, the act of giving is itself a reward, and the giver benefits as much as the receiver. So who should thank whom? And if the act or gift is truly worthy of mention, then 'Thank you' is inadequate.

The Indian may express gratitude with a phrase like "May you live a hundred years."

English Words Used Differently

hotel	restaurant (though big hotels are also hotels)
military hotel	non-vegetarian restaurant
gay	carefree, not homosexual
wheatish, fair	light-complexioned

Acronyms

NRI	non-resident Indian—a person of Indian origin ho lives abroad
STD	Standard Trunk Dialling
BJP	Bharatiya Janata Party

Commonly Used Indian Words

lakh	one hundred thousand
crore	ten million
panchayat	village level government
Sri, Srimati	honorifics, like Mr, Mrs
tiffin	a light meal, in the morning, or in the late afternoon
guru	teacher
pandit, ustad	maestro
raga	melodic scale in North and South Indian music

LEARNING INDIAN LANGUAGES

If you live, work, or travel extensively in rural areas, you will need to learn the language of that region, but even those who live in the big cities will find it useful. Unless you have a deep and abiding love for the place or some aspect of its culture, there is no need to achieve perfection. A vocabulary of five hundred words, and a grasp of simple grammatical structures will allow you to ask the price and understand the answer. More successfully than any other gesture you could make, learning the language of your Indian acquaintances communicates your admirable attitude of interest and involvement in India. Your willingness to make the effort to learn the language is taken as a mark of your respect for the whole culture. It is a powerful symbolic act that will win you appreciation and applause far beyond your meagre skills.

Sanskrit

The most widely spoken Indian languages can be divided into two families: the Indo-Aryan languages of the north, and the Dravidian languages of the south. The classical form of the oldest Indo-Aryan language, Sanskrit, is considered a sister-language to Latin, as they both derive from the same proto-language. A comparison of English and Sanskrit words illustrates this relationship: mother—*matar*, night—*nakt*, nose—*nas*, three—*thrini*, bind—*bandh*, teeth—*dent*.

The North Indian languages are related to Sanskrit in the same way that the Romance languages of Europe are related to Latin. But unlike Latin, Sanskrit is not a dead language—partly because it never was a living language, in the sense of being the vernacular, the language of daily life. It was, and continues to be, a language of religious observance and instruction all over India. At one time it was the language of the courts, of literature, drama and poetry.

Every once in a while, someone will write a play or poem in Sanskrit. But the role it once played in the intellectual life of India has been usurped by English. The study of Sanskrit is its own reward—it is elegant and precisely ordered, and opens the door to a vast literature—but no one really speaks it.

Hindi

The Indian propensity to divide and differentiate rather than unite and assimilate has resulted in two languages where there should be only one. Hindi and Urdu are one language with two scripts, two literary forms, and some vocabulary differences. The spoken languages are almost the same. But because Urdu is associated with Muslims, differences are exaggerated and encouraged, and continue to develop.

Hindi is not a difficult language to learn. The sentence structure is similar to that of Latin-based languages, which is not surprising since they are related. A speaker of English will have little difficulty with the sounds: no need to pout

If one were to consider Hindi and Urdu as one language, which is sometimes referred to as Hindustani, it would be understandable to about 50 per cent of the Indian population. Hindi or Urdu will enable you to reach more people than any other language except Mandarin.

as for the French 'u', recognise tonal differences as in Chinese, or make a whole bunch of 'n's, 'r's, and 'l's that sound all the same to the Western ear, as in Tamil and Malayalam. Hindi is written from left to right, in the Devanagari script, like Sanskrit. The formal variety is full of Sanskritised words, and Sanskrit words are also borrowed for scientific terms. This is what is spoken on Doordarshan, the national TV network; it sounds affected and haughty, and Indians themselves laugh at it and complain they can't understand it.

Max Mueller Bhavan, the German cultural institute, offers a very good short Hindi course. Private tutors are also available; word-of-mouth recommendation is the best way to find a good one. The important thing is to start using the language, and use it as much as possible. Your servants, the taxi-driver, the vegetable seller will all respond to your initiative to speak to them in their own language. Rather than using the language of power (English), you are meeting them on their own turf, as an equal. Unless you need to pull rank by using English in some specific situation, Hindi will get you better service, cheaper prices and more accurate information.

Tamil

In South India, Hindi is a political issue. If Hindi were adopted as a national language, it would put those who don't have Hindi as their mother tongue at an enormous disadvantage. At least with English, the reasoning goes, everyone starts off with the same handicap. In Tamil Nadu, the opposition to Hindi as the national language has been so vociferous and violent that it is no longer seriously considered.

English is more widely spoken in South India than in North India. Still, those living and travelling in the South may find it worthwhile to learn a little Tamil just for its public relations value. One young man got a lot of mileage out of 'Nalla ruji' ('Tastes great!'). He was always rewarded with numerous helpings of the choicest delicacies.

The Hindi lettering on a sigh is obliterated in Madras.

Tamil is more difficult to learn because of the pronunciation. It abounds in nasals and liquids; it has two different 'l' sounds, three different 'r' sounds, and five different 'n' sounds. The script is an elaborate maze of curves and squiggles. Although there is an equally long and extensive literary tradition in Tamil, it has not received the same study from foreign scholars as Sanskrit.

The foreigner who wishes to learn Tamil may have trouble finding a teacher; neither structured courses nor private tutors are so readily available as they are for Hindi. The best approach is to find a native Tamil speaker who is trained to teach some other language, whether this is English, French or German. Such a person can at least apply some principles of structured instruction to the teaching of Tamil.

NUMBERS

Even English-speaking Indians use the system of calculating large amounts in *lakhs* and *crores*. A *lakh* is a hundred thousand, and a *crore* is ten million. Newspapers, TV, radio, advertising always use these terms rather than the English ones, when referring to rupees.

One million is ten *lakhs*, and a hundred million is ten *crores*. Even when writing out the numbers, the Indian system is used:

- 1,00,000 instead of 100,000, so that it is clearly one *lakh*, not one hundred thousand;
- 1,00,00,000 instead of 10,000,000, so that it is one *crore*, rather than ten million.

Useful Numbers

one	*ek*
two	*do*
three	*teen*
four	*char*
five	*paanch*
six	*chhe*
seven	*saath*
eight	*aatt*
nine	*nau*
ten	*das*
eleven	*gyaaraa*
twelve	*baaraa*
thirteen	*teraa*
fourteen	*chaudaa*
fifteen	*pandraa*
sixteen	*solaa*
seventeen	*satraa*
eighteen	*attharaa*
nineteen	*unniiss*
twenty	*biis*
twenty-one	*ikkis*
twenty-two	*baaiis*
twenty-three	*taiis*
twenty-four	*chaubiis*
twenty-five	*pachiis*
fifty	*pachaas*
one hundred	*sau*

GETTING NAMES RIGHT

First names are not common currency, but the sign of true friendship. Even the wife, in traditional families, does not call her husband by name, but as 'so and so's father'. She will not even speak his name if asked, but give some clue like, "It sounds like the word for red (*lal*)."

Strangers are called *bhayya* (brother) or *bahanji* (sister). If they are much older, they may be addressed as *bapaji* (respected dear father), uncle, sir or *mataji* (respected dear mother), aunty, madam. These are the Hindi terms. The same terms are used in other Indian languages. The 'ji' suffix conveys respect and endearment. Especially in South India, men are often known to their colleagues only by their initials. My father was always K J among the other professors at his university.

First names and surnames do not follow the same conventions all over India. In North India, the system is more similar to the Western one, with a family name and a first name: Suresh Sharma is Mr Sharma to his colleagues, and Suresh to his friends. But in South India, the father's name and sometimes the name of an ancestral village are often initials, and one's given name is at the end. To take the example of my father, Dr K J Charles, the K J were the initials of his father's name, and Charles was, in a sense, both his first name and his last name. His mother called him Charles, and his students called him Dr Charles. But many Indians are choosing to arrange their names as 'first name then surname'.

The Indian equivalent to Mr and Mrs are *Sri* and *Srimati*. A foreign man may be addressed as sir, master, or *sahib* (pronounced saab, like the car) by servants and uncle by a friend's child. Colleagues may call him by his first or last name, and subordinates may append Mr to either name—Mr Steve, Mr Jackson. You may notice that your name is avoided altogether by those (especially younger women) who don't feel comfortable with any of these options.

The foreign woman may be addressed as madam or *memsahib* by servants and aunty by children. Male colleagues and subordinates may append Madam or Mrs before the first name (hers or her husband's) or last name—Madam Sylvia, Mrs Steve, or even Mrs Sylvia Jackson). Her Indian friends would, of course, use her first name.

PLEASE AND THANK YOU

An Indian who wants to be polite is likely to use the English please and thank you. They are well understood, so you can use them too. Nevertheless, politeness in Indian languages is not usually in a specific word, but in the form of the verb used, or in the way a request is worded. For example, a driver asking a rickshaw puller to get out of the way will start his sentence with "*Bhayya* (brother) …" . That makes the request polite.

There are Indian equivalents, but you'll be more likely to hear the terms at political rallies, on Doordarshan, and on Air India flight announcements than on the streets. The pure Hindi and Urdu equivalents for thank you are *dhanyavaad* and *shukriya*. Please is conveyed with *kripaya* or *meharbani se*. Sorry or excuse me is *kshama kijiyega* or *maaf kijiyega*.

In Tamil, the words are *nandri* for thank you, *dayavu sedu* for please and *mannichidingo* for sorry—but these words are more often heard in the movies than on the streets.

GREETINGS

In North India, *namaste* or *namaskar*, said with the palms-together gesture, is the standard greeting for both hello and goodbye. In Tamil Nadu, when meeting—morning, afternoon and night—the term is *vanakkam*. When departing, the guest says *poi varukiren*, meaning 'I'll go and come back' and the host says *poi varungal*, meaning 'Go and come back'.

Especially in Tamil, but also in Hindi and Urdu, this English transliteration of the words is the merest approximation, and if you do not get a native speaker to help you with the pronunciation, all your efforts to be polite will be wasted. When in doubt, stick to the English words; they are well understood in cities, even by rickshaw drivers.

Common Greetings in Hindi/Urdu are:

- Hindu greeting and response: *Namaste* or *namaskar.* (I pay my respects to you.)

- Muslim greeting: *Assalam 'alaikum*. (Peace be upon you.) Response: *Vaalaikum salaam*. (And peace be upon you also.)
- Sikh greeting and response: *Sat sri akal*. (Truth is eternal.)
- *Jii* is added to greetings, names, and the words for relatives, to convey respect: *namaste jii*; *mataji* (mother); Allison-*ji*
- *Achchhaa*: Right! Really! I see. Good. Okay.
- *Tthiig he*: Fine. Okay. All right.

INTRODUCTIONS

In any business situation, and even on many social occasions, Indians will want to know your professional or occupational designation and background. Don't hesitate to announce it. If you are introducing others to Indians, include their designation. A business card makes all this much easier, and is so much exchanged that you should always have some on hand. Even if you are not working, you will find it convenient to have on hand some business cards printed with your name, address and phone number.

Incidentally, any kind of information may be printed on the little rectangle. Don't act startled or ask for explanations when you see (on a card) that Mr So-and-So is a BA (failed). That he sat for the BA examination, even without passing, is an accomplishment which should not be overlooked.

BODY LANGUAGE
Avoiding Pollution and the Left Hand

The concepts of purity and pollution in the Hindu religion, especially as it relates to caste, may be rejected intellectually by many educated urban Indians and yet adhered to unconsciously in practice. Purity is an ideal state, quite apart from cleanliness. It is never actually attained, and the threat of pollution is ever-present. Some sources of pollution are so strong as to be hereditary—one is the stigma of untouchability passed on from generation to generation, whether or not the son performs the same degrading occupation as his father.

Objects that may become 'impure' through contact, such as a cup or a plate, are made to be discarded—the banana leaf plate and the clay teacup are some examples. The body is viewed as constantly moving between the pure and impure states; its secretions and excretions are impure, and contact with them is polluting. It is impure upon awakening, during sexual relations, after defecating, during three days of menstruation, after giving birth and when someone in the family has just died. The body is most pure right after bathing or after ceremonies of purification.

The Indian does not as a rule use toilet paper, and considers it a dirty habit. Rather, after using the toilet, water and the left hand are used to effect cleaning. Although the left hand is then scrupulously washed, it is believed to retain something of its polluting quality. Therefore, it should never be used to eat with, when eating with the hand.

A shopkeeper may refuse to accept the first payment of the day from the left hand, and ask you to switch the money to the right. Older people may insist you put out your right hand to receive a gift. Even non-Hindus observe this taboo, and although it is stronger in the south and among the more orthodox, it exists all over India.

Feet

After having walked the Indian streets, the custom of taking off the shoes at the door is a good hygienic practice. But like the left hand, the feet retain their impure quality however clean they may be.

The verse from the Rg Veda that tells us that the head of the primordial man gave rise to the high caste and his feet to the low caste expresses the Hindu view of the hierarchy that exists in the body itself. The most respectful form of salutation is to stretch out full length at the feet of the respected person. It says, 'I am like the dust on your feet.' This ceremonial salutation is performed before holy men or a deity in the temple. The more common form used by children to their parents, a wife to her husband, younger people to their elders, students to teachers, is simply to bend down and touch the feet, and bring the fingertips to the eyes.

The feet of others may well be worthy of respect, but one's own feet are to be kept firmly where they belong. While it is quite common to see Indians sit on chairs and sofas with

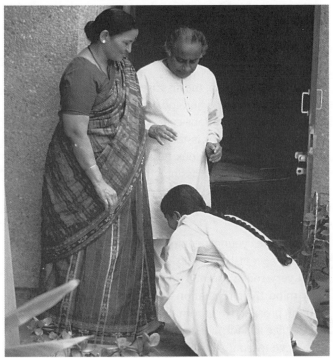

It is a gesture of respect to touch someone's feet.

their legs crossed, or one leg tucked under them, in imitation of the sitting posture on the ground, to raise the feet and place them on a desk, for example, is a mark of disrespect. It is equally uncouth to push something, especially an object worthy of respect such as a book, with the foot. When seated on the floor, don't stretch out your legs in front of you; if you really must stretch after sitting on the floor for a long time, make sure you do not point the soles of your feet at an image of a god, or at an older person.

While walking through a roomful of people seated on the floor, be careful not to step over a person, or an object such as a book, a musical instrument, or a plate of food. It is more polite, in a crowded room, to tap a person gently on the shoulder and say "Excuse me" so that they can move to let you manoeuvre past them than to step over someone. The older and more respected the person is, the more important is it not to step over them. If you do inadvertently touch someone with your foot, saying "Sorry" with a smile will remove any offence.

Kissing

Even on the big screen, the kiss used to be taboo. The movies usually show hero and heroine come within micrometers of actual lip contact without ever indulging in the real thing. No sex and no nudity is tolerated, and yet every manner of suggestive and salacious gesture and costume gets the message across embarrassingly loud and clear. The Indian mating dance takes place around trees and usually involves both participants rolling down a hill together, if possible soaking wet.

In real life, young people don't have much chance for courting, except in the big cities. The arranged marriage is still very much the norm in most strata of society. Girls must mind their reputation, for this will be a major issue with the prospective groom. Boys are awkward and unsure, and indulge in a form of verbal harassment, euphemistically called 'eve-teasing', for lack of any other way to interact.

The Evil Eye

All that is beautiful and attractive attracts the evil eye. The saying, 'Even a donkey, when it's suckling, is beautiful,' explains the special danger that young children are believed to face. The evil eye is tempted by compliments. Small children, besides wearing various amulets to ward off the evil eye, may also be marked by a huge black dot somewhere on their face, so that passers-by will look at them and think, 'How ugly' instead of 'How beautiful'.

One story of baby Krishna involves a strange woman (who turns out to be a demoness) getting permission from his mother to breastfeed him, since he looked so adorable. Children are much handled in India, being passed around, cuddled and caressed by everyone. Indian children get used to it, but your children may protest.

Indians, when meeting your small child, may make a circling movement around the child's head, and then crack their knuckles on their own head. This gesture means, 'I take all the evil influences attracted by your beauty on my own head.'

Body Space

In India, a woman may bathe at the communal pump in plain view, draped in one *sari* that somehow gets washed as well, and emerge at the end of the process, clean and dry and dressed in another *sari*, without compromising her own strict sense of modesty. And where the toilet is the field, the ditch or the riverbank, the railroad tracks or the sidewalk, this act too becomes a public one. Men with men, and women with women, go in groups to relieve themselves in the evening, as if going on a picnic.

A room of one's own is not possible for most Indians, even relatively wealthy ones, nor is it considered particularly desirable. Most Indians have slept every day of their lives with the lullaby of someone else's breathing. The Western notion of privacy would leave an Indian feeling very lonely indeed.

This is what often happens when East and West make contact: you go to the park and choose a spot as far away from everyone else as possible to have your picnic; an Indian family unrolls their mat within spitting distance. You go to the movie theatre, and sit equally far away from the only two people there; an Indian surveys the rows of empty seats, and chooses the seat right next to you. You board the train, and go to your assigned seat; five people are already seated in the space meant for four, and when you show your ticket, they simply shift closer to accommodate you as well.

More's to come. Your neighbours may then turn to stare at you with uninhibited curiosity, as if you were an exotic animal in the zoo. When you're already feeling uncomfortable from the close physical proximity of total strangers, they begin asking intrusive personal questions, starting with the ubiquitous "What is your good name?" and progressing to your nationality, marital status, work, salary, family and religion. It is difficult not to feel overwhelmed and harassed. There is very little you can do to keep the distance you feel comfortable with. It's better to accept that you might have to adjust, and keep a sense of humour.

The naturally friendly, curious Indian, sitting too close, staring too long and asking too many questions, is behaving in a polite and hospitable way to a lonely stranger, according to the standards of the Indian culture. Conversation is part ritual, part entertainment. After providing your name, your nationality and your purpose in coming to India, you can return to your book, or look out the window, or go to sleep. The formalities have been observed; no one's feelings will be hurt if you opt out of the entertainment part. When you get sick of answering questions, ask a few yourself.

Heat and Lust

A woman, on the other hand, may (correctly) sense that a man sitting uncomfortably close is obeying some other imperative than the norms of his culture. Indian men are brought up to keep their distance with women, and to treat all women as their own mother or sister, but they may feel these rules don't apply to foreign women.

An Indian man who stares, sits too close and behaves in an overly friendly manner to a woman is being obnoxious. True, it's a typically Indian brand of obnoxiousness, but it deserves a putdown just the same. Ignore the individual, because almost any form of polite rejection may be regarded as encouragement. If that doesn't work, don't hesitate to be rude and forceful. If that fails, threaten to get the police, station manager, or any other authority figure close at hand.

Even in the most crowded situations, any pressure that feels unnatural probably is. The surreptitious touch of breast or thigh may be provoked by provocative dressing, but even in the most modest costume you may encounter it. Indian women also complain about this form of harassment. The best reaction varies with the situation. If possible, move well away. If there's nowhere to go, step firmly on the instep of the offender and grind your heel down hard. If you're seated, stab him in the ribs with your elbow. And as long as you are not the only woman in the crowd, there is no need to be secretive; make a fuss and he'll have to slink away.

COMMUNICATING

The rules of cross-cultural communication bear repeating: It is not necessary to slow down your speech, turn up the volume, and use exaggerated hand gestures. Speak naturally, but don't pepper your speech with slang and jargon. "Way out in left field" makes no sense in a society that plays cricket, not baseball.

Avoid jokes until you know the culture well; you may unintentionally hurt or insult the listener. For example, telling a Polish joke may seem like a safe bet in a country with no Poles; but the Sardarjis, or Sikhs, are the butt of exactly the same kind of jokes in India, some so close as to sound like translations.

Stick to one idea per sentence, and make that as concrete as possible. Repeat important points in different terms. Remember this advice from a salesman, "Tell them what you are going to tell them. Tell them. Then tell them what you told them." Some listeners would rather miss what you said than have to admit they didn't understand it. When you're listening, ask politely for clarification whenever there is a word or phrase you don't understand, but don't interrupt and take the conversational lead away when the speaker pauses to find the right word.

Indians like to tell you what you want to hear, or rather, what they think you want to hear. The tailor who says it will be ready by Friday and the person who assures you that the place you are looking for is just ahead are obeying a proverb that says 'it is better to say something pleasant than something true.' Watch out for that kind of agreement or approval.

Most important, remember that what is not said is sometimes more interesting than what is said; pay attention to the non-verbal parts of any conversation—the silences, the tone of voice and the gestures. Silence may mean 'No', a certain kind of 'Yes' may mean 'No', and 'No' may mean 'Yes'. The body language will convey the real message.

> Language is an expression of culture; and even if the language is the same, the cultural assumptions and ways of structuring information differ. You may speak English, and your Indian friends, colleagues and workers may speak English, but both talking and listening provide many opportunities for misunderstandings.

DOING BUSINESS IN INDIA

CHAPTER 9

'Finally, I have to say that the most surprising aspect has
been the speed at which the folks in India adapt to Western
practices. They learn fast, really, really fast.'
—Sanjay Kumar

INDIA IS A VERY EXCITING PLACE to do business these days. Since 1991, when India's economic reform program began, it has increasingly opened itself to the world to become competitive in the global marketplace. Experts expect it to become the third largest economy in the world by 2025.

But each advantage to doing business in India seems to come with a matching disadvantage. The size of the Indian market—a middle class with purchasing power of 250 million—is offset by an equal number who eke out a living underneath the poverty line. True, labour costs are low, but then there is the poor infrastructure—electricity shortages, bad roads, delays at ports. No doubt you will find a sizeable pool of enthusiastic educated management and technical personnel, but you must first negotiate the labyrinthine bureaucracy.

The lesson of the previous government under Atul Bihari Vajpayee was that it was not sufficient that one or two small pockets of the economy experienced explosive growth, while the larger millions watched helplessly from the sidelines. The present government has turned its attention to the problems of poverty, poor infrastructure and unwieldy bureaucracy in its latest budget, while maintaining and strengthening the process of liberalisation. The prime minister, Manmohan Singh, said, "We must move away from a paradigm of incremental growth to a paradigm of exponential growth and growth into uncharted territory." There is in India a sense of tremendous optimism and energy.

BUSINESS ETIQUETTE

In business, as in every other aspect of Indian culture, there are enormous variations, and it is very difficult to generalise. There are the usual regional variations; just as North India and South India are markedly different in terms of climate, language, food, and dress, their business cultures are also different. Not only are there regional variations, there are differences in the way public sector and private sector companies work. Now added to the mix are the new industries like IT and telecom, which function quite differently from the older manufacturing companies.

Some differences are trivial—in the north, you may be served tea; in the south, coffee. Other differences are due to specific conditions: in the north, it cold in the winter, and therefore a suit and tie is the business dress of choice. In the summer, people may revert to shirt and tie, as is often the case in South India, where the weather is uniformly hot. But the most important differences are those that mark attitudes: the difficulty in making appointments with important people in the public sector is just one example of the working of a bureaucratic system, and it will also influence other aspects of the work relationship.

A young Indian businessman helped me to understand the differences through a useful paradigm of three Indias. The first functions in the 'Car Economy'. This is the India that you encounter in the cities. Business people have had prior exposure to Western business practices; IT, telecom and banking sectors belong to this India. Here business conditions are very similar to the developed countries.

The second India has a 'Motorcycle Economy'. It straddles cities and semi-urban areas. The industries are manufacturing related, and the conditions are somewhat more divergent from global practices. But companies in this sector are eager to do business, and are often aspiring to do it with foreigners.

Some businesses move through all three Indias: a friend who produces organic cotton vegetable-dyed garments has the weaving and dyeing done in the Bullock Cart Economy, the garments cut and sewn in the Motorcycle Economy and the finished product sold to the fashion industry in the Car Economy.

The third India practices the 'Bullock Cart Economy'. This is rural India, where 70 per cent of Indians still live and work, but it is not the India that most business people have to deal with. Agriculture or craft based products are to be found in this India. Business practice in the India of bullock carts requires a different outlook, and a whole new set of skills.

Using this simple, memorable model, you will be able to place all your business interactions in a proper context. And please approach the rest of the chapter keeping these three levels in mind: since the Car Economy is similar to Western business practice, I have geared my advice to Motorcycle and Bullock Cart Economies.

The Dabbawalla System

Every working day, in Bombay, the famous *dabbawalla* system ensures that about 100,000 home-cooked lunches packed in metal '*dabbas*' are picked up from the wives in their kitchens and delivered to the husbands working in their offices across the city's 60 km sprawl

The boxes go from the kitchens in the suburbs to the first sorting place, usually a train station, where the painted symbols—a yellow circle, a red cross, a blue square for example, determine where they go next, changing hands at least four times. They are transported, resorted, and transported through a series of moves by a relay of men carrying the *dabbas* on their heads until each box lands up at the office of the husband of the woman who cooked and packed it. Then the whole process is reversed so that the wife gets the empty lunch box back. This massive, intricate system involving more than 2000 men has been perfected and kept running for more than a hundred years. What Purolator does with a computer routing and tracking system, the *dabbawallas* manage with a few crude painted symbols.

Management schools study the *dabbawalla* system because it is a highly efficient operation that makes few mistakes; yet it was created by illiterate peasants, without computers, without technology and without MBAs.

NEGOTIATING SUCCESS

Business meetings in India are generally slower and more relaxed than in the West. Even an important scheduled meeting may start 10 or 15 minutes after the appointed time. Then there may be chit-chat, often about you—your family, your feelings about India, your travels. Tea and snacks may suddenly appear, carried in on a tray by the peon, and offered sometimes only to you.

Don't be taken aback if the person you've come to meet takes several phone calls, signs papers brought in by the secretary, gives orders to an underling, all during the course of your meeting. Indian people seem to have no problem in doing several things at once, and such actions do not express a lack of interest or attention to you.

Nor should you be surprised by digressions, personal questions, and discussion not directly related to your concern. The Indian needs to feel that there is a relationship that goes beyond business before making a decision. Questions like, "Where are you from?" and "How many children do you have?" are ways to place you within a social framework. The decision-making process involves more than pragmatic details; it involves understanding the situation as a whole, the context—therefore the digressions.

THE BOSS

The hierarchical nature of Indian society demands that there is a boss and that the boss should be seen to be a boss. In some offices, everyone may rise every time the boss enters the room. The person plays a role, and often the role is as important as any real work the person may do. The boss is as much a symbol of power and prestige as the sweeper is of degradation. The boss is the one who orders tea, makes all the decisions and accepts all the responsibility.

Everyone else just does as they're told, and even if they know the boss is 100 per cent wrong, no one will argue. It is difficult to get staff to express opposing viewpoints directly—that would be considered discourteous to the boss. They may simply go and do what they feel to be the correct thing, even if it is exactly the opposite of what was ordered. Sometimes, everything turns out all right because the Indian staff may know more about staff problems or problems of the infrastructure. If you are the foreign boss, you may not even find out that orders weren't followed—until something goes wrong. It is important to look for signs of the 'Yes' that means 'No', 'Maybe', and really 'Yes'. Indians are adept at telling you what they think you want to hear. This is for them a matter of politeness. You must find ways of allowing staff to express opposing viewpoints without going counter to their sense of the boss's absolute authority.

Accountability

Whenever you are sure that your way is the right way, demand that whoever objects accepts in writing the full responsibility for the outcome of not following your instructions.

It is important to make people write instructions down (or for you to give written instructions), so that it is not possible to later deny having heard any such instructions. Have a reporting system in the office, and circulate reports and memos, even to people not directly concerned, so that staff members cannot say "I didn't know." Complaints, requests and decisions should be given in writing.

Do make sure that you have communicated clearly without misunderstandings. There is a cultural reluctance to pursue questions with a white boss, and that hesitation must be overcome.

FOREIGN WOMEN WORKING IN INDIA

Foreign women working in the newer companies in cities, that is, in the Car Economy, reported a good working environment with no problems of harassment from male colleagues or problems with their women subordinates. They had no trouble establishing their authority; in fact they said they never had to. It was simply accepted. Two women said they actually had many more problems in their home country.

The psychoanalyst Erik Erikson wrote that Indians live in 'a feminine space-time' and perhaps this accounts for the ease with which these foreign women adjusted to India. What it comes down to is that the boss is the boss, whether male or female. The Indian subordinate accepts that a woman in a position of responsibility must be good at what she does, otherwise she wouldn't be doing it.

In the manufacturing sector and rural areas, there are fewer foreign women working in senior positions. Those who do so are more likely to encounter bias. Just like women on construction sites in the West, it will be slow process of familiarisation and education before the problem goes away.

BUSINESS ATTIRE

A suit and tie, despite the heat and intermittent air conditioning, is the norm, though trends are changing. In South India, a shirt and tie are normal and acceptable, but on some religious occasions, it is not unusual to find men dressed in traditional attire. For example, during the Ayyapa pilgrimage time, men wear black *dhotis* and go barefoot for a certain period before they start the journey to the shrine. There are other pilgrimages in the south which involve shaving the head. What may come as a surprise is that this is not necessarily the dress of the older man, who is accustomed to Western dress, having adopted it when it was a necessity in the business world, but of the younger man, who now feels the freedom to assert his 'Indianness'.

A Western man wearing Indian clothes is not acceptable in most business situations. The Indian shirt or *kurta*, though, is a very comfortable piece of clothing for hot weather and I have noticed a recent incarnation, a short version, with no collar, and therefore no tie, being worn with casual pants. This can look very smart, and may work in more casual offices.

For women doing business in India, it is advisable to err on the side of conservatism: if wearing a dress, make sure the knees and upper arms are covered, and that the neckline is quite high. Tailored pants and jackets are also acceptable for women. It is also more acceptable for women to wear Indian-style clothes such as the *salwar-kameez*—a two-piece outfit consisting of loose pants and long overshirt. This is convenient and very comfortable, as long as you take the time to find outfits that are appropriate. As a foreigner, it is hard to recognize the fashion sense of another culture, so it is easy to go into a shop and end up with outfits that are too dressy, too traditional or too cheap. It is

In hot weather, both sexes will be more comfortable in cottons and cotton blends. But remember that while the outside is hot, the inside may be cooled to Arctic temperatures. The key is to have pieces that can be taken off and put back on as needed.

better to stick to the clothes you know until your sense for Indian dress develops, or until you can get some knowledgeable Indian woman to help you. You will certainly have much to choose from.

THE WORKPLACE ENVIRONMENT

Three middle managers of a company meet with a foreign expert in his office to discuss the installation of a new computer. After much discussion, it is agreed that the best place for the computer is next to the switchboard. The only rearrangement of the office required is that a desk be moved so that the computer can be hooked up. All three managers leave. Two hours later, the desk still hasn't been moved. Three hours after that, still no change.

When asked, one of the managers explains to the foreign expert, "The peon is not here yet." The peon arrives. He is a thin, small, wiry man, barefoot, and wears a tattered uniform. The three managers show him the desk that has to be moved. They stand and watch while he struggles to single-handedly carry the desk out the door. The three managers offer him advice. Somehow or the other, the peon manages to manoeuvre the desk, which is more cumbersome than heavy, through the door. One of the managers now reports back to the foreign expert that the computer can be hooked up.

In the hierarchy of caste, the Brahmin is the highest; in the hierarchy of the body, the head is the highest. The high castes work with their heads and the low castes work with their bodies. One kind of work earns respect, the other is considered degrading. The foreigner working in India will encounter again and again the resistance that one group shows for the work of the other; from one side this resistance comes across as stupidity, from the other side, as laziness. It is neither. It is simply the strict adherence to the division of labour ordained by birth that Gandhi said has made Indians "the shortest lived, most resourceless and most exploited nation on earth."

In this chapter, problems are described first. Those who have read the earlier chapters will be prepared for these, and may even have an idea of likely solutions. Paths to effectiveness are offered only at the end of the chapter.

'Can't Dirty My Hands' Syndrome

The Rg Veda called the lowest caste 'two-footed cattle' and even today, the work of the poor is the work that is done by animals or machines in other countries. Nehru's comment, "With all respects to my people, I am compelled to say that we are not a hardworking nation," cannot possibly refer to the men and women and children who can be seen toiling day and night all over the country, doing jobs that are unsafe, unhealthy and unrewarding. Sometimes the work is heavy physical labour, often it is repetitive and dull. Cart pullers, cycle rickshaw pullers, construction workers and stone breakers all work long and hard for a daily wage that hardly meets the needs of survival. Women work twice as hard, often pregnant or breastfeeding while doing the same physically demanding tasks as the men, and then going on to do the cooking, cleaning and washing at home.

These are not the people the foreigner is likely to be working with in India, but it is wise to remember that they exist, and that they are the majority, before cursing the inefficiency and laziness of the Indian worker.

The office peons are not there just to bring tea; rather they are there as symbols to the elevated position of the man who can order them to do so. The more powerful the man, the more peons he has to order around. Unlike peons, educated members of the office staff, who speak English and are so familiar with Western ideas, sometimes convey the impression of working on Western terms. But it will not take the foreigner long to find out that this is little more than a veneer, and that underneath the surface is a person with a very different system of values.

The almost pathological aversion to physical labour displayed by Indians, and especially by a certain type of Indian male office worker, is one of the most frustrating ways that the caste system continues to exert its grip on daily life in India. Lifting, carrying, cleaning, fetching, cleaning the toilets,

People instead of machinery.

as well as digging the earth and tending the soil, are still, despite Gandhi's attempts to change all that, activities that demean the person who does them. Therefore any amount of inconvenience and discomfort arising out of inaction is preferable to such an action.

A cup of coffee spilt on the floor in the morning by the male secretary remains there until the office cleaner comes in the evening. When the company needs an interface between the computer and the electronic typewriter, the office manager will phone and phone for days rather than pick it up himself, because that would be beneath him. The peon is summoned from the corridor by the buzzer at the desk to bring the file that is on the shelf just behind the desk. The clerk would rather push the buzzer and wait than get up, turn around, reach up and lift down the file.

Given India's population, this strict division of labour makes a certain amount of sense. Why employ one person to do a job when you could just as well employ five people to do it? Greater efficiency of that kind would cause a whole set of other problems. If the office staff got their own tea, moved their own desks and cleaned up after themselves, what would the chaprasis and peons and sweepers do? Which is not to say that this is an ideal solution: rather, there is a problem, and Indians deal with it this way.

Women Workers

A foreigner working in the garment industry told me this story. Someone in his all-male office spilt a cup of coffee. No one cleaned it up the whole day; ants came, it got spread around by people walking through it, and by the time the cleaner arrived, it was a big mess. He said, "That's why my office is now predominantly female."

Women at all levels are less rigidly hierarchical, and more willing to do whatever needs to be done. They must function like that in their own homes, doing the washing, cooking and so on if the servant doesn't show up. They bring that same flexibility and practicality to the office.

People I interviewed maintain that women also make more loyal staff members, and are more concerned with finding a good working environment; they cannot be bought with a 50 rupees pay increase. This may be an over-generalisation, for surely not all women are paragons. What is certainly true, however, is that hiring women has far-reaching implications. Development workers have found that, at all levels, positive changes in the lives of women are transferred to the whole family. When a man gets more money, it may be spent on drinking, gambling or consumer goods for his own use, such as transistor radios. When women get more money, the money is usually spent on food, clothing and school fees for the children.

Communicating Ideas of Quality

One of the main reasons that multinational companies come to India is the abundance of cheap labour. But there is a price to be paid for working in a society that has what economist John Kenneth Galbraith called 'private affluence and public squalor'. Even if companies pay an equitable wage by Indian standards, workers still must cope with their lack of basic communication skills that the government is not able to help them overcome.

Take the weaver who practises a craft that has a long history of excellence in India and can thread complicated patterns of peacocks and parrots and elephants on his loom. Nevertheless, he makes errors in the weaving of simple placemats and whole orders have to be discarded because not one piece is the standard size. Another batch is wasted because the napkins and the placemats were dyed separately, and the two shades of blue are different.

The traditional craftsperson makes things of beauty and utility for a known market; the potter knows the use of pots, the weaver sees the final product being worn, the carpenter makes the plough for the farmer, who repays him with grain. The artisan knows the market well. When the needs of the market change, the artisan is able to change the product to meet that need. In traditional handmade goods there is no need for a particular uniform standard. Neither do the raw materials, vegetable dyes, hand-spun threads, handmade looms and so on conform to any industry standard.

The problem becomes how to explain to people whose concerns are so different that when another family in another land sits down to dinner, it is very important to them that all the placemats are exactly the same size and the same shade. Most workers at the bottom level are illiterate. Their concerns are with the bare necessities of life. Matching placemats does not figure in their reckoning.

The worker at this level is also struggling with too many children and a living and working environment of flies, filth, stench and no running water or electricity, is harassed at every turn by the weather, communal problems, moneylenders and the need to follow the rituals of religion.

And on top of all this, the foreign buyer comes along and says, "But the blues don't match!" The weaver will not share that concern or understand the obsession with such a minor thing. How does that matter? So the dye colours will vary from lot to lot, one shade of blue different from the other.

Quality control is one of the most serious problems facing the Bullock Cart Economy. But quality control as an abstract notion is unlikely to be effective. It must be made concrete, in terms understood by the potter or the weaver or the carpenter or the illiterate factory worker. Imposing what seems like an arbitrary numerical measurement is not enough. It must be a process of educating the worker in the ways of a foreign market.

The fact that many low level workers cannot read or write means that training manuals are ineffective. Assistants and apprentices usually learn on the job, with no systematic training. Access to tools and materials that have never been used before is therefore useless without the proper training sessions. Tools and equipment in India are anyway in short supply. Instead of cranes and tractors and earth movers,

The boss has to conduct regular quality checks.

you have people and pulleys and ropes. Safety standards are pathetically low.

But in the Car Economy, safety standards, efficiency, and quality control have been shaped by the competitive forces of the international marketplace, and now match those of the rest of the world. Indian companies have won international awards for quality and design.

BUSINESS SCHEDULES AND FAMILY
The Indian business is often a family one. Even for the relatively rich, the threat of poverty is real and the natural instinct is to protect one's job and interests. People outside the family are not to be trusted, so no one else is allowed to do the work when the head of the family is away. The head of the family usually keeps a tight control by limiting information, even to his own family members. He is the only one who knows prices and materials, and when he has gone to the village to arrange the marriage of his nephew, it may not even be possible to get relevant information, much less the finished product.

It is the prime responsibility of the man to marry children off, perform birth, death, and other ritual ceremonies, and take care of aged parents and destitute relatives. Auspicious days, and births and deaths, cannot be predicted much in advance and play havoc with schedules, which may become even more erratic at the times of harvest and planting. A promise of delivery in eight weeks means 'eight weeks, provided nothing else comes in the way'.

WORKING IN SCHOOLS AND COLLEGES
The Guru
The unquestioning acceptance of the authority figure is also a feature of the teaching profession. Indian students are taught that the teacher is the *guru*, a term that expresses far more respect than what Westerners mean by the term 'teacher'. *Guru* used to mean a spiritual teacher, someone akin to a god. But even the teacher of economics or biochemistry, as an imparter of knowledge, belongs to the same tradition, and is worthy of respect.

Segregation by Caste and Sex

Students in the technical disciplines may be equally at conflict when asked to perform a physical task. The professor teaching a course in video production to a group of Indian graduate students found that it was actually the driver who unloaded and set up all the equipment for an outside shoot, including plugging in the lights and mounting the camera on the tripod: equipment that cost thousands of dollars and for which he had absolutely no training. The professor was so impressed with the driver, who was young, talented and eager to learn, that he tried to arrange for

While students in the bigger urban universities may be used to free and easy communication between the sexes, smaller, more traditional colleges away from the big cities will still keep young men and women separate, if not in physical terms, certainly by societal strictures.

him to be admitted to his video production course. But the same system of caste that insured that he did all the work, insured that he was kept from gaining any status for it.

THE BUREAUCRACY

The Indian bureaucracy can be right out of Kafka: old musty offices piled with dusty files, reluctantly turning ceiling fans disturbing 20-year-old papers, dark, smelly corridors going nowhere, and mole-like petty officials in safari suits, toadies currying favour and barefoot peons forever bringing tea.

At the immigration office, you are told, "You cannot get a visa without having your press accreditation." At the press office, you are told, "You cannot get your press accreditation without having a visa." Catch 22 is nothing compared to what you are likely to become mired in when you try to find your way in the maze and tangle of Indian rules and regulations.

The government initiated a major programme of economic reform, which promised deregulation, delicensing and a streamlining of procedures to make investment and trade and manufacturing in India more efficient and competitive in the world economy. As part of this reform, the rupee became partially convertible in March 1992, and is now fully convertible. The reforms were a desperate response to the International Monetary Fund and the World Bank, which were threatening to withdraw loans and aid unless India took some drastic measures. In practical terms, all that was promised has not yet been achieved. It is helpful to have someone on your side who can understand the new regulations, especially how the statutes of the Central government relate to State legislation, which can be markedly different from state to state.

Dealing with the Bureaucracy

International firms have to get used to dealing with the Indian bureaucracy, which can be hostile and unwieldy, with various departments at the national and state levels working at cross purposes, and unaware of decisions taken elsewhere in the system. Use an Indian intermediary. Foreigners are apt to have less patience. Bring an Indian colleague, or hire someone whose job it is just to get the various stamps and seals and letters of permission. If you are the boss, it's often your presence that's important, so that the negotiations can take place at the top level—an underling will only be able to meet with an underling. But once you have gained access to the necessary 'higher-up', the two of you may only need to exchange pleasantries while your assistants get down to details. At that point, let the Indian do the talking.

Trade Unions

Indian trade unions are very powerful organisations linked to political groups and politicians. In disputes, the trade unions provide legal assistance for workers. Their goal is to bring private sector employees to the level of government workers, who have many benefits, like shorter working hours, health care, and pension schemes. Be prepared to meet with problems when you try to make changes in the interests of higher production that involve streamlining overstaffed companies or shortening the traditional tea breaks.

WAYS TO BE EFFECTIVE

The foreigner working in India must be prepared to deal with different problems at different levels. At the bottom, the problems of poverty, illiteracy, malnutrition, and caste restrictions affect all aspects of work. Quality control requires the greatest vigilance and cannot be achieved without arranging workshops and training sessions that take into consideration the worldview of the worker. Never ever take for granted that workers are properly trained in the correct use of equipment, or that proper equipment exists in the first place.

Corruption

You should be aware that bribery is illegal in India and the one who bribes is as culpable as the one who accepts the bribe. Nevertheless, an inflexible and righteous decision never to be involved in such iniquitous activity may make it difficult to do business in India. People say it usually involves only trifling amounts, drops of oil to speed up and smoothen the working of an ancient and rusty machine.

Persistence and patience in the face of refusal can be as effective as money on the final outcome, but if you have no time or patience, the other solution is to hire someone to get the work done: there are always people in the middle when there's a lot of money at stake. It can be a dirty game, so get someone who can play it and still be straight with you.

Setting an Example

To some extent, this is a carryover from the British colonial mentality. If you are the boss, you have certain advantages (and unpalatable though this sounds, if you are white your judgement may be given greater validity).

In the situation with the three office managers and the desk, if the foreign boss had walked over and lifted one end of the desk, the three office managers would have immediately moved to help. So in some cases you can use your position as pressure to do things unconventionally. Your willingness to do whatever needs to be done yourself, loading stuff onto the truck, picking up parts, getting your own files, will provide a powerful incentive to your staff to follow that example.

The boss will be forgiven a great many eccentricities and lapses of etiquette. But even the slightest physical abuse, like pushing someone or grabbing someone by the shirt, is unacceptable. Lose your control and you will immediately lose your authority. It is much more advantageous to keep smiling. Petty officials, clerks and customs officers who start off cold and officious respond with warmth to a friendly enquiry and a smile.

Making Adjustments

Remind yourself that everything takes a lot longer in India. Efficiency is not necessarily achieved by adopting the most direct solution: sometimes a circuitous route gets you to your goal more quickly. The heat makes this a physically taxing environment for you and your staff. The problems of infrastructure are not going to go away any time soon. Patience is the primary rule.

INDIA AT A GLANCE

CHAPTER 10

'India happens to be a rich country inhabited
by very poor people.'
—Prime Minister Manmohan Singh.

Official Name
The Republic of India

Capital
New Delhi

Flag
Three equal horizontal bands, with orange on the top, white in the middle, and green on the bottom, with a navy blue twenty-four spoked *chakra*, or wheel, a Buddhist symbol, in the centre

Time
GMT + 5.5 hours

Telephone Country Code
91

Land
Total: 3,287,590 sq km (1,269,345.6 sq miles)
Land: 2,973,190 sq km (1,147,955.1 sq miles)
Water: 314,400 sq km (121,390.5 sq miles)

Highest Point
Kanchenjunga: 8,598 m (28,208.7 ft)

Major Rivers
Ganga, Yamuna, Godavari, Krishna, Mahanadi, Narmada, Tapti, Brahmaputra, Kaveri

Climate
Mainly tropical in Southern India but temperatures in the north range from sub-zero degrees to 50 degrees Celsius. There are well defined seasons in the northern region:
- winter (December–February)
- spring (March–April)
- summer (May–June),
- monsoons (July–September)
- autumn (October–November)

Natural Resources
coal (fourth-largest reserves in the world), iron ore, manganese, mica, bauxite, titanium ore, chromite, natural gas, diamonds, petroleum, limestone

Population
1.027 billion

Ethnic Groups
Indo-Aryan 72 per cent, Dravidian 25 per cent, Mongoloid and others 3 per cent

Religion
Hindu 80 per cent, Muslim 14 per cent, Christian 2.4 per cent, Sikh 2 per cent, Buddhist 0.7 per cent, Jains 0.5 per cent, others 0.4 per cent

Languages
English is the most important language for national, political, and commercial communication, and as such is recognised as an associate language. Hindi is the national language and primary tongue of 30 per cent of the people, but is not spoken at all in some parts of the country. Bengali, Telugu, Marathi, Tamil, Urdu, Gujarati, Malayalam, Kannada, Oriya, Punjab, Assamese, Kashmiri, Sindhi, Sanskrit are

official languages. Hindustani, a popular variant of Hindu/ Urdu, is spoken widely throughout northern India. India has 24 languages, each spoken by a million or more persons and numerous other languages and dialects, for the most part mutually unintelligible

Government
Federal Republic

Administrative Divisions
25 states and seven union territories*; Andaman and Nicobar Islands*, Andhra Pradesh, Arunachal Pradesh, Assam, Bihar, Chandigarh*, Dadra and Nagar Haveli*, Daman and Diu*, Delhi*, Goa, Gujarat, Haryana, Himachal Pradesh, Jammu and Kashmir, Karnataka, Kerala, Lakshadweep*, Madhya Pradesh, Maharashtra, Manipur, Meghalaya, Mizoram, Nagaland, Orissa, Pondicherry*, Punjab, Rajasthan, Sikkim, Tamil Nadu, Tripura, Uttar Pradesh, West Bengal

Currency
Indian Rupee (INR), 100 paise—1 INR. Coins in use: 10 paise, 25 paise, 50 paise, INR 1, 2 and 5. Currency notes INR 5, 10, 20, 50, 100, 500 and 1,000

Weights and Measurements
India has officially adopted the metric system; lengths are measured in metres and kilometres; weights are measured in grams and kilograms

Gross Domestic Product (GDP)
US$ 3.319 trillion (2004 est.)

Industries
Textiles, chemicals, food processing, steel, transportation equipment, cement, mining, petroleum, machinery, software

Exports
Textile goods, gems and jewellery, engineering goods, chemicals, leather manufactures

Imports
Crude oil, machinery, gems, fertilizer, chemicals

Railways
Indian Railways is the largest rail network in Asia, and the second largest under single management in the world. More than 14,000 trains, about 8,000 of which are passenger trains, run every day, covering 63,140 km (39,233.4 miles)

Ports and Harbours
India currently has 11 major ports and 184 minor/intermediary ports along its 7517 km long coast line. The major ports are Kandla, Mumbai, Mormugao, New Mangalore, Kochi, Tuticorin, Chennai, Vishakhapatnam, Paradip, Kolkata, and Haldia

Airports
333 altogether, 234 with paved runways

Common Abbreviations

- AC: Air-conditioned
- CM: Chief Minister
- FIR: First Information Report
- I.A.S. officer: A member of the Indian Administrative Service, an important bureaucratic position
- ISD: International calls
- pp number: For those who do not have a telephone, the number of a neighbour who will call them to the phone

Typical Use of English Words
English word: Indian usage
- auto: autorickshaw
- backside: at the rear
- black: money paid for which no receipt is given
- Don't mention: You're welcome
- fair: light-skinned
- homely: good at household management
- hotel: restaurant

- lodge : cheap hotel
- military hotel: non-vegetarian restaurant
- petrol: gasoline
- retiring room: waiting room in railway stations
- white: money paid that is legally accounted for
- wine shop: liquor store, which does not sell wine at all

FAMOUS PEOPLE
Mohandas Karamchand Gandhi
Born on 2 October 1869 in Porbandar, India, Mohandas Karamchand Gandhi is honoured by Indians as the father of the Indian Nation, because he was instrumental in freeing India from British rule. He used the principal of nonviolent resistance and civil disobediance, called Satyagraha. He was assassinated on 25 January 1948, by a Hindu fanatic.

Jawaharlal Nehru
The first prime minister when India gained its freedom in 1947, Jawaharlal Nehru was the architect of modern India as a secular democracy, building a country with a free press, an independent judiciary, a commitment to civilian oversight of the army and overall egalitarianism. He was a charismatic leader on the world stage, who pursued staunchly socialist economic policies and a foreign policy of 'non-alignment'.

Rabindranath Tagore
Rabindranath Tagore was a scholar, freedom fighter, writer and painter. He won the Nobel prize for literature in 1913, for his collection of poems, 'Gitanjali'. He has written 35 plays and 12 novels, numerous short stories, some of which have provided the inspiration for films by Satyajit Ray and other modern filmmakers. One of his poems, set to music, is the Indian national anthem.

M S Subbhalakshmi
M S Subbhalakshmi was a charming and gifted musician who became known as the nightingale of Indian music. Both Gandhi and Nehru enjoyed the pure timbre of her voice.

Because of her early work in films, she was one of the most popular and best-loved of Indian musicians.

Indira Gandhi

The third prime minister and the only child of Jawaharlal Nehru, Indira Gandhi was groomed for a political career when she was just 13 years old. Indira was the leader of a resistance group, the 'Monkey Army' (*Vanar Sena*) made up of young teenagers fighting for Indian Independence. She was assassinated on 31 October by her Sikh bodyguards, to avenge the storming of the Golden Temple in Amritsar, which she had ordered because of terrorist activities in the temple precincts.

Amartya Kumar Sen

A man so affected by his experiences as a ten-year-old during the Bengal famine that his study of economics was concerned with the underlying causes of famines and poverty, Amartya Kumar Sen's contributions to economic theory offer a new philosophy of development. He won the Nobel prize in Economics in 1998.

Subrahmanyan Chandrasekhar

A Nobel Laureate in Physics and one of the greatest astrophysicists of modern times, Subrahmanyan Chandrasekhar is noted for his work in the field of stellar evolution: he was the first to theorise that a collapsing massive star would become an object so dense that not even light could escape it—now known as the Black Hole. He demonstrated that there is an upper limit (known as 'Chandrasekhar Limit') to the mass of a White Dwarf star.

Arundhati Roy

Arundhati Roy became the first Indian woman to win the Booker prize, which she won in 1997 for *The God of Small Things*. Now, she is better known for her social activism, especially the anti-nuclear movement, and environmental issues.

Satyajit Ray
Satyajit Ray was a renowned film director from West Bengal, best known for the *Apu* trilogy, noted for its realistic portrayal of everyday life in rural India. He made 28 full length feature films and a few documentaries. On his deathbed, he received a Lifetime Achievement Oscar for his contribution to cinema.

Jamshedji Tata
Known as the grandfather of Indian Industry for the visionary nature of his business acumen, Jamshedji Tata started the Indian Institute of Science in Bangalore, the Hydro Electric Project in Bombay, and the Taj Hotel in Bombay. The name Tata is everywhere in India now, and the city of Jamshedpur is named after him.

Phoolan Devi
Phoolan Devi, known as the 'Bandit Queen', began life as a low-caste, illiterate, abused young woman, but then took to banditry and led a gang of desperadoes. Finally, after the revenge-style killings of 22 men who had allegedly been involved in her gang-rape, she surrendered, went to jail for 11 years, and then became a member of Parliament, fighting for the oppressed. She was murdered in July 2001 by masked gunmen.

PLACES OF INTEREST
Agra and Fatepur Sikri
Agra has the Taj Mahal, but 37 km (23 miles) away and also exquisitely beautiful is the ghost city Fatehpur Sikri, built by Akbar as his capital, and then abandoned because there was no source of water.

Ajanta and Ellora
The caves of Ajanta were Buddhist monasteries, and their painted interiors tell the story of the life of Buddha. Close by in Ellora are the finest examples of cave-temple architecture, hewn into the sides of the basaltic hills; most remarkable is the magnificent Kailasa temple, the largest

The magnificient Taj Mahal draws huge crowds
each day, all eager to see its splendour.

monolithic structure in the world. Both are UNESCO World Heritage Sites.

Khajurahao

The exquisite pink sandstone temples of Khajuraho mark the culmination of the northern Indian or Nagara style of temple architecture. They are most famous for the stone depictions of erotic love—men, women and even animals in every possible combination—but it is the vibrant, sensuous carvings of all aspects of life that are so compelling, as well as the play of proportion and scale in foreground and background.

Madurai

This is one of the oldest cities in India, having been a centre of trade since the 6th century BC. The Meenakshi temple complex is a stunning example of Dravidian architecture, with a 'thousand pillared' hall.

Jaisalmer

Jaisalmer is like an exquisite mirage in the desert. Once on the camel trade route between India and Central Asia, it is full of havelis with carved golden yellow sandstone facades, built to house the rich merchants of a bygone era.

Corbett National Park

Located at the base of the Himalayas in Uttar Pradesh, this is the oldest national park in Asia and the first tiger reserve. Because of the variety of habitats within its 521 sq km (201.2 sq miles), you can see tigers, Asiatic elephants and about 600 species of birds. You can go deep into the forest on elephant back, which is a thrill in itself.

Fort Cochin (Kochi)

When pepper was such a precious commodity that it was called 'black gold', Cochin had the monopoly on its trade and attracted Jewish, Arab and Christian traders. Just across the water from the bustling mainland city of Ernakulam, it is a serene and charming old-world refuge. You will find a

16th century Jewish synagogue, and some of the best antique shops in India.

Thanjavur
The great Brihadishwara temple of the Chola period is probably the greatest example of the *dravida* style of temple-building, with its mountain-like *vimanas*; and the bronzes of the deities are testaments to the brilliance of the Chola sculptors and their skill in wax resist metal casting.

Darjeeling Himalayan Railway
The Darjeeling Himalayan Railway is one of the most spectacular narrow gauge steam railways of the world. Opened in 1881 to connect the plains of West Bengal with Darjeeling, it applied bold, ingenious engineering solutions to the problem of establishing an effective rail link across a mountainous terrain of breath-taking beauty. It climbs to a height of 7400 ft (2,255.5 m), the highest on the Indian Railways route, and the second highest in the world.

CULTURE QUIZ

SITUATION 1

You've invited a few people for dinner. You are dressed and waiting, the table is laid, the souffle has just been popped into the oven. No sign of any guests. Long after the souffle has sagged beyond redemption, when you've given up hope and changed into your pyjamas, your guests arrive. Not only that, one has brought her aged mother, who speaks not a word of English, and another has brought his house guests, who just happen to be Indian royalty. What do you do?

Ⓐ Turn off all the lights and pretend you're not home.

Ⓑ Receive your guests in your haughtiest manner, being just barely polite so that they realise your plans have been upset. Be sure to mention the souffle and all the trouble you've gone to.

Ⓒ Throw on your silk dressing gown, and greet your guests graciously, as if this is how you organise all your dinner parties. Make sure everyone has plenty to drink, and then set about making a whole new souffle.

Comments

The Indian hostess is gracious in the face of any eventuality; this is the quality you must cultivate to have successful parties in India, for you will be faced with just about every unexpected situation possible. But just to make things easier on yourself next time, don't expect anyone to turn up earlier than an hour late; don't cook something that must be served on the dot, and don't set the table for a sit-down dinner.

In the situation above, you would of course choose **Ⓒ**, relaxed in the knowledge that no one expects to eat for a couple of hours. Tell your friend that of course she could bring her mother along without asking, and then go bask in the glory of a real Maharajah, who will surely invite you to visit his summer palace in the hills.

SITUATION 2

Your maidservant is still breastfeeding her three-year-old child on demand. You decide to be helpful and give the child a glass of milk whenever your own children have some. But instead of gaining weight, the child gets thinner, and has constant diarrhoea. What do you do next?

Ⓐ Keep on giving her milk. After all, your children thrive on it.

Ⓑ Stop giving her milk, or anything else.

Ⓒ Try giving her a little yogurt.

Comments

Children in India who have built up an immunity to various germs may find packaged milk, which Westerners have no trouble with, too hard to digest. Intolerance to milk usually doesn't include yogurt, as the bacteria in the fermentation process break down milk proteins into a more digestible form. It is a good idea to keep an eye on the health of servants and their children, if only in your own best interests. In the situation here, **Ⓑ** is the best option. The child's mother knows best.

SITUATION 3

You are in a shop in the main bazaar area, and when you come out onto the street, you realise it is later than you thought. You head out for the main road, but in the darkness end up in the maze of narrow lanes, hopelessly lost. There isn't a taxi or autorickshaw in sight. Suddenly, everything looks very threatening and strange. What now?

Ⓐ Scream at the top of your lungs.

Ⓑ Keep on going. You'll eventually come to the main road somehow.

Ⓒ Look around for help. Find an older, respectable-looking person of the same sex and explain your problem in English.

Comments

Male or female, in an Indian crowd, unless it is a religious riot, you are quite safe. If you can speak the language, go ahead, but now is not the time to use the only six words you know. Speak English, and I can almost guarantee that you will be helped. Someone who doesn't speak it will find you someone who does. You will be taken by the hand and led to the main road. My only caution is that a woman should be wary of accepting a ride with a single male under 80 years of age. If you feel confident enough that you can handle the situation, ask to be dropped at a big hotel, rather than at your home. (This way, you preserve your privacy.) Do not offer money to those who have helped you; if someone really went out of their way, then take down the address and send a thank you card. Otherwise, just a thank you is enough, for, as your benefactors may tell you, 'it was their duty'.

SITUATION 4

You are driving from a big city to a popular scenic spot on the main highway. It's time for lunch and the children are hungry. How can you avoid dysentery and still get something to eat?

Ⓐ Look out for a Western-style 'restaurant', air-conditioned if possible.

Ⓑ Buy cookies and bottled drinks from a roadside stall.

Ⓒ Watch where all the big trucks are parked, and pull in there.

Comments

Western-style restaurants outside the big cities often have only the vaguest notion of things like sandwiches, pizza or soup. Nor is the presence of a menu and a waiter any guarantee of cleanliness. If you want to avoid the sugar-induced hyperactivity likely to be brought on by cookies and soft drinks, choose **Ⓒ** and head for the roadside eateries patronised by Indians.

Drivers of big trucks always know which one has the best food. The cooking is simple, but every bit of it is right in front

of you so you can see what's going on. There will be one or
two pots of vegetable and lentil stews that have been on the
fire since early morning, so every germ is cooked out. These
are served with wholesome unleavened breads piping hot
from the clay oven. You must not drink the water, but that
is equally true of the Western-style restaurant.

SITUATION 5

As an afterthought while leaving the house, you say to your
maid, "… and tell the driver to wash the car." When you get
back, the maid is in tears, the driver hands you his letter
of resignation, and of course the car has not been washed.
What went wrong?

Ⓐ The driver is not permitted by his union to wash cars.

Ⓑ The maid misunderstood, and asked the driver to wash
the carpets, which understandably, he felt was beyond the
scope of his duties.

Ⓒ You had a sudden lapse, and forgot that your driver is a
50-year-old high-caste BA (Failed) male chauvinist p—,
while your maid is hardly 20, low-caste, and not very
diplomatic.

Comments

You may come to believe that the more servants you have, the
less work gets done, because of the time taken making sure
that things run smoothly between them. It is best whenever
possible to give orders directly to the person concerned. Even
then, you may be called in to mediate over small things, like
tea, phone privileges and so on, that seem to get blown up
out of all proportion. Try not to let your personal likes and
dislikes cloud the picture: in India, age, caste, sex, job and
education definitely affect a person's standing, and nothing
you can do is going to change all that.

SITUATION 6

You are trying to get through some paperwork so that you
can import some equipment. The clerk at Customs says you
can't get customs clearance without the import certificate.

The clerk at the Import and Export Licences Bureau says you can't get the import certificate without the customs clearance. Neither clerk has heard of Catch 22. Will you have to shuttle back and forth between these two offices for the rest of your term in India?

Ⓐ Yes, unless you commit hara-kiri.
Ⓑ Yes, until you figure out which one to bribe.
Ⓒ No, because you ask an Indian friend to help you.

Comments
Ⓒ is an option you could use. But if you have the clout to go higher, the impasse can be quickly resolved. Make an appointment at the highest level open to you, making sure to take a clever Indian subordinate to actually handle the details, and explain your problem to the person in charge. Then sip tea and exchange pleasantries while the papers go down the line and come back up again, with the necessary stamps.

SITUATION 7
While visiting a village in South India, you decide to take an evening stroll through the paddy fields. As you walk, squatting figures all around you stand up, looking decidedly uncomfortable. Should you be worried?

Ⓐ No, they're just stretching their legs.
Ⓑ Yes, they're muggers, just waiting for the unsuspecting foreigner.
Ⓒ Not really, but you should still get out of there as quickly as you can.

Comments
The fields around a village are often the toilets, and late evening is the time that people set off with their pots of water to answer nature's call, so to speak. You have interrupted them in the middle of an important bodily function, which in all modesty they cannot complete until you leave the area. Make your exit as gracefully as possible, but don't bother to wave.

SITUATION 8

An Indian friend takes you visiting. At each and every house, as soon as you enter, the hostess comes with a tray, with glasses of juice, or lemon squash, or just plain water. When she offers it to you, you

ⓐ ask, "Has this water been boiled and filtered?"

ⓑ pray silently to the patron saint of hepatitis, cholera and dysentery, and gulp it all down.

ⓒ take a glass, but never actually take a sip. Lift it up, put it down, bring it almost to your lips, but stop because you just thought of something to say. Carry on like that until your visit is over.

ⓓ say, "My friend has told me already about your excellent South Indian coffee. Would it be too much trouble for you to make that instead?"

Comments

There is no good solution: your choice is to be rude, sick or a perfect hypocrite. People who are aware of the dangers of untreated drinking water will usually make a point of telling you that it has been boiled—if they don't tell you it is, then it probably isn't. So asking only points out the inadequacy of the offering. At the same time, it seems rather silly to get seriously ill just to be polite. It's better to be a hypocrite. But if you can't manage that, then take the onus of blame on yourself for being an unfortunate foreigner with a strange and sensitive stomach. Everyone will sympathise.

DO'S AND DON'TS

DO'S

- Be aware of the behaviour of others around you in social situations and use this as a guide to your own behaviour.
- Remove your shoes when entering a temple, a Sikh *gurudwara* or mosque and in many cases, when entering someone's house.
- Speak English clearly and without slang and idiomatic expressions in order to be easily understood.
- Treat elders with special respect.
- Find out about the food and drink restrictions of your guests when you invite them for meals.
- Dress appropriately for the event you are attending.
- Bring a gift when visiting someone; it is not expected, but will be appreciated.
- Carry small change.
- Use the shopkeeper's interest in making the 'first sale of the morning' to get yourself a good deal.
- Make the purchase once the shopkeeper has accepted your price following bargaining.
- Dress more conservatively outside the major urban areas.
- Take precautions to make sure that drinking water is safe.
- Take normal precautions with money and valuables.

DON'TS

- Use the left hand to eat, hand over food, money, gifts or important documents.
- Treat religious ceremonies as entertainment, though music and dance may sometimes be part of the ceremony.
- Answer personal questions that make you uncomfortable, but find a polite way to avoid them, as in most cases, no offence is meant.
- Smoke without first asking if it is acceptable, especially at religious celebrations.
- Show excessive physical signs of affection with members of the opposite sex in public.

- Shake hands, hug or kiss someone of the opposite sex as a greeting, unless the contact is initiated by the Indian person.
- Wear Indian garments in inappropriate ways; such as wearing the *salwar* without the *kameez* on top, or the *sari* blouse and underskirt without the *sari*.
- Take every invitation to 'drop in anytime' at face value.
- Expect Indian guests to show up exactly on time and don't be absolutely punctual yourself, except for official events.

GLOSSARY

USEFUL PHRASES IN HINDI AND TAMIL

English	Hindi	Tamil
Excuse me	*Maaf kiijye*	*Maaniyungal*
Good bye	*Namaskar*	*Poi varukiren*
How are you?	*Aap kaise hain?*	*Yeppadi irukkireergal?*
Do you understand?	*Kyaa aap samjhate hain?*	*Puriyudhah?*
I understand	*Main samajh gaya (male)/gayi (female)*	*Yenakku purikirathu*
I don't understand	*Main samjha (male)/samjhi (female)*	*Yenakku puriyavillai*
I don't want...	*Mujhe nahin chahiye*	*Vendam*
I need...	*Mujhe chahiye*	*Vendum*
I want to go to...	*Mujhe...jaana hai*	*Naan...kku poga vendum*
It doesn't matter	*Koi baat nahiin*	*Parravaa-illai*
Thank you	*Dhanyavaad*	*Nandri*
What is the price?	*Iska kya daam hai?*	*Vellai yenna?*
Where can I get...?	*Mujhe kahan... milega*	*Yengay... kadaikkum*
Where is (this person/thing)?	*...Kahan hai?*	*...Yengay irukkirar/ rukkirathu?*

RESOURCE GUIDE

> **Please Note**
> In india, telephone numbers are in a contant state of flux and change fairly often. For this reason, they are not included in this list. The exceptions are for emergencies numbers which are permanent. We suggest that you check the websites listed for more updated details on phone numbers.

VISAS

Business visas or tourist visas are adequate for short stays in the country, but if you plan to work in India, you will have to apply for an employment visa from the Indian Embassy in your home country. It is difficult to convert a tourist or business visa to an employment visa in India. You will most likely have to leave the country in order to do this. Do apply at once for a multiple entry visa if you intend to do this.

Information on Indian visas, as well as application forms, and links to the Indian embassies and consulates of various countries is available at http://passport.nic.in/visa.htm

REGISTRATION

If you intend to stay for more than six months at a stretch, you will have to register your presence in India within 14 days at the Foreigner's Regional Registration Office (FRRO). When you go to the FRRO to register yourself, please make sure that you are carrying the following documents:

- Photocopy of your passport
- Photocopy of initial visa
- Four photographs
- Details of residence in India
- If your age is anywhere between 16–60 years, an HIV test report from an institution recognised by the World Health Organisation is required.

Depending on the kind of visa you have, there may be additional support material you need. FRRO addresses in the 4 metropolitan cities of India are:

- Hans Bhawan, Bahadurshah Zafar Marg, ITO
  New Delhi
- Tata Press Building, 2nd Floor, 414 S.V Marg
  Mumbai
- 237, A.J.C. Bose Road
  Calcutta
- Shastri Bhawan Annexe, 26, Haddow Road
  Chennai

In all other places, the District Superintendents of Police act as Foreigners' Registration Officers. When you leave the country, these certificates of registration should be surrendered to the immigration officer at the port/check post of exit from India. You can also surrender the certificate, just prior to departure, to the FRRO who issued the certificate to you, but in this case, you must get a receipt from the FRRO which you can show to the immigration authorities.

RECORDS
Children may need to show past medical records in order to prove that they have been immunized when they are admitted to school in India. Being able to produce school records will ease the process of admission.

SHIPPING DOCUMENTS
If you are bringing your household belongings into the country, shipping documents are necessary for clearing the items through customs. In order to be allowed to do so, you must show you have been residing outside India for at least two years and plan to stay in India, with the proper visa, for at least one year. Your shipping agent, if a good one, will definitely bear the brunt of the tedious work, but for the final step, you must be present with your passport.

USEFUL WEBSITES
- http://www.khoj.com
  A directory of Indian sites
- http://www.123India.com
  Provides news about movies, music, Bollywood, government ministries and politics

- http://www.theory.tifr.res.in/misc/index.html
  This page of the website of the Tata Institute of Fundamental Research has links to all the useful Mumbai sites you might need, including railway, telephone, restaurants, Air India
- http://www.indiantravelportal.com
  Gives links to hotels, tours, travel packages all over India
- http://www.explocity.com/info/Listinghomepage
  Has information on all the major cities, including restaurants, shopping, nightlife, etc
- http://www.bangaloreit.com
  Useful website of the Department of IT and Biotechnology, Karnataka, with everything you need to know about Bangalore
- http://www.bsnl.co.in/onlinedirectory.htm
  Provides online directories for all the major cities, as well as links to each state
- http://www.mtnl.in/index.htm
  Provides links to phone directories and services for Delhi and Mumbai
- http://mtnldelhi.in/
  Delhi directory, phone services, applications etc
- http://mtnlmumbai.in/
  Mumbai directory, phone services, applications etc.
- http://phonebook.bol.net.in/

EMERGENCY NUMBERS
- Police   100
- Fire   101
- Ambulance   102
- International call assistance 187
- Traffic police   103
- Railway Enquiry General   131

HOSPITALS
Hospitals and Clinics in Mumbai (Bombay)
- **Breach Candy Hospital and Research Centre**
  60 Bhulabhai Desai Road Breach Candy
  Mumbai-400026

- **Hinduja Hospital**
  Veer Savarkar Marg Mahim
  Mumbai-400016
- **Jaslok Hospital and Reseach Centre**
  Chakravaty 15 G Deshmukh Marg Peddar Road
  Mumbai-400026
- **Bombay Hospital Trust**
  12 New Marine Lines
  Mumbai-400020

Hospitals and Clinics in Calcutta
- **Woodlands Nursing Home**
  8/5 Alipur Road
  Calcutta-27
- **The Bellvue Clinic**
  9 Loudon Street
  Calcutta-17

Hospitals and Clinics in Delhi
- **All India Institute of Medical Sciences**
  Ansari Nagar
  New Delhi-29
- **Apollo Hospital**
  Sarita Vihar Mathura Road
- **Sir Gangaram Hospital**
  Rajinder Nagar
  New Delhi-60

Hospitals and Clinics in Chennai (Madras)
- **Apollo Hospital**
  21 Greams Lane
  Chennai-6
- **Devaki Hospital**
  148 Luz Church Road Mylapore
  Chennai-4
- **Malar Hospital**
  52 First Main Road Gandhinagar Adyar
  Chennai-20.

- **Willingdon Hospital**
  21 Pycrofts Garden Road
  Chennai-6
- **Tamil Nadu Hospital**
  439 Cheran Nagar Perumbakkam
  Chennai 601302

HOME AND FAMILY
Schools in Mumbai (Bombay)

- **Bombay International School**
  Gilbert Building Babulnath 2nd Cross Road
  Mumbai-7
- **Campion School** (for boys)
  13 Cooperage Road
  Mumbai-3
- **Bombay Scottish School**
  Veer Savarkar Marg
  Mumbai-16

Schools in Calcutta

- **St. Xavier's** (for boys)
  30 Park Street
  Calcutta-16
- **Loretta House** (for girls)
  7 Middleton Road
  Calcutta-16
- **La Martiniere** (for boys)
  11 Dr. UN Bramhachari Street
  Calcutta-17
- **La Martiniere** (for girls)
  Rawdon Street
  Calcutta-16

Schools in Delhi

- **The American Embassy School**
  Chandragupta Marg, Chanakyapuri
  New Delhi-21

- **The British School**
  San Martin Marg Chanakyapuri
  New Delhi-21
- **The German School**
  2 Nyaya Marg Chanakyapuri
  New Delhi-21
- **The Japanese School**
  61C Defense Colony
  New Delhi-24

Schools in Chennai (Madras)

- **Abacus Montessori School**
  50/1D Thirumalai Nagar Annex
  3rd Main Road Perungudi
  Chennai-96
- **American International School**
  Chennai 8 Murray's Gate Road
  Chennai-18
- **Harrington House School**
  21 Dr. Thirumurthi Nagar Main Street
  Nungambakkam High Road
  Chennai-34
- **Sishya**
  15 Second Street Padmanabha Nagar Adyar
  Chennai-20

Boarding Schools

- **Woodstock School**
  Musoorie Uttar Pradesh 248179
- **Kodaikanal International School**
  P.O. Box 25 Kodaikanal
  Tamil Nadu 624101
- **Hebron School**
  Lushington Hall Ootacamund
  Nilgiri Hills 643001

HOTELS
- http://www.indiahotels.com
- http://www.heritagehotels.com
- http://www.indiatourism.com

ENTERTAINMENT AND LEISURE
Restaurants
- http://www.dinerpages.com/india/india.htm
- http://www.india123.com
  Has city guides for all the major cities with some restaurants
- http://www.whereincity.com
  Allows you to search by city for restaurants
- http://www.world66.com/asia/southasia/india
  Has reviews
- http://www.world66.com/asia/southasia/india
- http://www.virtualtourist.com/travel/Asia/India
  Has reviews written by travellers
- **Dhanraj Restaurant**
  23 Linking Road Bandra
  Mumbai-400050
- **Dastar Khanwane Karim**
  Nizamuddin West
- **Kolkata**
  6A Chowringhee Place
  Calcutta
- **New Woodlands Hotel**
  72-75 Dr. Radhakrishnan Road Mylapore
  Chennai 600004

Libraries
- **American Library**
  Marine Lines
- **Asiatic Library**
  Town Hall
- **British Council Library**
  Nariman Point
- **Bharatiya Vidhya Bhavan**
  Chowpatty

- **David Sasson Library**
  M G Road
- **University Library**
  K P Patil Marg
- **American Center Library**
  38A Jawaharlal Nehru Road
  Calcutta 700071
  A popular library with the student and research community.
- **Asiatic Society Library**
  1 Park Street
  Calcutta 700016
  The library of the Asiatic Society has a large collection of over 100,000 printed books, periodicals and rare manuscripts.
- **Connemara Public Library**
  Pantheon Road
  Chennai-600008

Bookshops
- **Landmark**
  Apex Plaza
  Chennai-600034

Magazines
Frontline
- Has excellent photo essays and articles by eminent writers on a variety of topical issues. It comes out fortnightly.

India Magazine
- Comes out monthly with well-written articles on aspects of Indian culture, but occasionally suffers from overkill.

India Today
- Published fortnightly, uses a slick international news magazine format, comparable to *Time* and *Newsweek*, to provide up-to-date and politically unbiased reports on what's happening in India. Extremely readable, with excellent photographs.

Sruti
- The definitive magazine on South Indian music and dance. It comes out monthly with lively, informed articles on the most fascinating aspects of the art forms. It is definitely a must for anyone interested to be on the inside of the Carnatic scene. Now it handles Hindustani music, too. If you can't find it at bookshops, write to Sruti at 276-B, J.J. Road, Chennai-18.

Cultural Organisations
- **National Centre for the Performing Arts**
  Nariman Point
  Mumbai-21
- **The Bombay Natural History Society**
  Hornbill House Shahid Bhagat Singh Marg
  Mumbai-23
- **The Asiatic Society of Bombay**
  Town Hall
  Mumbai-1
- **Triveni Kala Sangam**
  205 Tansen Marg
  New Delhi-1
- **India International Centre**
  40 Max Mueller Marg Lodi Estate
  New Delhi-3
- **Academy of Fine Arts**
  Cathedral Road
  Calcutta-71
- **Nandan (for good films)**
  1/1 AJC Bose Road
  Calcutta-20

Tamil Language Institutes
- **The International Institute of Tamil Studies**
  Central Polytechnic Campus Adyar
  Chennai-113

Department Stores

- **Spencers**
  Plaza, Mount Road
  Chennai-02
- **Akbarally's**
  45 Veer Nariman Road
  Mumbai-23
- **Asiatic Departmental Store**
  73 Veer Nariman Road
  Mumbai-20
- **West Side**
  77 Commercial Street
  Shivajinagar Bangalore
- **Atlantic Stores**
  2A Shakespeare Sarani
  Kolkata
- **Globus**
  South Extension, Part II.
  New Delhi

Provision Stores

- **Steakhouse**
  13/8 Jorbagh Market
  New Delhi-3
- **Modern Bazaar**
  Shop 49 Basant Lok Community Centre
  Vasant Vihar
  New Delhi-57
- **Nilgiris Dairy Farm**
  58 Dr Radhakrishnan Road
  Chennai
- **Puspa Shoppe**
  1 Lattice Bridge Road Adyar
  Chennai-20
- **Mark's Supermarket**
  Ashutosh Mukherjee Road.

Clubs

- **Bombay Gymkhana Club**
  Mahatma Gandhi Road
  Mumbai-1
- **The Breach Candy Swimming Bath Trust**
  66 Bulabhai Desai Road
  Mumbai-26
- **The Tollygunge Club**
  120 DP Sasmal Road
  Calcutta-33
- **The Saturday Club**
  7 Wood Street
  Calcutta-16
- **The Bengal Club**
  1/1 Russel Street
  Calcutta-16
- **The Delhi Gymkhana Club**
  2 Safdarjung Road
  New Delhi-11
- **Chelmsford Club**
  Raisina Road
  New Delhi-1
- **The Madras Club**
  Chamiers Road
  Chennai-28
- **The Madras Gymkhana Club**
  1 Anna Salai (Mount Road)
  Chennai-2
- **The Madras Boat Club**
  Madras Boat Club Road
  Chennai-28
- **Indo American Association**
  10 Nandanam Main Road Nandanam Extension
  Chennai 600035

Volunteer Organisations

- **Mother Theresa Nirmal Hriday**
  54A Lower Circular Road
  Calcutta-16.

- **Mobile Creche for Working Mothers' Children**
  Section 4 DIZ Area Raja Bazaar
  New Delhi-1
- **Working Women's Forum**
  55 Bhimasena Garden Street Mylapore
  Chennai-4
- **Udavum Karangal, Centre for Humane Services**
  460 NSK Nagar
  Chennai-106

Social Organisations

Hash House Harriers uses the excuse of running to get people together, and then have a few beers. It's a fun way to meet people, even if you hate running and beer. Each Hash is different: the proportion of expatriates to Indians, families to singles, men to women, varies in each city. In India at the moment, there are Hash House Harriers in Chennai, Mumbai, Delhi, Hyderabad and Bangalore. Get addresses and telephone numbers, which change as expatriates leave, through the British, Australian or American Embassies or Consulates.

There are also many women's clubs and associations, like the American Women's Association, the British Women's Club and so on. In Chennai, where there are few foreigners, there is the Overseas Women's Club, with women from all the different nationalities. Phone numbers and addresses keep changing, and embassies, high commissions and consulates can provide up-to-date information.

FINANCIAL SERVICES

- **Narayanan's Consulting**
  23 Sir CV Raman Road Alwarpet Chennai-18
  The company has branches located at:
- 238 Hindustan Kohinoor Complex LBS Marg Vikhroli
  Mumbai-1
- 664 17 D Cross Indira Nagar II Stage
  Bangalore 39

FURTHER READING

LANGUAGE

The Treasury of Indian Expressions. Ed. Vijaya Ghose. New Delhi: CMC Ltd, 1992.

- Explains words and phrases relating to all aspects of Indian culture: adornment, food, holy places, nature are just some of the 21 chapters. This book is both a convenient reference and beautifully illustrated.

SERIOUS READING

An Area of Darkness. V S Naipaul. Vintage, 2002.
India—A Wounded Civilisation. V S Naipaul. Vintage, 2003.
India—A Million Mutinies Now. V S Naipaul. Penguin, 1992.

- V.S. Naipaul has written three books on India, all intense, literate records of his own private journey. In the first two, *An Area of Darkness* and *India—A Wounded Civilisation*, he discovers an India that bewilders and saddens and angers him. But in the latest, *India—A Million Mutinies Now*, he turns a more compassionate eye upon the subcontinent, and finds an India 'greater than the sum of its parts', the mutinies he speaks of being 'the beginning of a new way for many millions, part of India's growth, part of its restoration'.

A History of India (Vol. 1). Romila Thapar. Penguin, 1990.
A History of India (Vol. 2). Percival Spear. Penguin Books, 1990.

- Meant for readers with a general interest in India. Both volumes skilfully weave the various strands of India's history into a whole that reveals the 'inner meaning' of the transformations that led to the development of modern Indian society. The first volume covers the period up to the coming of the Moghuls; the second volume takes it from there up to independence and Nehru's government.

The Speaking Tree. Richard Lannoy. Oxford University Press, 1971.

- A Western anthropological eye turned on various aspects of Indian society, including caste, family and religion. It is readable and sensible, yet scientific, at the same time avoiding jargon and esoterica.

Sources of Indian Tradition, Volumes 1 and 2. Ed. Ainslie T. Embree and Stephan Hay. Columbia University Press, 1988.
- Excellent books for occasional reference, they give an authentic taste of Indian thinkers without requiring the reader to plough through every word. A succinct commentary ties everything together and establishes a context.

The Penguin Guide to the Monuments of India—Volume I: Buddhist, Jain, Hindu. Dr George Michell. Penguin Books, 1990.
The Penguin Guide to the Monuments of India Volume II: Islamic, Rajput, European. Philip Davies. Penguin Books, 1990.
- These are well written, comprehensive handbooks on all the major monuments and sites in India, organised in two volumes according to architectural style, and within each book according to area, with black and white photographs, maps and building plans.

JUST FOR FUN

R.K. Narayan's novels and short stories set in the fictional South Indian town of Malgudi are pure delight. His charming, funny characters are unforgettable and as real as any Indians you'll meet. You'll get more insight into the workings of the Indian mind from a Narayan book than from any authoritative text on the subject. Titles include *Under the Banyan Tree and Other Stories, Swami and Friends*, *The Guide*, *The Financial Expert*, *The Man-eater of Malgudi*, and *A Vendor of Sweets*. His books are published by Penguin Books and Indian Thought Publications, Mysore.

A Corner of a Foreign Field: The Indian History of a British Sport. Ramachandra Guha. Pan MacMillan, 2002.
- Much more than a history of cricket in India, it is more of a history of India through the lens of cricket. Caste, religion, politics are all naturally part of the story.

Folktales from India. Ed. A.K. Ramanujan. Pantheon, 1994.
- This wonderfully translated collection of oral tales from 22 Indian languages is very readable. The stories are funny, witty, sad, mysterious and romantic, and full of the vitality of India's folk culture.

EPIC

The Mahabharata of Vyasa. Trans. P. Lal. New Delhi: Vikas Publishing, 1980.
- Condensed from Sanskrit and transcreated into English by P. Lal, who recommends it 'for an age that breeds dry thoughts in a Waste Land'.

Many Ramayanas: The Diversity of a Narrative Tradition in South Asia. Ed. Paula Richman. University of California Press, 1991.
Questioning Ramayanas: A South Asian Tradition. Ed. Paula Richman. University of California Press, 2000.
- Through the story of Rama and Sita and their exile in the forest, and the many variations in the telling of that story, the essays collected here reveal so much about Indian culture.

COOKBOOKS

The Art of Indian Vegetarian Cooking. Yamuna Devi. Century, 1987.
- This book has not only 520 recipes carefully adapted to the Western kitchen, but also background material on the history of Indian vegetarianism, a description of culinary techniques, a glossary and lovely illustrations. The dishes do not use onions or garlic. Unfortunately the choice of recipes is restricted by the religious beliefs of the author, a follower of the International Society for Krisha Consciousness. Some very delicious Indian dishes have been omitted from the book.

CHILDREN'S BOOKS

Seasons of Splendour. Madhur Jaffrey. Trafalgar Square Publishing, 1995.
- A beautifully illustrated book of some popular myths and legends of India. Especially helpful are the stories that go with the major festivals.

ABOUT THE AUTHOR

Gitanjali Kolanad, born in 1954, grew up partly in India and partly in Canada, and has lived in the USA, Singapore and Germany as well. She has been involved in the practice, performance and teaching of Bharata Natyam for more than 30 years, travelling to major cities of North America, Europe and Asia. She has travelled extensively all over India, both as a tourist and while working with volunteer organisations. Ms Kolanad is married to a journalist and has two sons, and divides her time between Toronto and Chennai.

INDEX

Titles in the CULTURESHOCK! series:

Argentina	Hong Kong	Paris
Australia	Hungary	Philippines
Austria	India	Portugal
Bahrain	Indonesia	San Francisco
Barcelona	Iran	Saudi Arabia
Beijing	Ireland	Scotland
Belgium	Israel	Sri Lanka
Bolivia	Italy	Shanghai
Borneo	Jakarta	Singapore
Brazil	Japan	South Africa
Britain	Korea	Spain
Cambodia	Laos	Sweden
Canada	London	Switzerland
Chicago	Malaysia	Syria
Chile	Mauritius	Taiwan
China	Mexico	Thailand
Costa Rica	Morocco	Tokyo
Cuba	Moscow	Turkey
Czech Republic	Munich	Ukraine
Denmark	Myanmar	United Arab
Ecuador	Nepal	Emirates
Egypt	Netherlands	USA
Finland	New York	Vancouver
France	New Zealand	Venezuela
Germany	Norway	Vietnam
Greece	Pakistan	

For more information about any of these titles, please contact any of our Marshall Cavendish offices around the world (listed on page ii) or visit our website at:

www.marshallcavendish.com/genref